IMAGES
of America

TENNESSEE'S ARABIAN HORSE RACING HERITAGE

Andra Kowalczyk

ARCADIA
PUBLISHING

ISBN 978-0-7385-4390-1

Published by Arcadia Publishing
Charleston SC, Chicago IL, Portsmouth NH, San Francisco CA

Printed in the United States of America

Library of Congress Catalog Card Number: 2006934706

For all general information contact Arcadia Publishing at:
Telephone 843-853-2070
Fax 843-853-0044
E-mail sales@arcadiapublishing.com
For customer service and orders:
Toll-Free 1-888-313-2665

Visit us on the Internet at www.arcadiapublishing.com

To the pioneers of Arabian horse racing,
from Tennessee and elsewhere.

IMAGES
of America

TENNESSEE'S ARABIAN HORSE RACING HERITAGE

ON THE COVER: Taken in May 1937, the cover image depicts the historic importation of six Arabian mares from Poland prior to their delivery to Gen. Jacob McGavock Dickinson's Travelers Rest (as it was spelled then) Arabian Stud in Tennessee. (Courtesy of Travellers Rest Plantation and Museum, Nashville, Tennessee, from collection donated by Peggy Dickinson Fleming.)

Contents

ACKNOWLEDGMENTS

Without the contributions from individuals and organizations, I could not have achieved this project. To Travellers Rest Plantation and Museum in Nashville, I owe many thanks for the use of photographs from what must be one of the most significant collections left by a pioneer breeder of Arabian horses, Gen. Jacob McGavock Dickinson. All the photographs in chapter one are from the Travellers Rest collection donated by Dickinson's daughter, Peggy Dickinson Fleming. Thanks also to the Albert Gore Research Center on the campus of Middle Tennessee State University, whose equestrian collection from Margaret Lindsley Warden has been an invaluable resource to me. The family of Dr. Sam Harrison of Loudon, Tennessee, Arabian horse racing promoter and horse breeder, contributed photographs from their personal albums, reinforcing the amateur, grassroots beginnings of this sport of Arabian horse racing. All photographs in chapter three, unless otherwise noted, are from the Harrison family collection.

INTRODUCTION

The Arabian horse since ancient cultures has embodied the ideal war mount: agile, efficient, and of unsurpassed stamina. In Middle Eastern deserts, the breed evolved into a small, thrifty, tough horse, capable of thriving in an environment of sparse water and food. In relative isolation, the Arabian horse's attributes, including speed, became fixed. Proof of the breed's genetic prepotency exists in the blood of all light horse breeds, as Europeans acquired so-called "hot-blooded" Arabian stallions for crossing on their "cold-blooded" native stock in the Old World. The influence of the Arabian horse perhaps was most profound in England, where aristocrats began acquiring Arabian stallions for breeding horses for racing alone. The selective breeding for speed soon created a new type of horse—taller, narrower, and longer than the Arabian horse—and by the early 18th century, the Thoroughbred horse was considered its own distinct breed, specifically for racing.

All modern Thoroughbred horses trace to at least one of the three most used Arabian stallions imported to England: the Byerly Turk, imported in 1689; the Darley Arabian, 1704; and the Godolphin Arabian, 1730; as they are historically known, each bearing the eponymous title of its owner. Traditionally horse racing, called the Sport of Kings, has been characterized by wealth, exclusivity, and government connections both in England and in the American colonies. From the Colonial period into the 20th century, Americans of a privileged society sought to emulate British class traditions and customs, in part, via the breeding and racing of Thoroughbred horses. The Arabian horse was still valued for upgrading stock, both Thoroughbreds and other breeds. It was not until the late 19th century that horse breeders in America desired to preserve the purebred Arabian horse.

The Columbian Exposition in Chicago in 1893 introduced visitors to exotic places, sights, and sounds. The fair's Syrian exhibit, complete with Arabian horses from the desert performing an exciting "Wild East" show, enjoyed great popularity. Twenty-eight horses from the Syrian exhibit were sold at the end of the fair, and a handful of horse breeders fancied the idea of breeding purebred Arabian horses in America. By 1908, an Arabian Horse Club was founded. Many of the owners of Arabian horses, including cavalry colonel Spencer Borden and political cartoonist Homer Davenport, championed the tough, thrifty breed for use by the U.S. cavalry. This idea was met with resistance, as army officers preferred the taller Thoroughbred. Also there were strong political ties between the army and the Thoroughbred Jockey Club.

The necessity of purchasing thousands of horses during World War I caused Congress to establish an army horse-breeding program. In 1919, the new U.S. Army Remount Board, consisting of army and civilian horsemen, recommended methods and regulations for supervising the breeding of horses, in the hands of public caretakers, for army use. The breeding program had a two-pronged purpose: to improve the quality of American horses and to maintain in peacetime horses that could be called up to service in case of an emergency. The army instituted a series of annual endurance races, open to the public, for testing equine performance.

Overall, the results of these endurance rides, from 1919 to 1922, provided strong evidence supporting the Arabian as the horse of choice: they required 50 percent less feed than larger horses, and they suffered only a 15 percent lameness rate, compared to up to 90 percent for Thoroughbreds. The Arabian horses also lasted longer, recovered more quickly, and carried more weight proportionally. The attention from the U.S. Army would later have repercussions in the development of Arabian horse racing in America.

By 1922, in the United States, there were approximately 300 Arabian horses, 4,000 Morgans (an American breed created with the inclusion of Arabian ancestors), and 16,000 Thoroughbreds. By 1927, the number of horses registered with the Arabian Horse Club in the United States had risen to 639, and by 1936, the number had edged up to almost 700.

Gen. Jacob McGavock Dickinson, owner of the Travelers Rest Arabian Stud in Nashville, Tennessee, was a primary contributor to the growth of the breed's population in America as well as a pioneer of a racing sport that did not exist officially until 1959. On his goal to preserve the purebred Arabian horse, he superimposed the desire to test his stock for racing athleticism as an indicator of general health and substance. His efforts can be considered the foundation of Arabian horse racing.

One

PRESERVATION

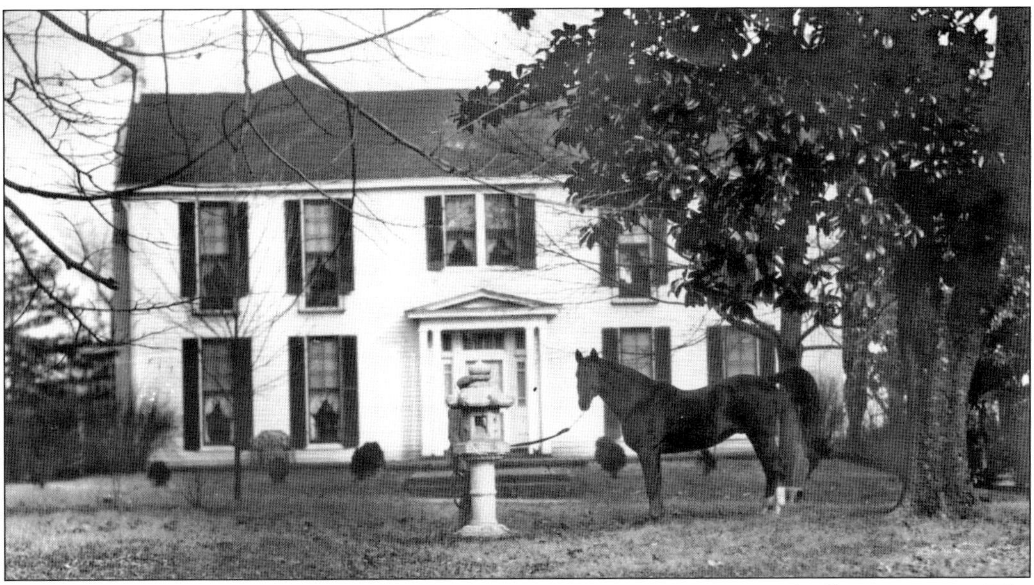

Judge John Overton established Travellers Rest Plantation in 1799 in Nashville, Tennessee. The 2,300-acre estate took its name from the reprieves in Overton's career as a circuit judge traveling many exhausting miles on horseback. Travellers Rest Stud became renowned for the production of Thoroughbred racehorses, fancy Saddlebred riding horses, and Standardbred trotters. The plantation passed through generations of the Overton's descendants, coming to his great-grandson (by marriage) Jacob McGavock Dickinson Jr. in 1929. As the size of the estate had been parceled up over the years, Dickinson's purchase included a small farm and the residence, which he once termed an old-fashioned Southern farm. By family background, Jacob McGavock Dickinson Jr. was predisposed to law practice, military service, and horse breeding. His father, a prominent Nashville businessman, had been a teenaged cavalryman for the Confederate army before becoming a successful lawyer and judge in Chicago and Secretary of War under Pres. William Howard Taft. J. M. Dickinson Jr.'s mother was Martha Maxwell Overton, a granddaughter of Judge John Overton, founder of Travellers Rest Stud.

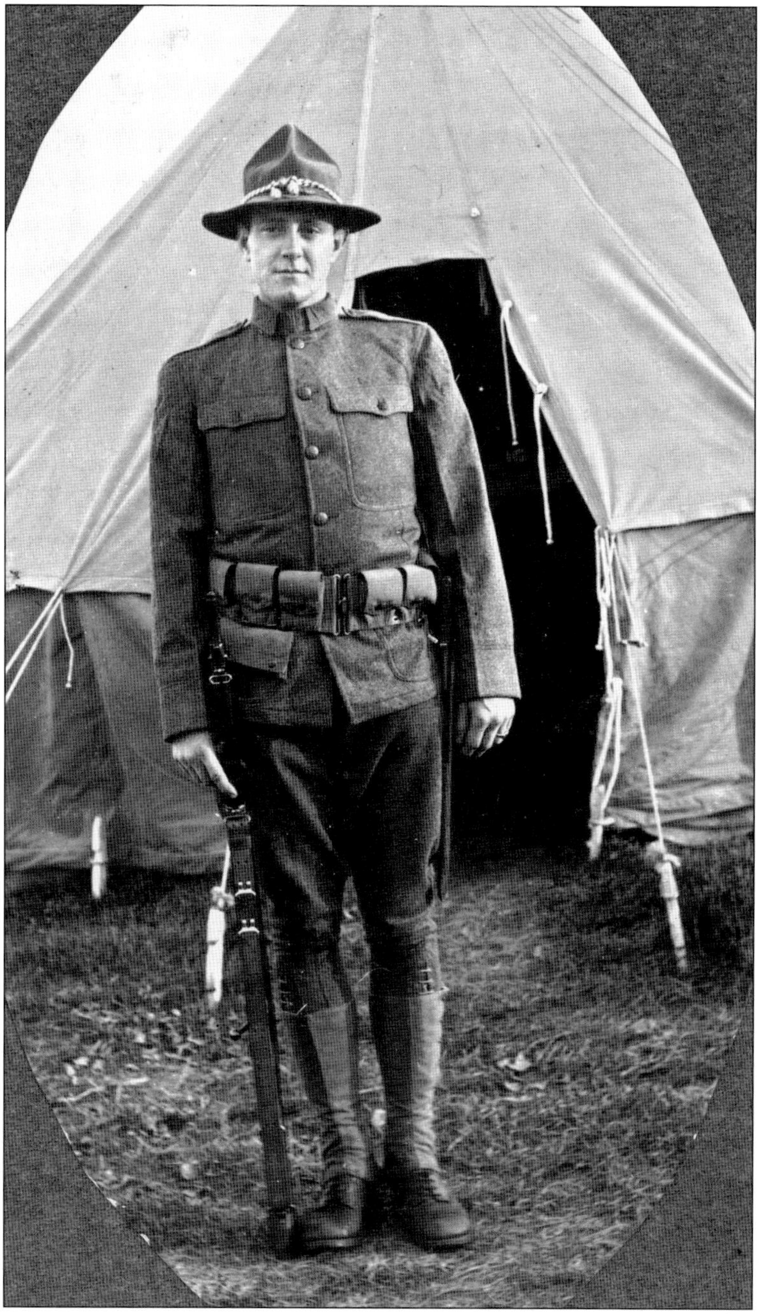

Jacob McGavock Dickinson Jr. followed ancestral footsteps, attending Harvard Law School and serving in the 43rd Rainbow Division in France during World War I, in charge of all the division's horses. Dickinson's military career also included time on the Mexican border in 1916 as a member of Battery C of the 1st Illinois Field Artillery. Later, during World War II, Dickinson was commissioned by the State of Tennessee to organize a home guard while the state's National Guard was serving in war. He attained the rank of brigadier general. Other positions of civil service include chairmanships of both the Selective Service of Williamson County, Tennessee, and the state alcohol control board.

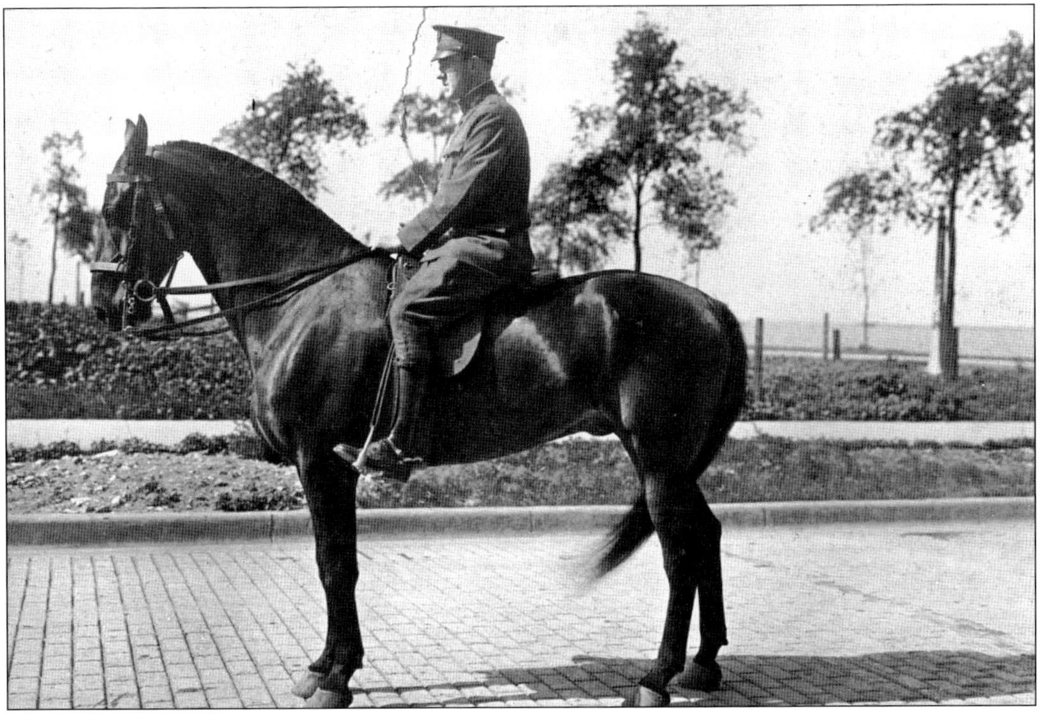

After World War I, Dickinson practiced law in Chicago. In 1928, Dickinson and his wife, Margaret, relocated the family to Travelers Rest in Nashville, where he resumed the stud's tradition of Saddlebred horse breeding. In researching the stud's history, Dickinson found a reference to an Arabian mare named Santa Fe, raising his curiosity. He began studying the Arabian horse in English and several foreign languages, learning that the Arabian horse is the progenitor of all riding horse breeds, including the Thoroughbred and Saddlebred in the United States. He refocused Travelers Rest Stud on preserving purebred Arabian horses. Dickinson learned, too, of a growing criticism among American horsemen for the purebred Arabian horse, which he attributed to simple ignorance and romantic myth. He devoted Travelers Rest to producing beautiful and usable horses, accessible to the middle-class buyer.

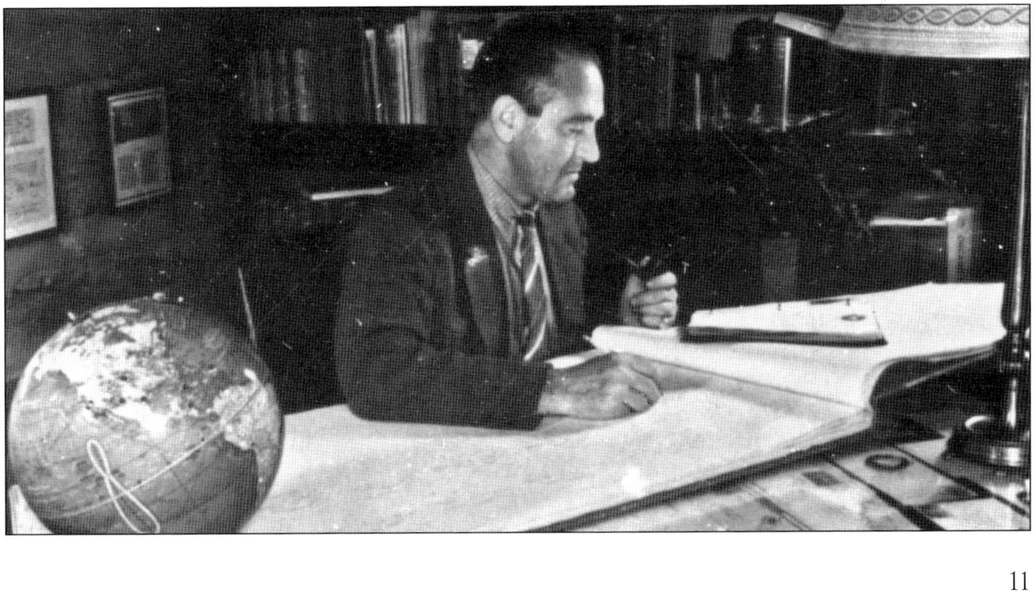

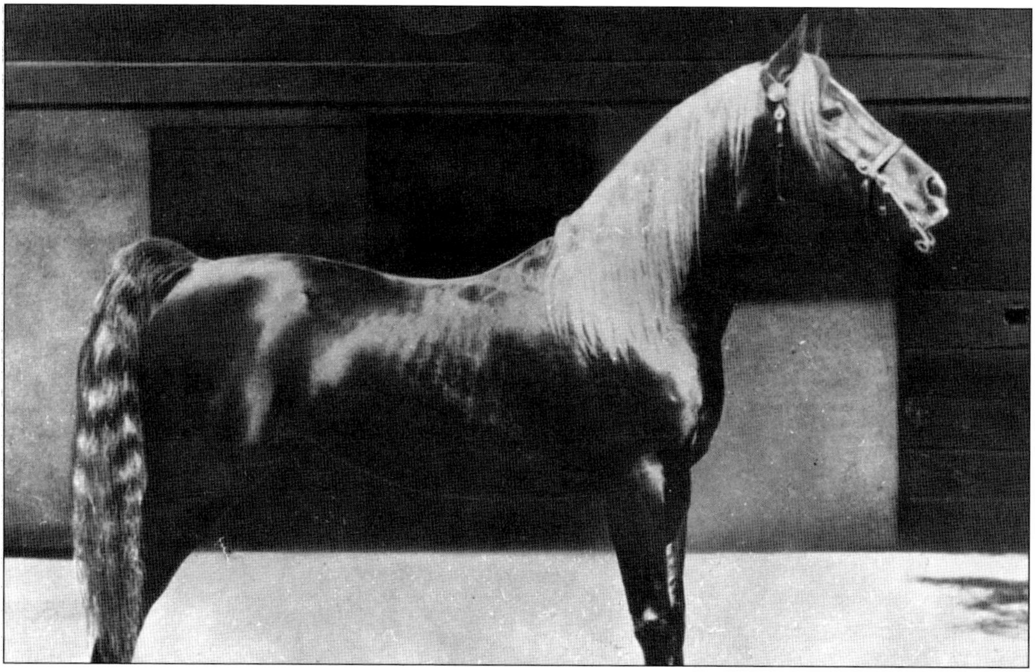

Dickinson began selecting horses for his Arabian stud in 1930, purchasing several from the W. K. Kellogg Ranch in California. The copper-red stallion Antez was a favorite riding horse of Kellogg's because of his even temperament. Kellogg credited the good-natured stallion with saving his life on a trail ride. Dickinson was able to acquire Antez for $5,000 and shipped him to Tennessee, where he was soon used for breeding.

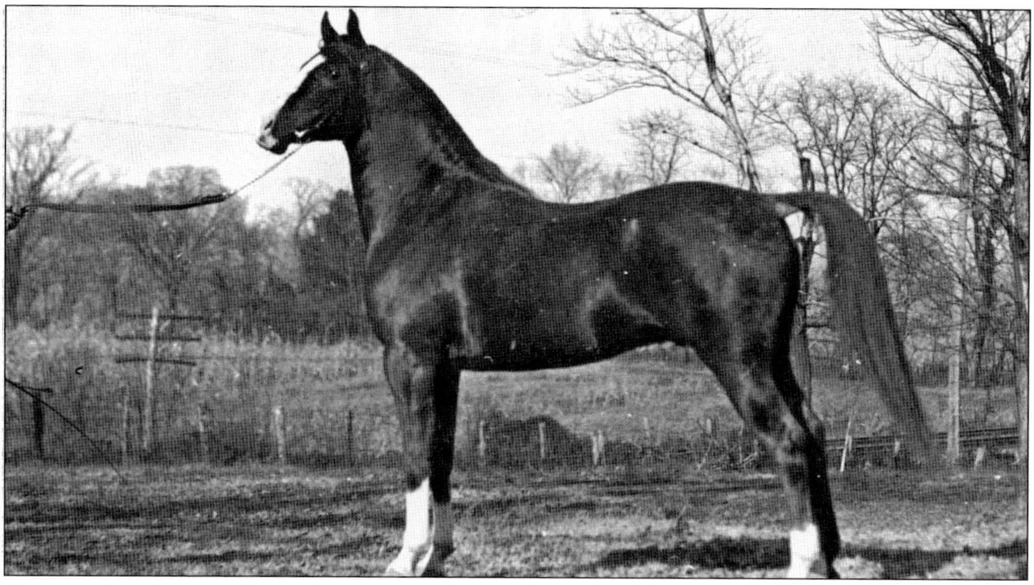

Travelers Rest's second breeding stallion during the early 1930s was Bazleyd, a chestnut stallion born in 1928 at W. R. Brown's Maynesboro Stud in New Hampshire. At a time when most Arabian horse owners were located on either coast, Dickinson, in Middle Tennessee, began growing Travelers Rest Stud into the largest Arabian horse operation in the country. He acquired Bazleyd in 1931 and used the horse for breeding until 1936.

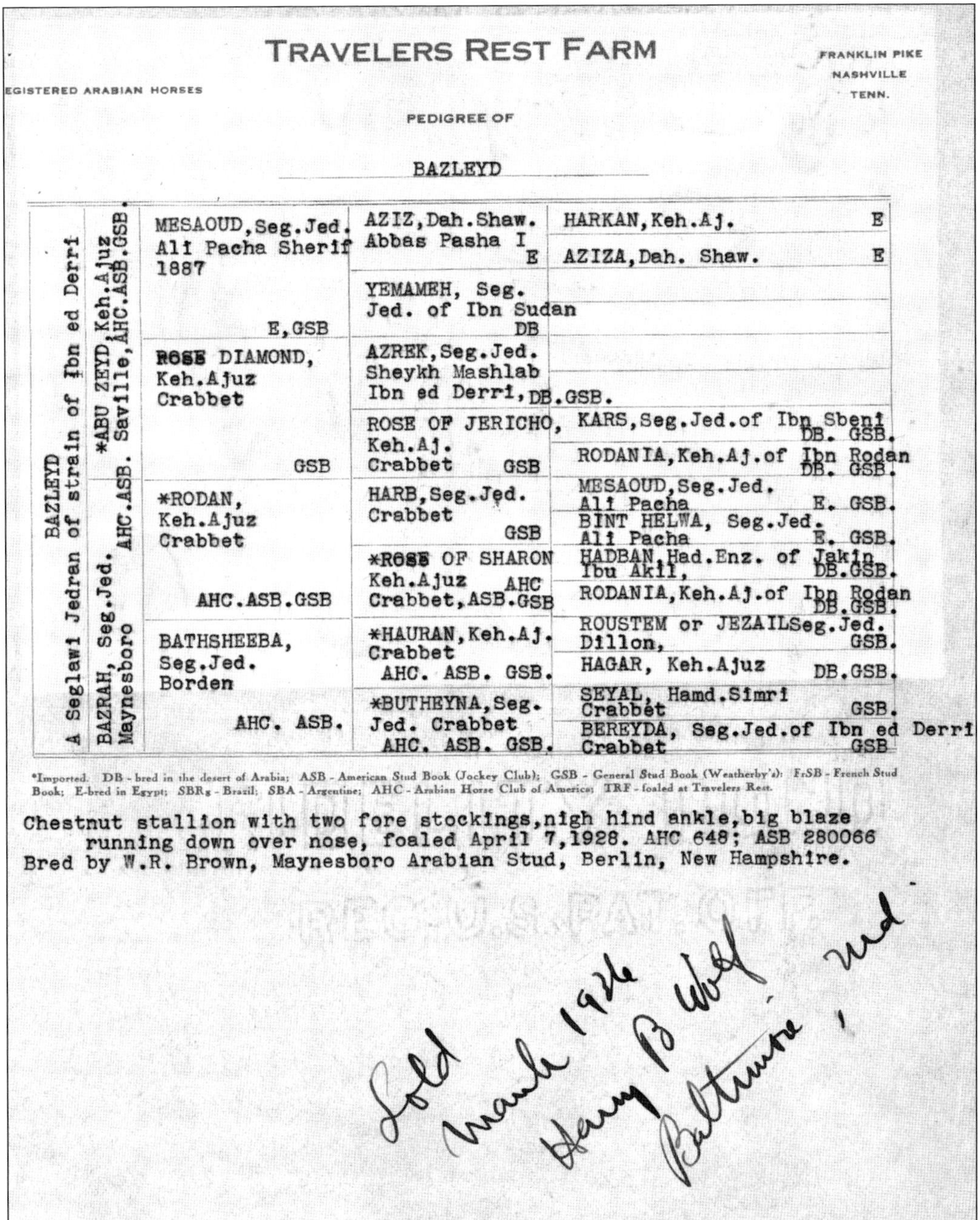

TRAVELERS REST FARM

EGISTERED ARABIAN HORSES

FRANKLIN PIKE
NASHVILLE
TENN.

PEDIGREE OF

BAZLEYD

BAZLEYD A Seglawi Jedran of strain of Ibn ed Derri	*ABU ZEYD, Keh.Ajuz Saville, AHC.ASB.GSB.	MESAOUD, Seg.Jed. Ali Pacha Sherif 1887 E, GSB	AZIZ, Dah.Shaw. Abbas Pasha I E	HARKAN, Keh.Aj. E AZIZA, Dah. Shaw. E
			YEMAMEH, Seg. Jed. of Ibn Sudan DB	
		ROSE DIAMOND, Keh.Ajuz Crabbet GSB	AZREK, Seg.Jed. Sheykh Mashlab Ibn ed Derri, DB.GSB.	
			ROSE OF JERICHO, Keh.Aj. Crabbet GSB	KARS, Seg.Jed.of Ibn Sbeni DB. GSB. RODANIA, Keh.Aj.of Ibn Rodan DB. GSB.
	BAZRAH, Seg.Jed. Maynesboro AHC.ASB.	*RODAN, Keh.Ajuz Crabbet AHC.ASB.GSB	HARB, Seg.Jed. Crabbet GSB	MESAOUD, Seg.Jed. Ali Pacha E. GSB. BINT HELWA, Seg.Jed. Ali Pacha E. GSB.
			*ROSE OF SHARON Keh.Ajuz AHC Crabbet, ASB.GSB	HADBAN, Had.Enz. of Jakin Ibu Akil, DB.GSB. RODANIA, Keh.Aj.of Ibn Rodan DB.GSB.
		BATHSHEEBA, Seg.Jed. Borden AHC. ASB.	*HAURAN, Keh.Aj. Crabbet AHC. ASB. GSB.	ROUSTEM or JEZAILSeg.Jed. Dillon, GSB. HAGAR, Keh.Ajuz DB.GSB.
			*BUTHEYNA, Seg. Jed. Crabbet AHC. ASB. GSB.	SEYAL, Hamd.Simri Crabbet GSB. BEREYDA, Seg.Jed.of Ibn ed Derri Crabbet GSB

*Imported. DB - bred in the desert of Arabia; ASB - American Stud Book (Jockey Club); GSB - General Stud Book (Weatherby's); FrSB - French Stud Book; E-bred in Egypt; SBRs - Brazil; SBA - Argentine; AHC - Arabian Horse Club of America; TRF - foaled at Travelers Rest.

Chestnut stallion with two fore stockings, nigh hind ankle, big blaze running down over nose, foaled April 7, 1928. AHC 648; ASB 280066
Bred by W.R. Brown, Maynesboro Arabian Stud, Berlin, New Hampshire.

Sold March 1936 Harry B Wolf Baltimore, Md

Bazleyd, foaled in New Hampshire, was the product of parents imported from England, where Arabian horses had been used to develop the Thoroughbred racehorse beginning in the late 17th century. Bazleyd's pedigree documents his pure Arabian breeding. A horse's "papers" accompany him each time he is sold to a new owner.

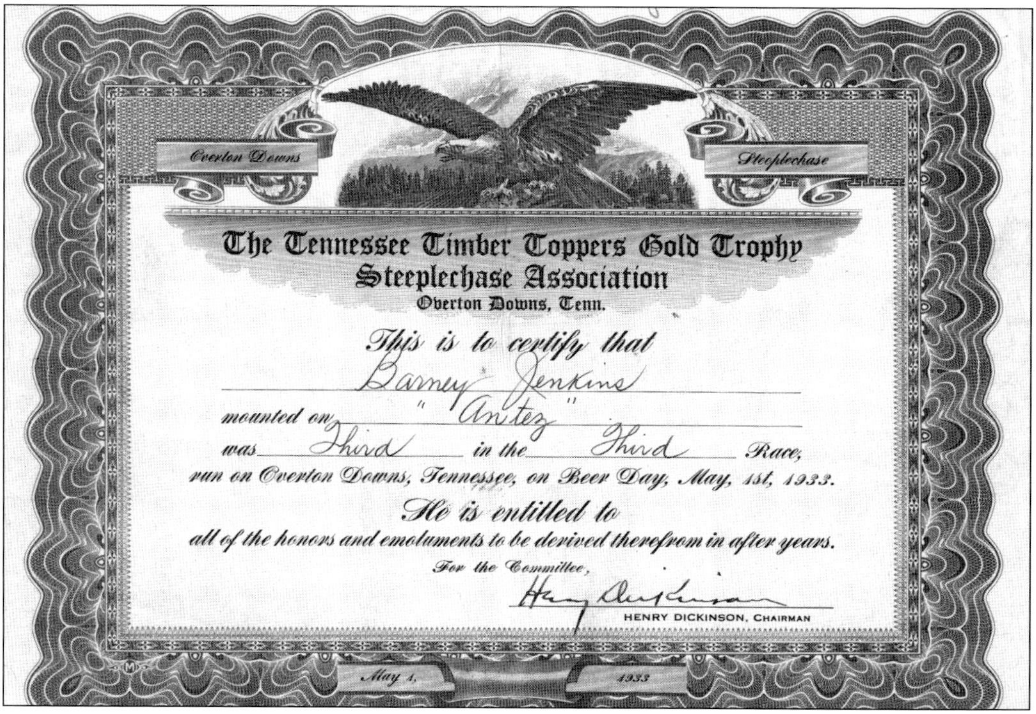

Overton Downs — Steeplechase

The Tennessee Timber Toppers Gold Trophy Steeplechase Association

Overton Downs, Tenn.

This is to certify that Barney Jenkins

mounted on "Antez"

was Third *in the* Third *Race,*

run on Overton Downs, Tennessee, on Beer Day, May, 1st, 1933.

He is entitled to

all of the honors and emoluments to be derived therefrom in after years.

For the Committee,

Henry Dickinson

HENRY DICKINSON, CHAIRMAN

May 1, 1933

In May 1933, for sport, Dickinson entered Antez and another of his Arabian horses, Kaibab, in a race with seasoned Thoroughbred racers. Though Antez was much smaller and had no formal race training, he finished a strong third to the two racehorses. Both of his Arabian horses received certificates of performance from the Tennessee Timber Toppers Gold Trophy Steeplechase Association.

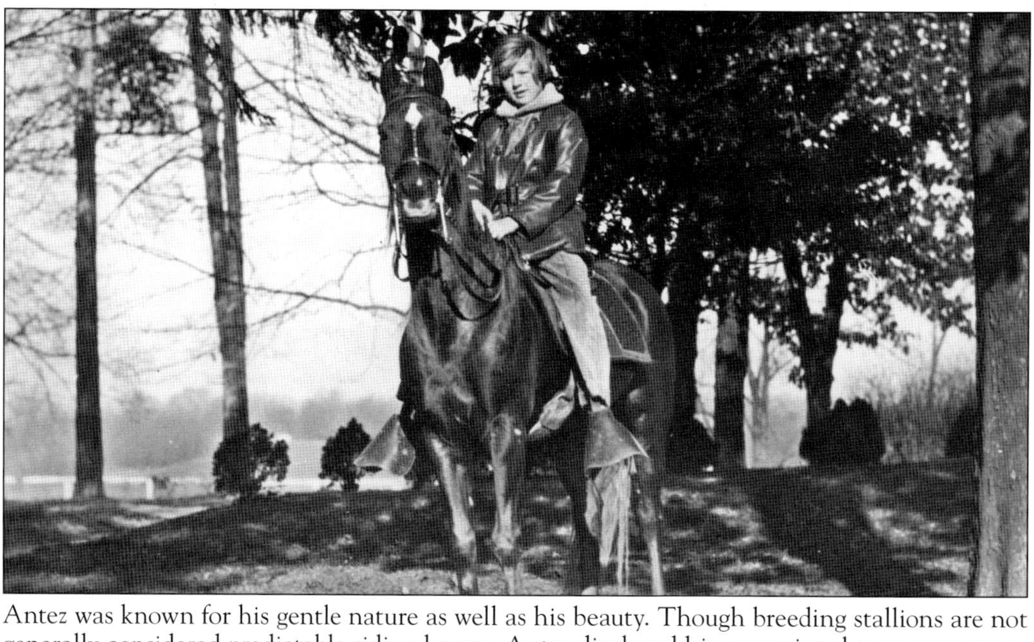

Antez was known for his gentle nature as well as his beauty. Though breeding stallions are not generally considered predictable riding horses, Antez displayed his exceptional temperament as the personal mount of Dickinson's 13-year-old daughter Margaret (Peggy).

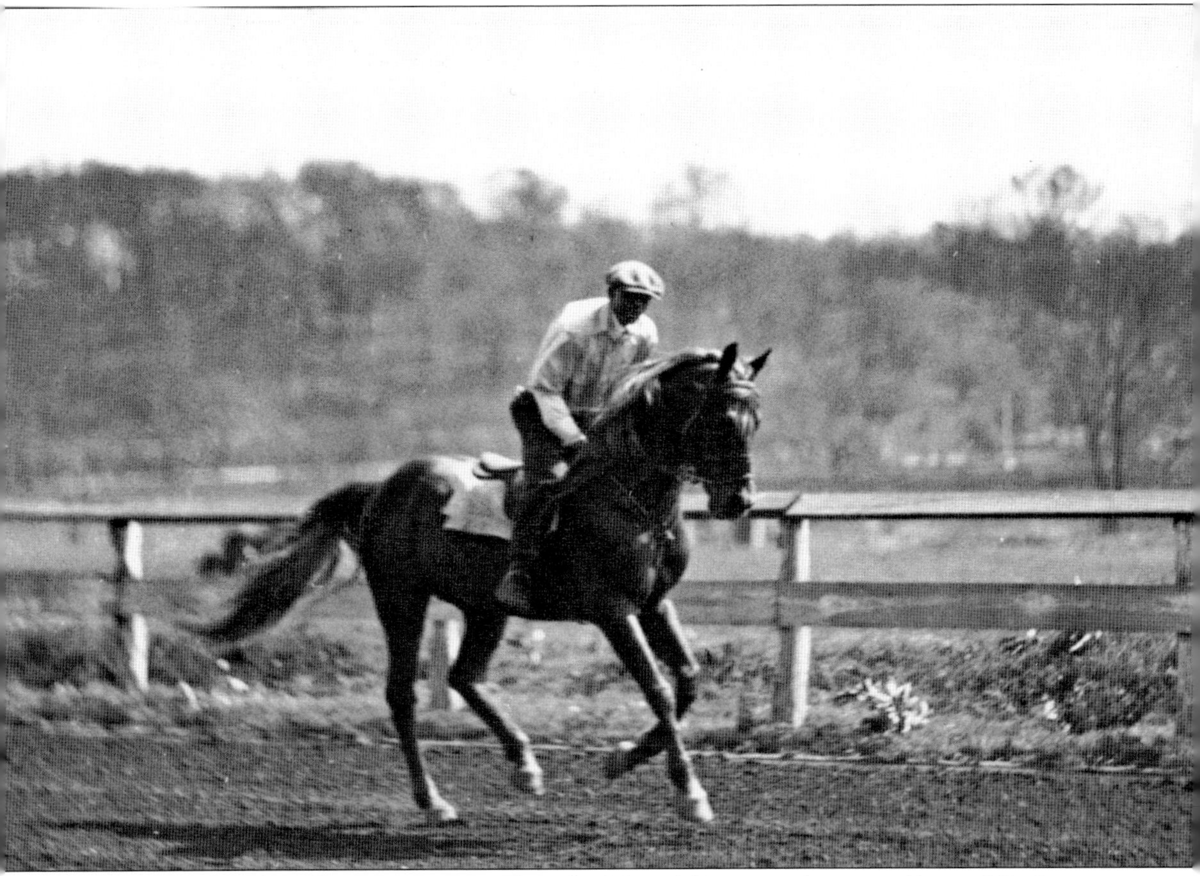

Though no Arabian horse races existed in the United States at the time, General Dickinson had compiled a list of record times for Arabian horses in other countries, mainly Egypt and Poland. Convinced of Antez's speed, Dickinson arranged for the horse to be tested in timed trials at several distances on May 23 and 31, 1933. At Nashville's Cumberland racetrack, ordinarily used for Standardbred trotting races, the speed tests were conducted under the auspices of the National Trotting Association. Antez was tested at one-half mile, three-quarter mile, and 1,200 meters, distances selected for comparison to standing records. Antez equaled a world record of 51 seconds at the half-mile and clocked impressive times at other distances too. After the trials, the half-mile track was measured and actually was nine and one-half feet over. Antez's rider for each timed test was Bernie Silver.

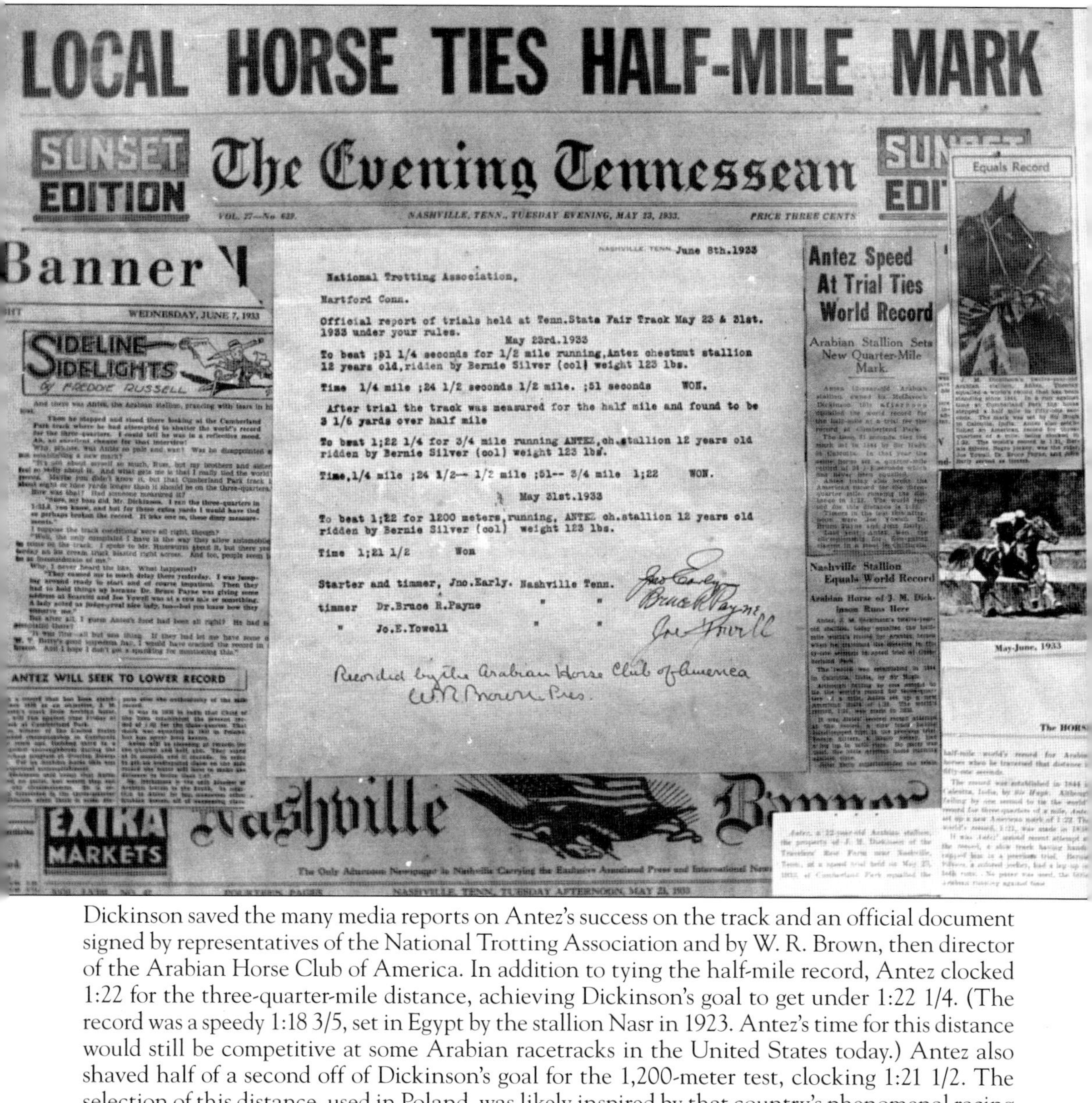

NASHVILLE, TENN. June 8th.1933

National Trotting Association,

Hartford Conn.

Official report of trials held at Tenn.State Fair Track May 23 & 31st. 1933 under your rules.

May 23rd.1933

To beat ;51 1/4 seconds for 1/2 mile running,Antez chestnut stallion 12 years old,ridden by Bernie Silver (col) weight 123 lbs.

Time 1/4 mile ;24 1/2 seconds 1/2 mile. ;51 seconds WON.

After trial the track was measured for the half mile and found to be 3 1/6 yards over half mile

To beat 1;22 1/4 for 3/4 mile running ANTEZ,ch.stallion 12 years old ridden by Bernie Silver (col) weight 123 lbs.

Time,1/4 mile ;24 1/2-- 1/2 mile ;51-- 3/4 mile 1;22 WON.

May 31st.1933

To beat 1;22 for 1200 meters,running, ANTEZ ch.stallion 12 years old ridden by Bernie Silver (col) weight 123 lbs.

Time 1;21 1/2 Won

Starter and timmer, Jno.Early. Nashville Tenn.

timmer Dr.Bruce R.Payne " "

" Jo.E.Yowell " "

Jno Early
Bruce R Payne
Joe Yowell

Recorded by the Arabian Horse Club of America
W.R. Brown Pres.

Dickinson saved the many media reports on Antez's success on the track and an official document signed by representatives of the National Trotting Association and by W. R. Brown, then director of the Arabian Horse Club of America. In addition to tying the half-mile record, Antez clocked 1:22 for the three-quarter-mile distance, achieving Dickinson's goal to get under 1:22 1/4. (The record was a speedy 1:18 3/5, set in Egypt by the stallion Nasr in 1923. Antez's time for this distance would still be competitive at some Arabian racetracks in the United States today.) Antez also shaved half of a second off of Dickinson's goal for the 1,200-meter test, clocking 1:21 1/2. The selection of this distance, used in Poland, was likely inspired by that country's phenomenal racing stallion Kaszmir, who clocked 1:21 in 1932.

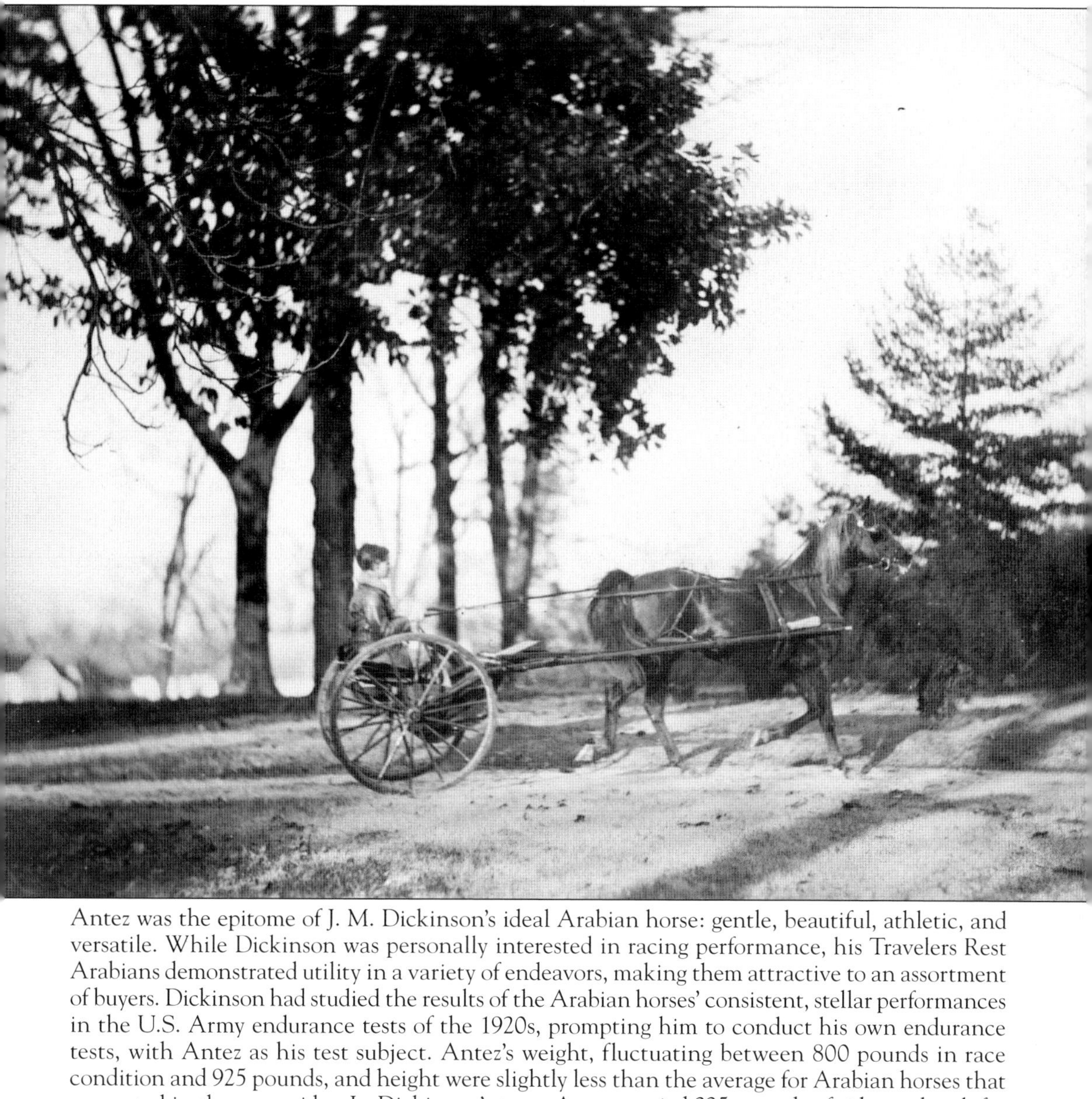

Antez was the epitome of J. M. Dickinson's ideal Arabian horse: gentle, beautiful, athletic, and versatile. While Dickinson was personally interested in racing performance, his Travelers Rest Arabians demonstrated utility in a variety of endeavors, making them attractive to an assortment of buyers. Dickinson had studied the results of the Arabian horses' consistent, stellar performances in the U.S. Army endurance tests of the 1920s, prompting him to conduct his own endurance tests, with Antez as his test subject. Antez's weight, fluctuating between 800 pounds in race condition and 925 pounds, and height were slightly less than the average for Arabian horses that competed in the army rides. In Dickinson's tests, Antez carried 225 pounds of rider and tack for 12 hours straight, five days in a row, over hilly terrain and country roads. This weight was carried by horses in the 1922 army. Dickinson noted the little horse was game for more.

W. R. BROWN, PRESIDENT
BERLIN, N. H.

A. W. HARRIS, VICE-PRESIDENT
CHICAGO, ILL.

H. S. GREGORY, SECRETARY-TREASURER
BERLIN, N. H.

The Arabian Horse Club of America

(Incorporated)

Office of the President
BERLIN, N. H.

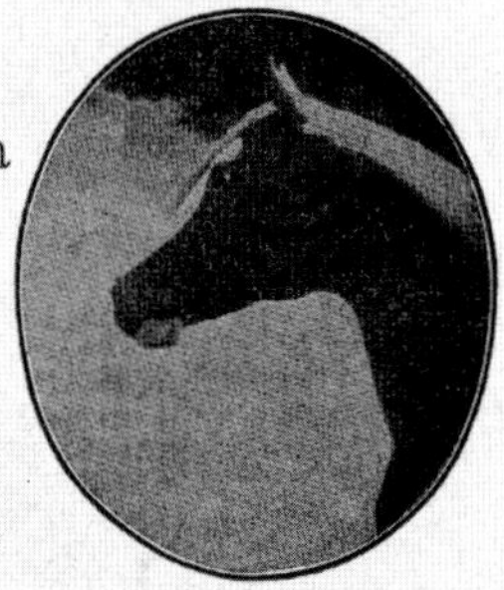

Directors
W. R. BROWN
BERLIN, N. H.
W. H. KELLOGG
POMONA, CALIF.
A. W. HARRIS
CHICAGO, ILL.
RAYMOND C. FORCE
SAN LEANDRO, CALIF.
J. M. DICKINSON
NASHVILLE, TENN.

November 10, 1934.

O F F I C I A L   S H O W   R E C O R D S
of
B A Z L E Y D
and
HIS PRODUCE

At the request of Mr. J. M. Dickinson, owner of Travelers Rest Farm, Nashville, Tennessee, I certify that the records of the Arabian Horse Club of America show that the following prizes have been won by Bazleyd and his produce:

1932
OHIO STATE FAIR

First Prize Arabian Stallion	BAZLEYD
Second Prize Three Gaited Arabian	BAZLEYD
Champion Arabian Horse of the Show	BAZLEYD

1933
NATIONAL ARABIAN HORSE SHOW
TENNESSEE STATE FAIR

Champion Arabian Stallion	BAZLEYD	
Third Prize Five Gaited Arabian	BAZLEYD	
Third Prize Arabian Colt or Filly	GAYZA,	daughter of Bazleyd
Four Prize Arabian Colt or Filly	JU-DHAR,	son of Bazleyd
Fifth Prize Arabian Colt or Filly	GUTNE,	daughter of Bazleyd

1934
NATIONAL ARABIAN HORSE SHOW
TENNESSEE STATE FAIR

First Prize Five Gaited Arabian	BAZLEYD	
Champion Arabian Colt or Filly	JAGAI,	son of Bazleyd
Fifth Prize Arabian Colt or Filly	GAYZA,	daughter of Bazleyd
First Prize Weanling Arabian	JAGAI,	son of Bazleyd
Third Prize Yearling Arabian	GAYZA,	daughter of Bazleyd
Fourth Prize Yearling Arabian	JU-DHAR,	son of Bazleyd
Second Prize 2 or 3 Year Stallion or Mare	GUTNE	daughter of Bazleyd

Berlin, New Hampshire, November 10, 1934.

Hubert S. Gregory
Secretary.

THIS PAPER, SUBSTANCE 24, IS MADE FROM 100% BROWN COMPANY ALPHA FIBRE

Bazleyd was apparently not a subject of General Dickinson's race tests, though he did earn the title National Champion Arabian Stallion in both 1933 and 1934. Dickinson kept Bazleyd's show record, and that of some offspring, on the official letterhead of the Arabian Horse Club of America, founded in 1908.

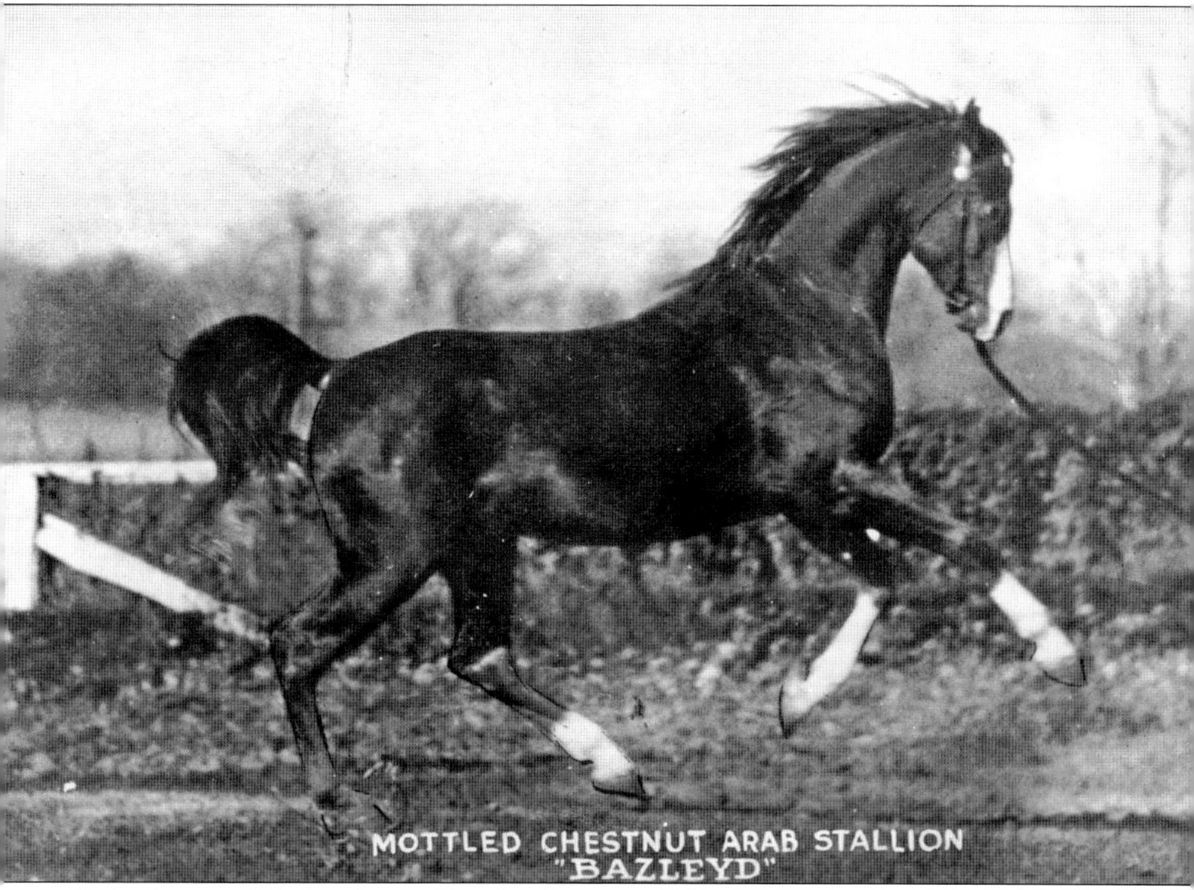

Bazleyd was used for breeding at Travelers Rest from 1931 to 1936, when he was sold to a new owner in Maryland. Dickinson was willing to part even with his champions, always looking to incorporate fresh bloodlines, which was not easy, given the small Arabian horse population in America at the time.

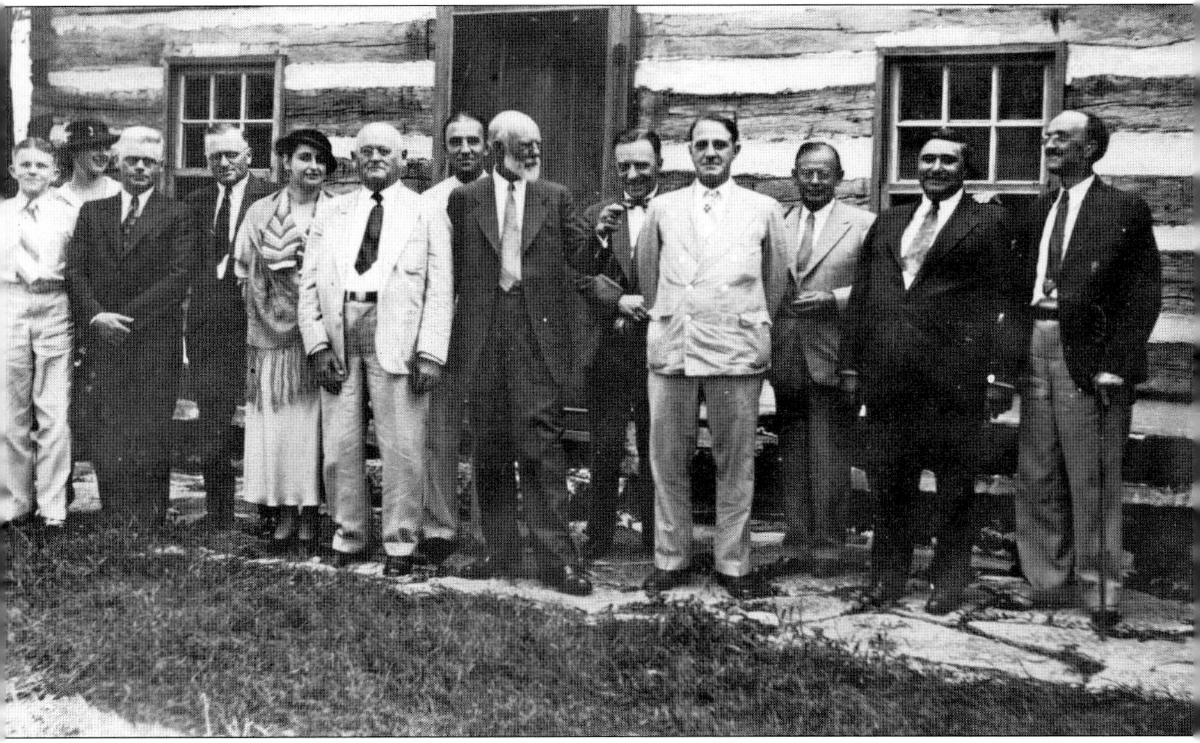

In 1933, the small Arabian horse community assembled in Nashville when General Dickinson arranged for the Tennessee State Fair to host a national Arabian horse show. Dickinson is right of center in the light-colored, buttoned, double-breasted suit. To his right, centered in front of the doorway, is Albert Harris, who competed on Arabian horses in the army's annual endurance rides of the 1920s. Challenging horses' soundness, stamina, and agility, the tests were dominated by Arabian horses, leading to the incorporation of the breed into the army's horse breeding program. To the right of Harris, in the unbuttoned, light-colored suit, is Will K. Kellogg, of cornflake fame. Kellogg introduced thousands of spectators to the Arabian horse at his Pomona, California, ranch, where his Arabian horses performed tricks and drills for Sunday crowds. Kellogg even sent a team of performance horses to the Nashville show, including Jadaan, equine star of the silent film *The Son of the Sheik*, starring Rudolph Valentino.

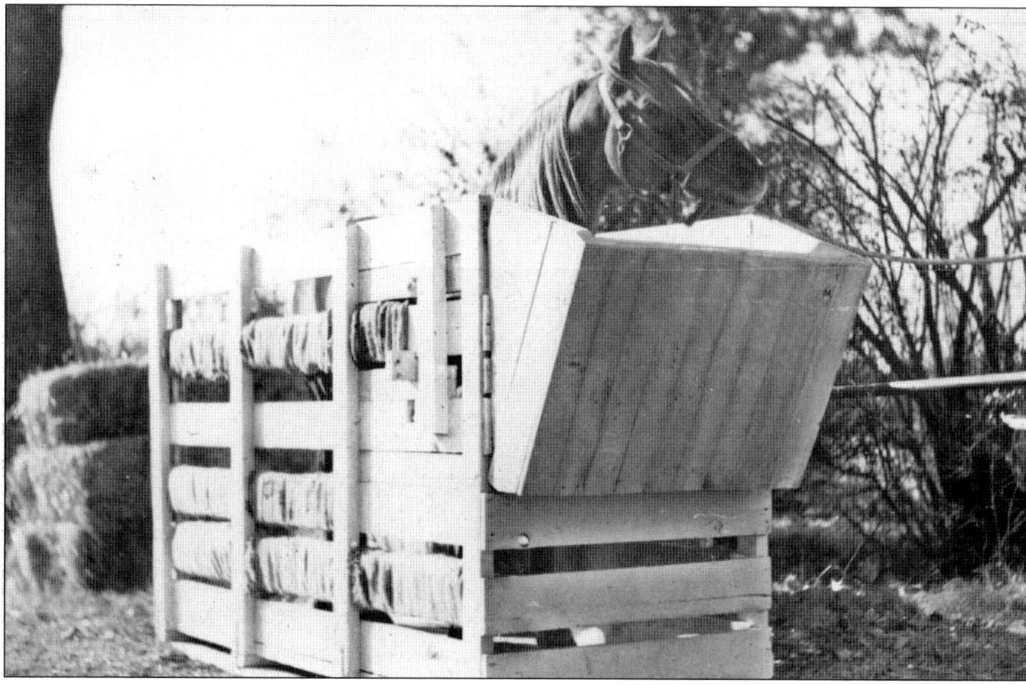

As Travelers Rest Arabian Stud was operated as a business, rather than a hobby, not even the local horse hero Antez was immune to sale. Crated for shipment to Poland in 1934, the stallion bears his usual look of interest in activity around him. The horse had an individual presence that was readily captured in photographs. In Poland, an article on Antez's racing accomplishments ran in the prominent horse magazine *Jezdiec I Hodowca* (translated "The Horseman and the Breeder") in 1933. Horse breeders there utilized racing to test the quality of breeding stock. Antez was used for breeding by Count Potocki in 1935 and Count Rostwordwski in 1936, opening the door between Travelers Rest (as well as the United States) and one of the most respected countries for breeding of Arabian horses.

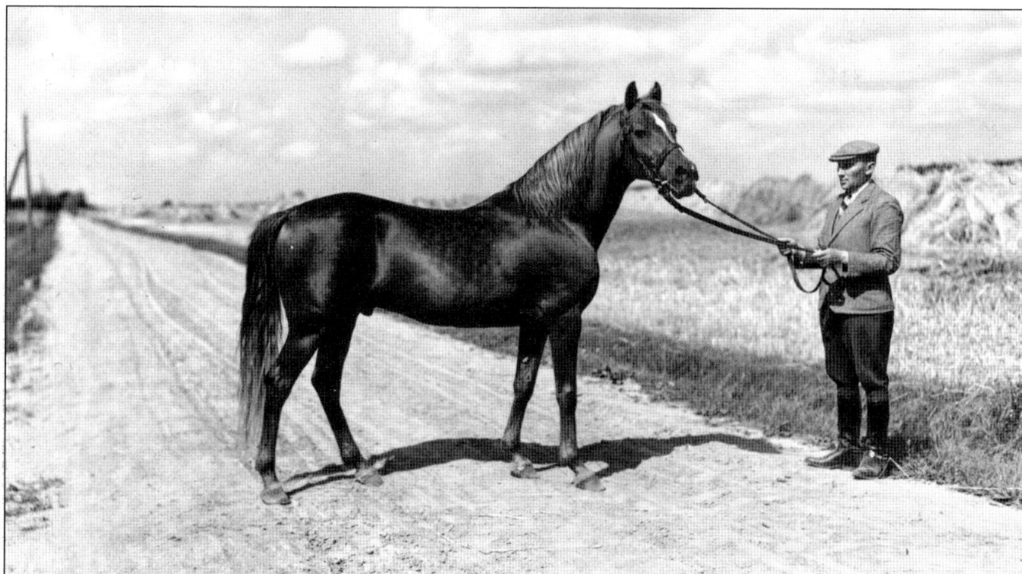

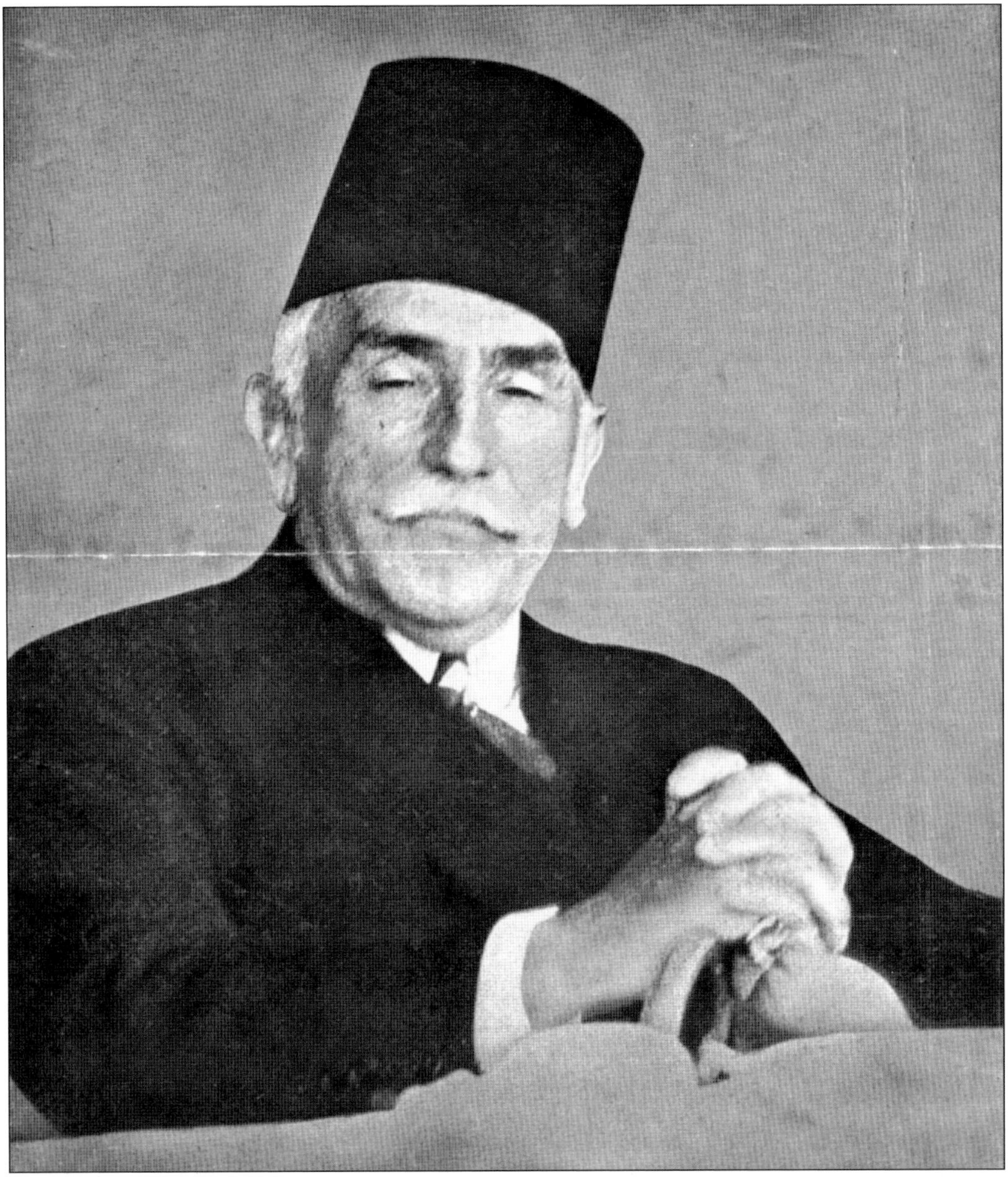

The Egyptian prince Mohamed Ali Tewfik was the breeder of a handful of Arabian horses that came to Dickinson's Travelers Rest by way of their importer, W. R. Brown. Brown imported several of the prince's horses in the 1930s, including the grey mare *Hamama (the asterisk denotes importation to the United States) and the outstanding race stallion *Nasr (mentioned above).

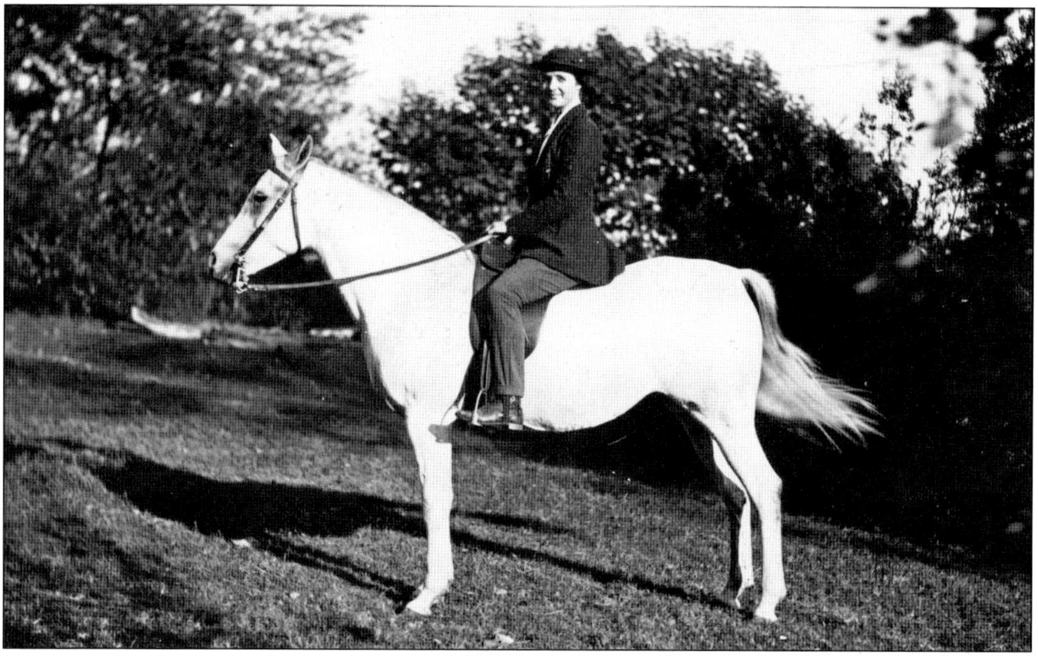

*Hamama is shown here with General Dickinson's daughter Marge. At the National Arabian Shows of 1933 and 1934 at the Tennessee State Fair, *Hamama won several championships titles. General Dickinson was not long without a proven Arabian racehorse following Antez's departure to Poland. He acquired the grey stallion *Nasr from W. R. Brown. *Nasr was the Arabian record holder for not only the three-quarter mile, but also for the distance of one-and-a-quarter mile, at 2:20, a time he set in Egypt in 1924. For Brown, *Nasr won the Reserve Champion Stallion title at the 1933 National Arabian horse show held in Nashville. He repeated this honor at the 1934 show for Travelers Rest, newly under Dickinson's ownership. He went on to sire many Travelers Rest foals.

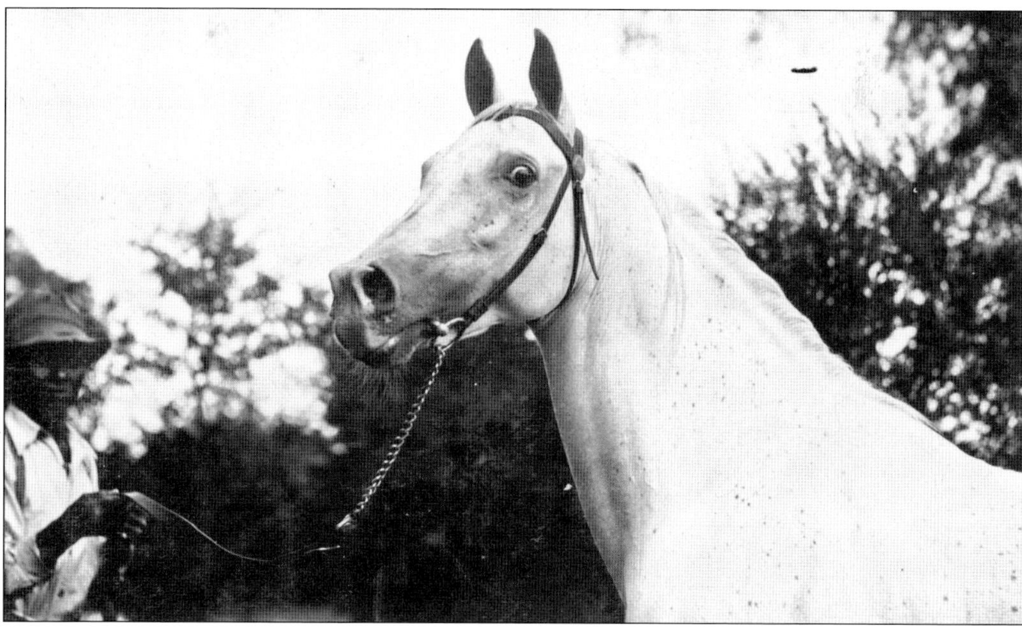

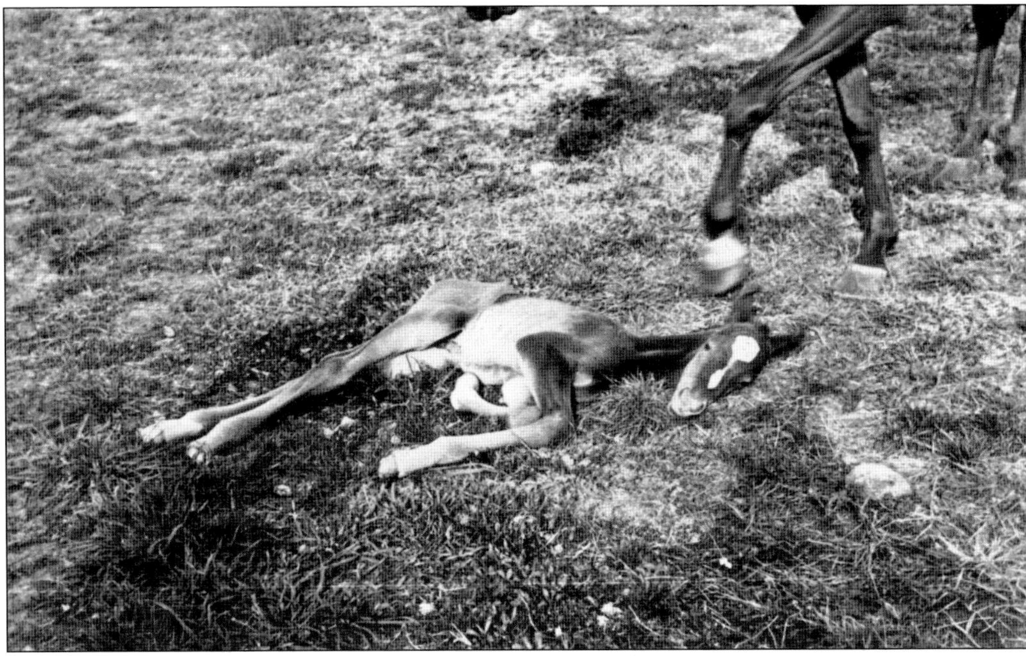

Pictured here is the 1937 newborn colt Bady, sired by *Nasr. Bady was sold to South Carolina that same year as a weanling. Also pictured is a pasture at Travelers Rest, filled with a herd of young horses. Dickinson set uniform prices for all weanlings of the same sex: $400 for colts, $700 for fillies, even when some could command higher dollar. The majority of his clients were middle- and working-class ranchers, farmers, and pleasure riders. Between 1930 and 1949, Dickinson bred 274 horses, sold to buyers in 40 states and 13 foreign countries. Dickinson documented the accomplishments of Travelers Rest Arabians in his yearly *Catalog of Travelers Rest Arabian Horses*. These books, no longer in print, were invaluable collections of historical information about the breeding of Arabian horses in foreign countries and in the United States.

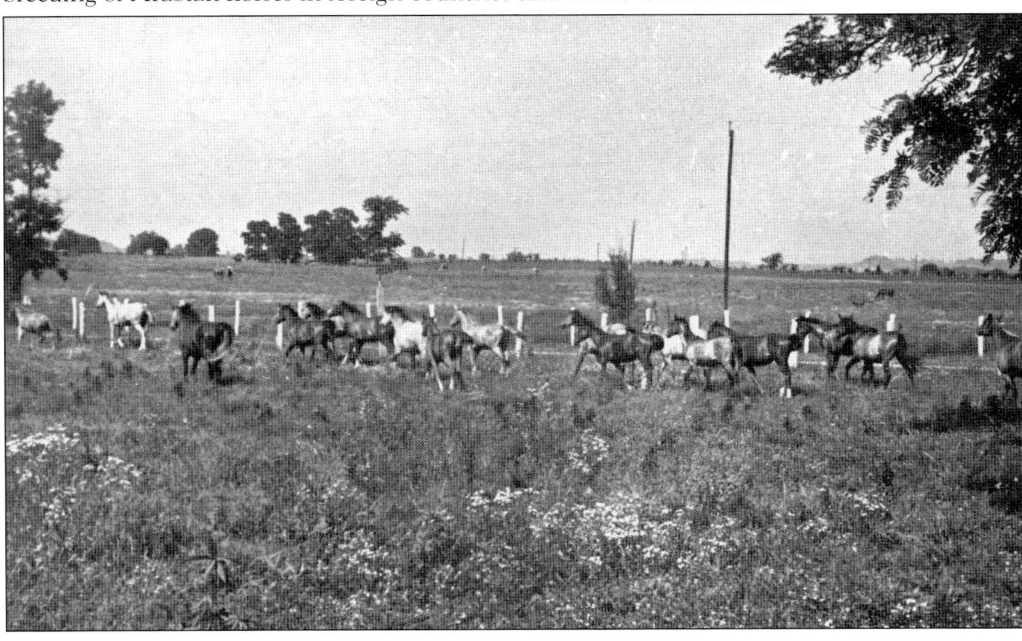

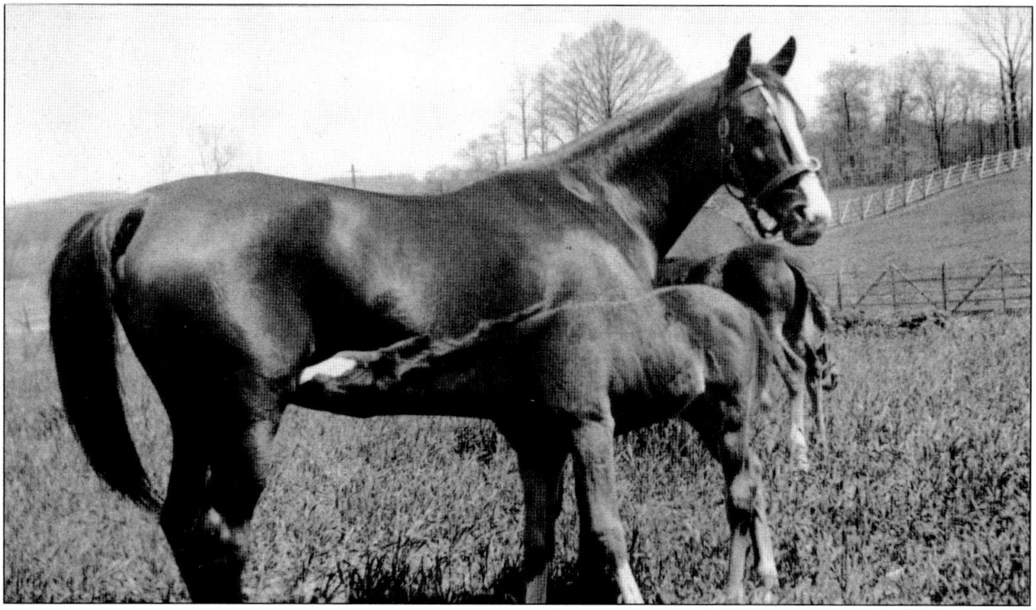

The chestnut mare *Exochorda was bred by the Royal Agricultural Society of Egypt. Originally named Leila II, she was raced in Egypt under the name Marquita and was imported to the United States in 1931 by a Dr. Heberman. Dickinson noted that the mare's parents were also racehorses, which likely attracted his interest in adding her to the Travelers Rest broodmare band. *Exochorda's 1932 filly was Suleika, bred by Heberman.

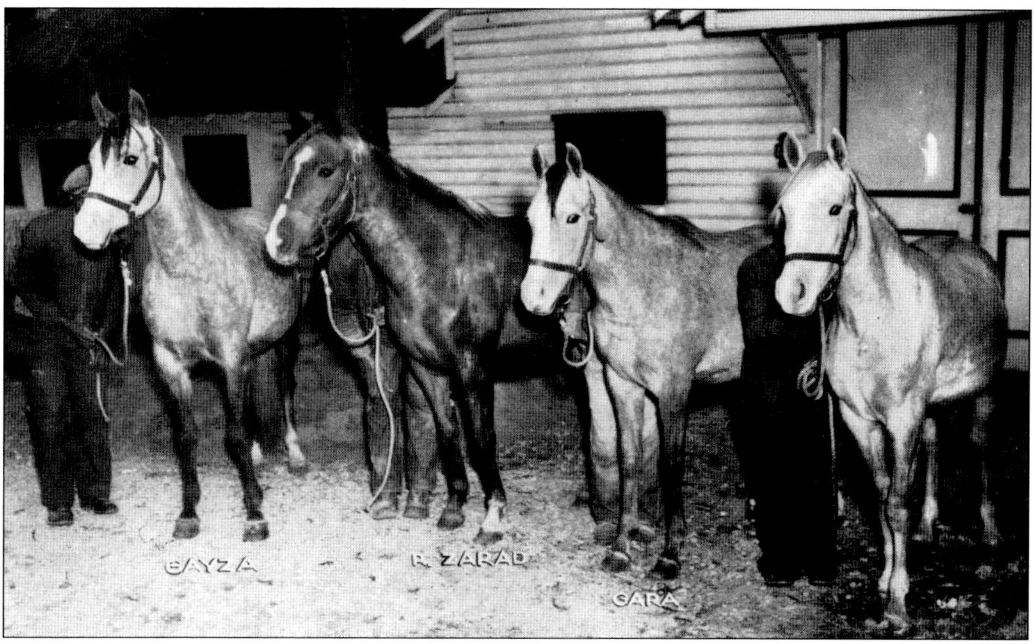

From left to right are Gayza (1933), R Zarad (1933), Gara (1935), and Jellaby (1935). These four young horses were exported to England in 1936, demonstrating Dickinson's international influence. Gayza and Gara were sired by the stallion Bazleyd. Jellaby was the product of Egyptian imports *Nasr and *Hamama. All four horses had winning show records in Europe, and Jellaby also earned a living as a dispatch mount during World War II.

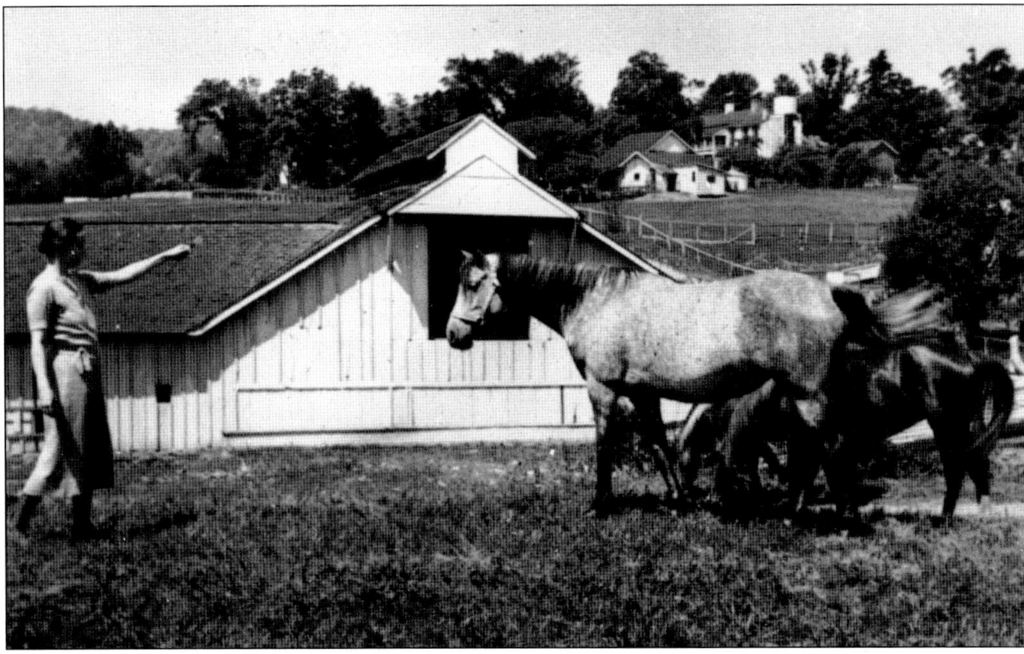

Here are two views of the Travelers Rest farm: the main residence and outbuildings in the far background and a panorama that includes Walter Jones in the background. Also a small dwelling can be seen, perhaps the residence of farm help. Travelers Rest changed in appearance and location over the centuries of its existence. The original home built by Judge Overton underwent several additions and removals during the first half of the 19th century. As the acreage accompanying the home had decreased over the years, there was not enough land to accommodate General Dickinson's flourishing Arabian horse breeding operation. The family and horses moved to another location outside of Nashville on Del Rio Pike. In 1946, Dickinson sold the historic Travelers Rest and moved his Travelers Rest Arabian Stud to Santa Barbara, California.

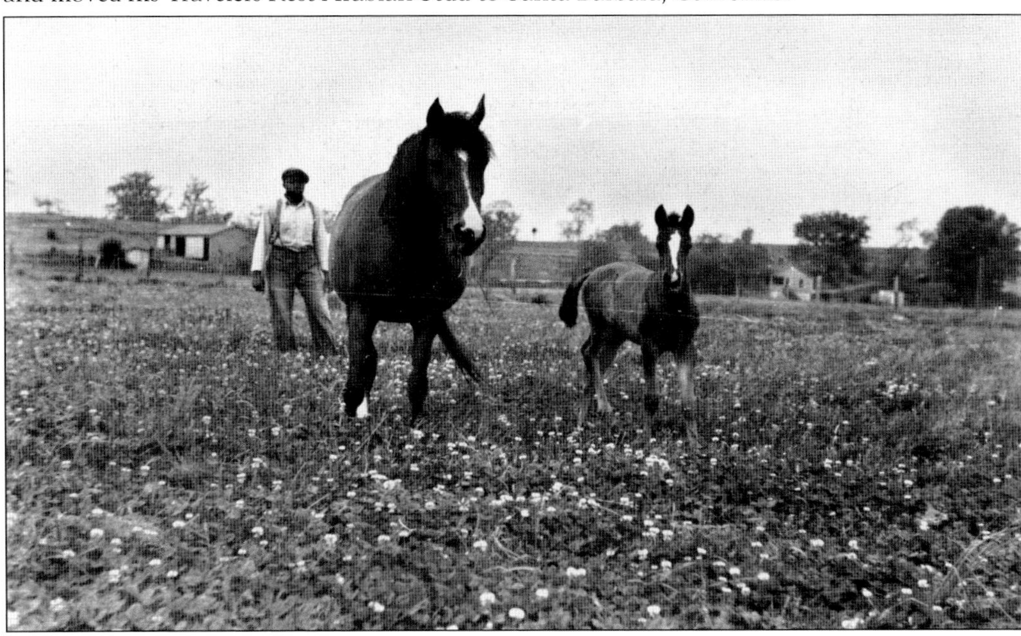

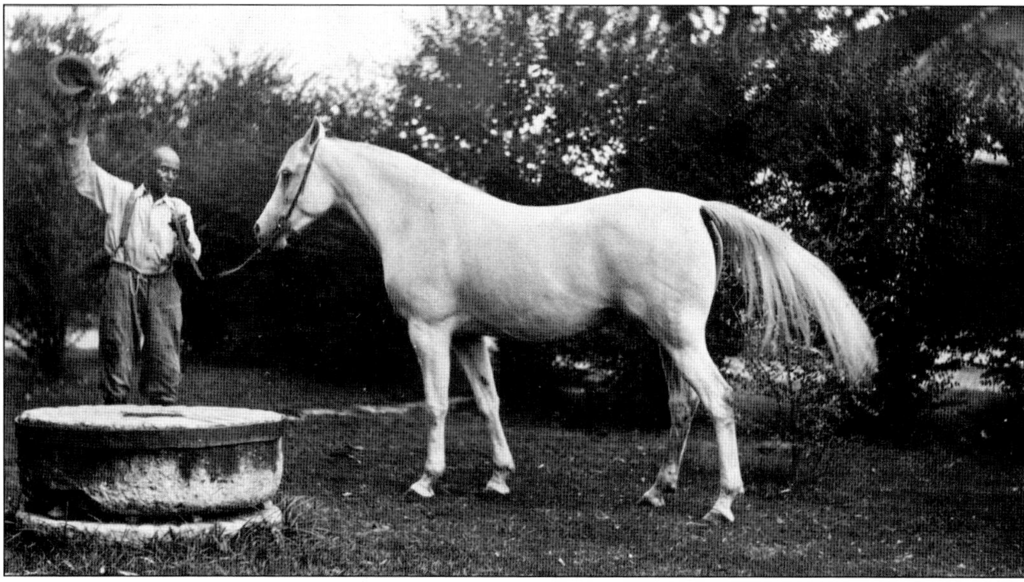

Historically, in the antebellum South, a slave could elevate his position through his horsemanship. These skills were desirable to horse breeders, such as Dickinson, into the 20th century. Sandy Hughes was a respected and admired trainer for Travelers Rest, and General Dickinson introduced him to visitors as his friend. At the time, African Americans were not allowed to show, however. So Travelers Rest Arabians were shown by other riders, including Dickinson's daughter Peggy. The Dickinson children called Hughes "Uncle Sandy," and he taught them how to ride. From left to right, the Dickinson family is William, Maxie, McGavock, Rufus, Margaret, Peggy, and Edith. Hughes moved to California when Dickinson relocated there. At the age of 86, Uncle Sandy helped establish the new farm before returning home to Tennessee.

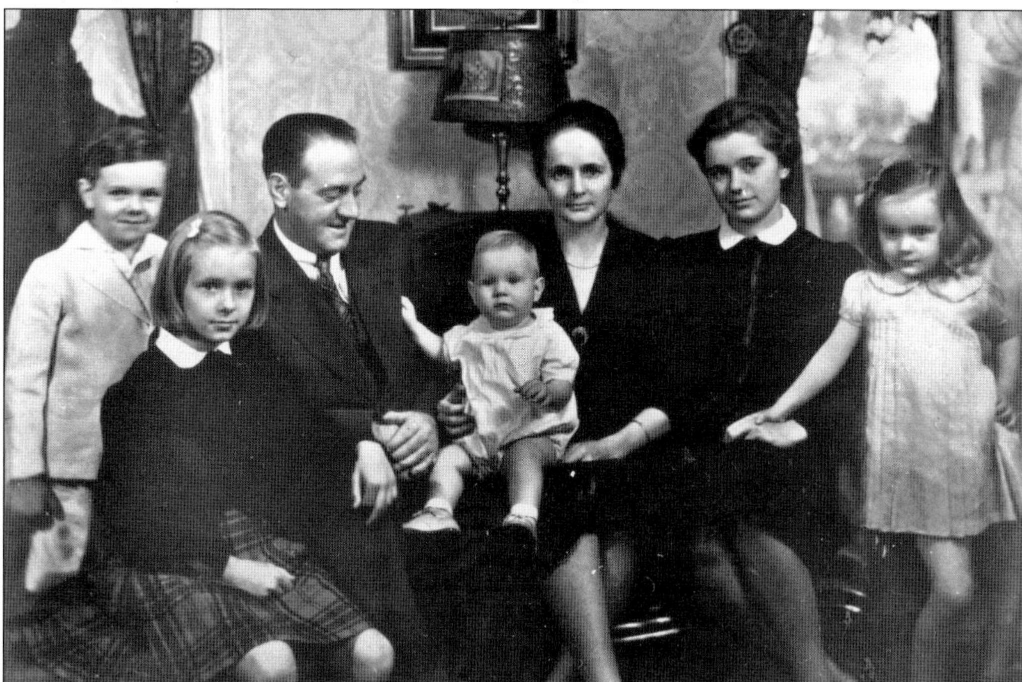

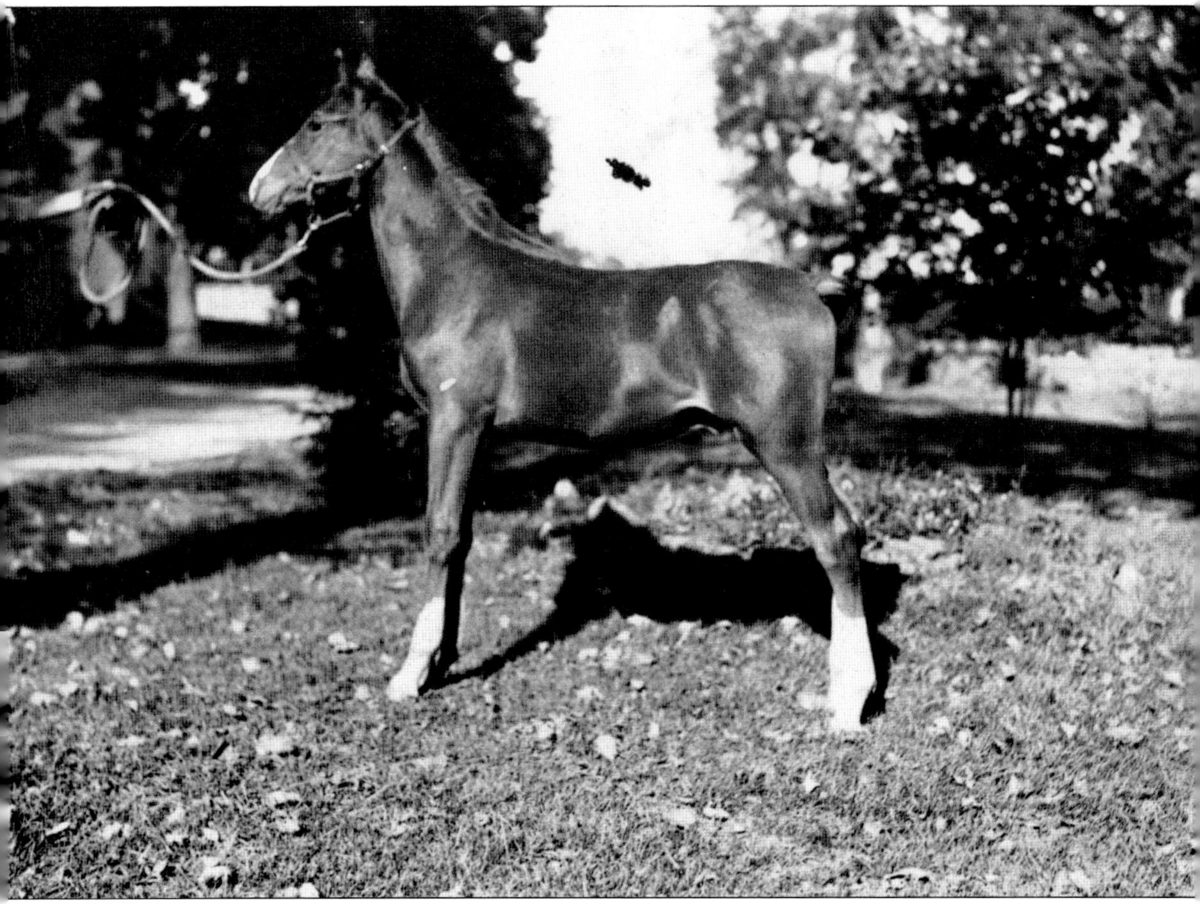

The young colt Khyber is in an awkward stage. He developed into a beautiful and useful stallion. He was sold to the U.S. Remount Service during World War II and was appreciated for his versatility. Khyber's sire was Kaibab, Antez's stablemate entered in the 1933 Timber Toppers race. Years after the closing of Travelers Rest Arabian Stud, Dickinson's legacy as a pioneer of Arabian horse racing came through Khyber. Under other ownership, Khyber sired Kinchi, who was bred to Subic, a Travelers Rest mare herself. The resulting filly, Kapaphal, later produced Ghami (1961), who raced successfully in 1968 after Arabian racing became an officially sanctioned sport. Another son of Khyber was Gudea, bred by Dickinson and born at Travelers Rest. Gudea was grandsire of Speed Queen, a winner of her two races in 1970, as well as her brother Speed King.

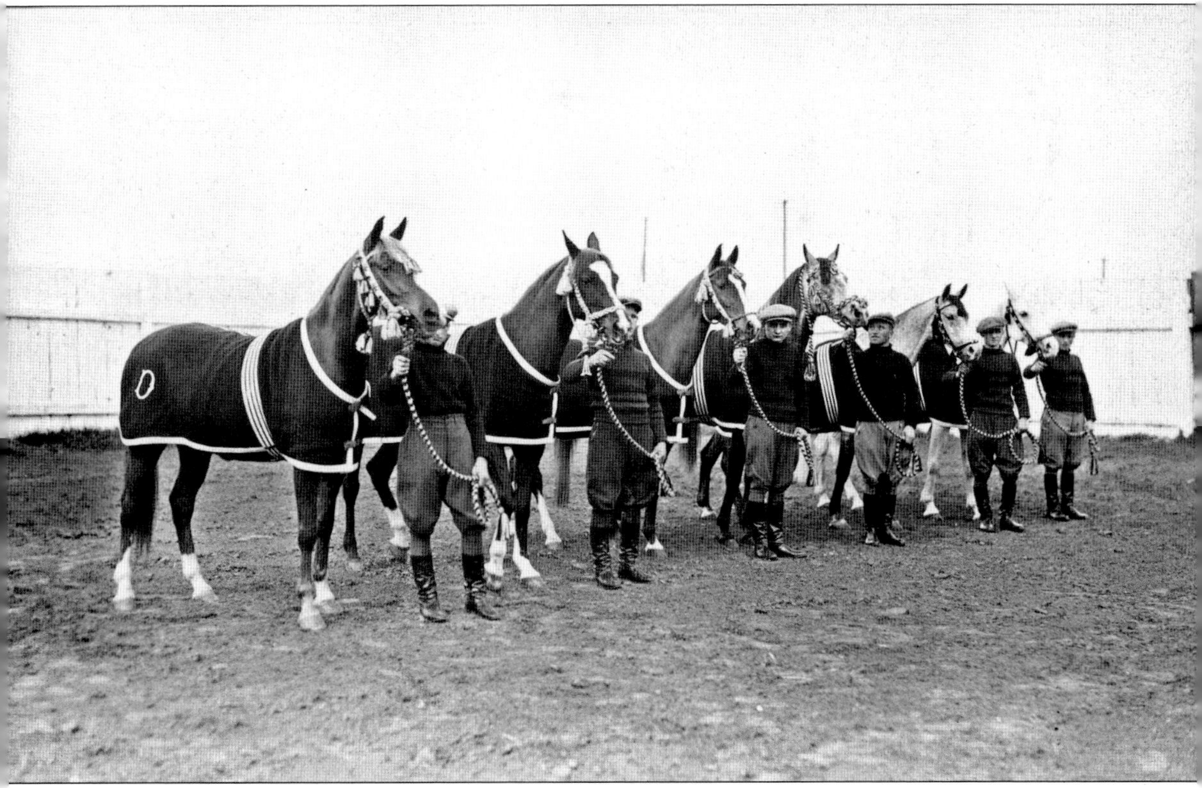

General Dickinson's business dealing with Poland in 1934 (the selling of Antez) was reciprocated in 1937. Through his regular correspondence with Arabian horse breeders there, Dickinson had cultivated a source of new bloodlines of historic lineage and proven racing ability. He and his family traveled to Hoboken, New Jersey, to greet the shipment of six Arabian mares on the SS *Batory*. Four of the mares were in foal, two to Antez. The implication of the purchase was two-fold: Dickinson was the first person to bring Polish Arabian horses to the United States, expanding the available gene pool of the breed here; additionally, the importation of mares proved significant by 1939, when Poland came under German attack. As Europe became embroiled in World War II, Germany confiscated horses from several countries, including Poland, to breed "superhorses" for war. Thus Dickinson's importation effectively prevented the loss of important bloodlines. The mares were Przepiorka, Lassa, Nora, Liliana, Mattaria, and Niwka.

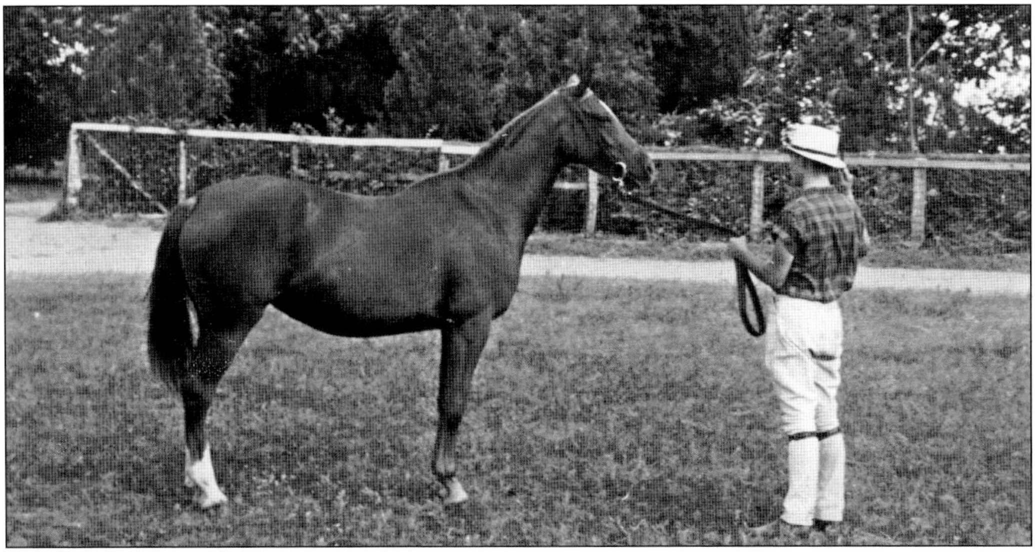

*Przepiorka was a chestnut mare from the esteemed Polish state stud farm Janow-Podlaski. Her sire, Almanzor, was a leading sire of racehorses in Poland. For Travelers Rest, *Przepiorka produced foals by several different stallions, including the Egyptian racehorse *Nasr. One colt of this mating, Ptolemy, later sired the horse Hampton, who raced once, winning, in 1962 during the fledgling years of Arabian horse racing in the United States.

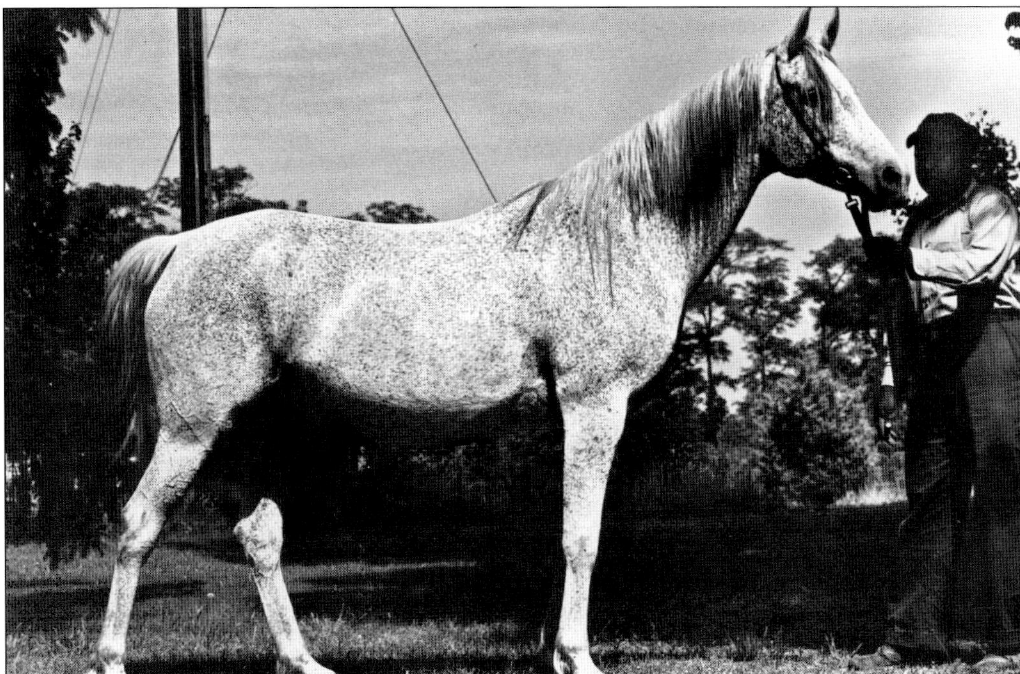

*Niwka was a grey mare from Janow-Podlaski whose sire, Fetysz, was valued for his athleticism. In Poland, *Niwka was trained for racing. Bred to Dickinson's Egyptian racer *Nasr, *Niwka produced Tirs, grandsire of Rickmar Hondio, who achieved success in the early days of American Arabian racing at the Ohio state fairgrounds. *Niwka also produced Subic, previously mentioned as the grandam of another racing descendant of Travelers Rest bloodlines (see Khyber).

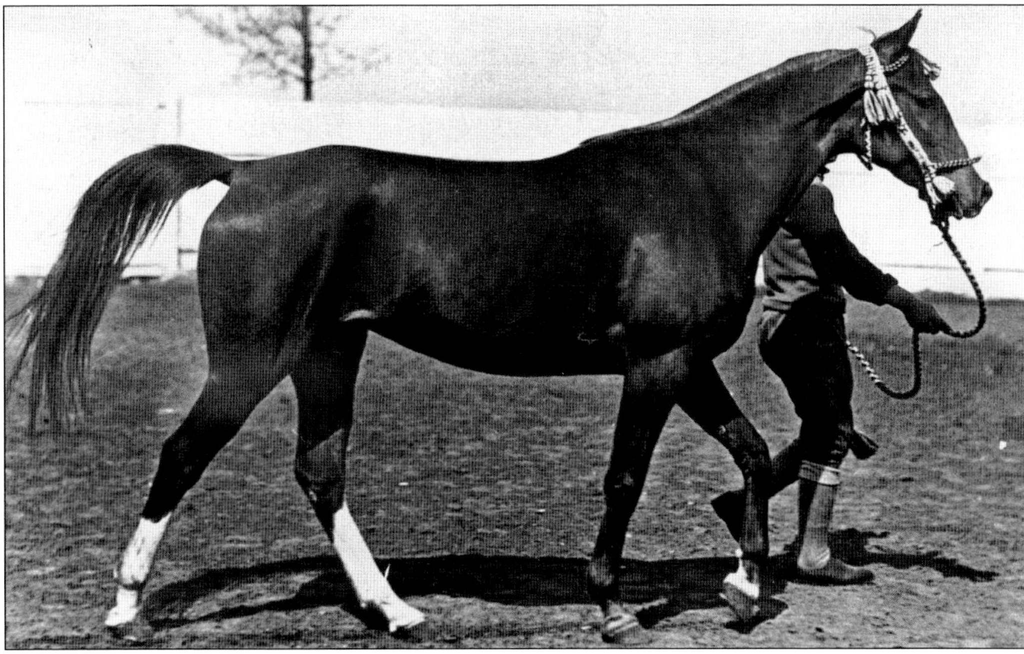

*Nora, from Janow-Podlaski, represented the successful racing bloodlines of her sire, Hardy, who was undefeated for two seasons. Five Hardy sons were confiscated by Germany during World War II. *Nora was imported in foal to Lowelas, a prominent Polish stallion who had five sons seized by Germany. *Nora's foal was named Janow, honoring the preeminent Polish state stud. Janow later sired the mare Serdecka, who produced several early American racers.

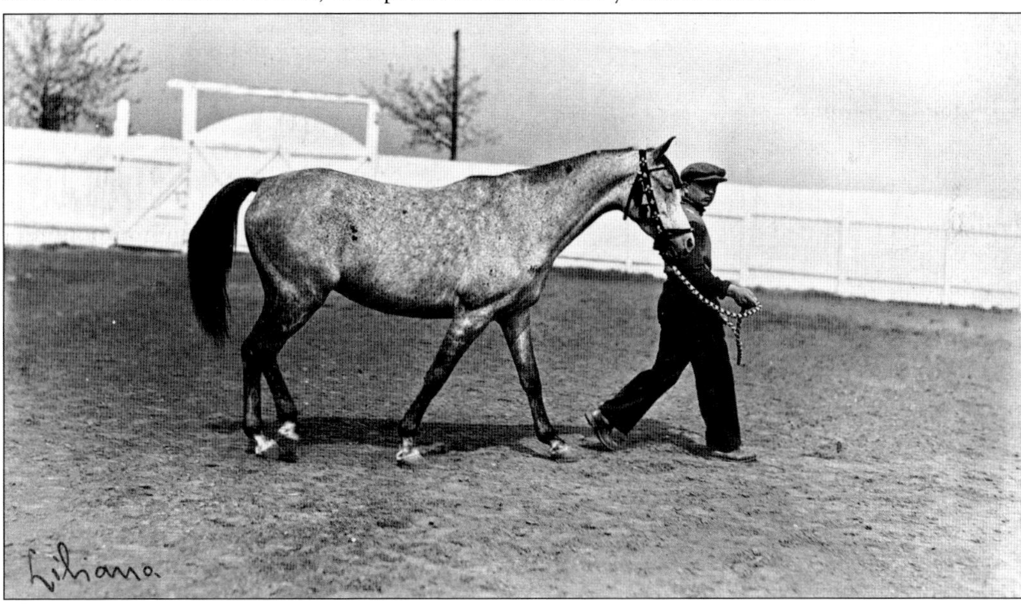

*Liliana was a small, grey mare who came from the private estate of Jana Kleniewskiego at Zagloba-Opole. She arrived in foal to the former Travelers Rest stallion Antez. The resulting filly was named Sielanka. *Liliana later produced the stallion Lwow (named for a Polish city), whose son Ibn Lwow was among the group of horses entered in the first official Arabian horse race, held in 1959 (see next chapter).

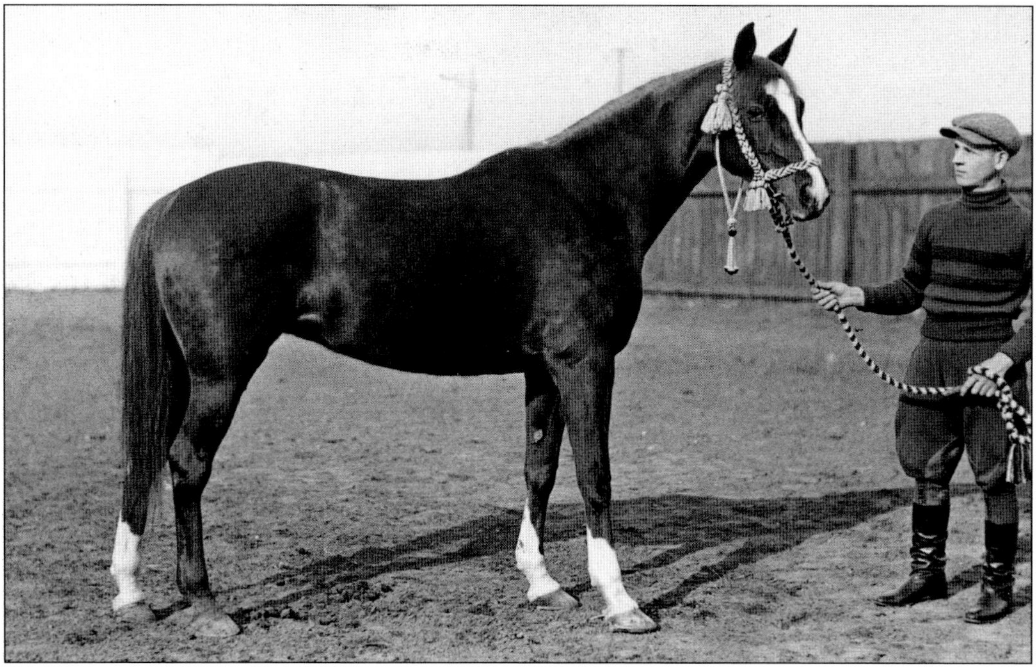

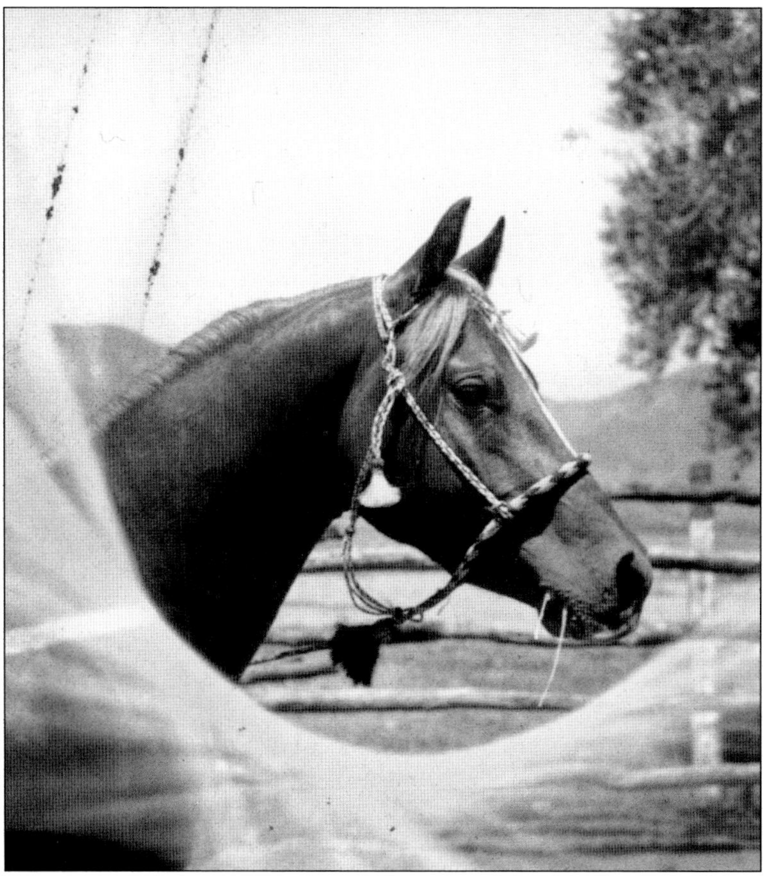

*Lassa was a large chestnut mare sired by Koheilan I, leading sire of race winners in Poland. Dickinson wrote to Janow-Podlaski director Stanislaw Pohoski, lauding the mare's great success in the showring in the hands of 10-year-old Maxi Dickinson. After Travelers Rest ceased breeding operations, *Lassa sold to Mrs. Bazy Tankersley, owner of Al-Marah Arabian farm, as well as the organizer of the first official Arabian horse race, held in Maryland in 1959. *Latif was *Lassa's son by Antez, imported in utero from Poland. *Lassa also produced Laab, a 1960s racer.

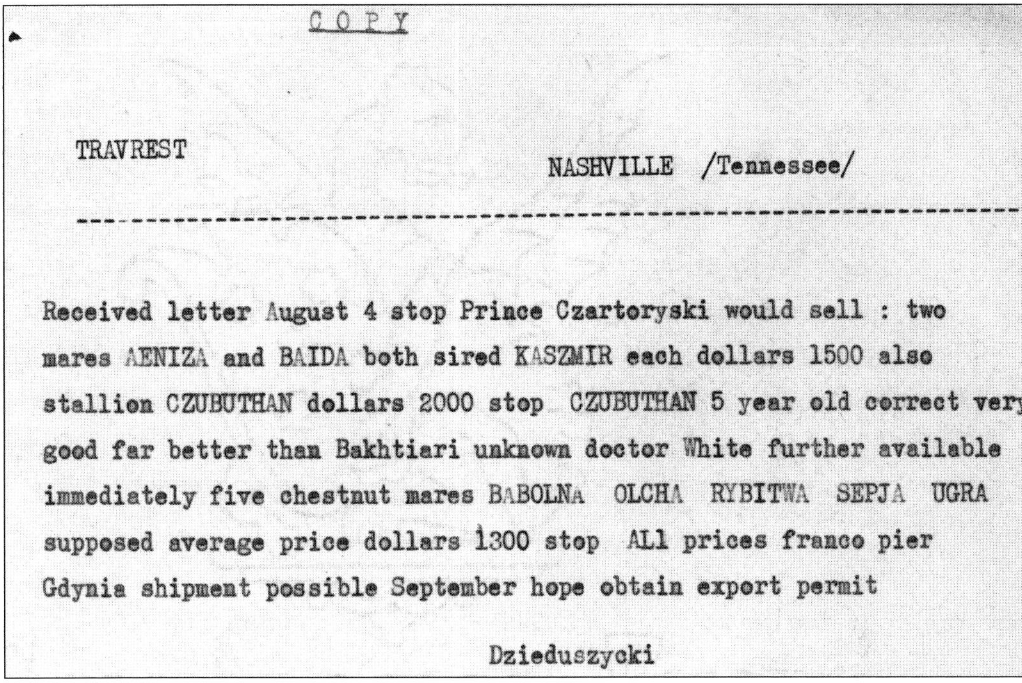

COPY

TRAVREST

NASHVILLE /Tennessee/

Received letter August 4 stop Prince Czartoryski would sell : two mares AENIZA and BAIDA both sired KASZMIR each dollars 1500 also stallion CZUBUTHAN dollars 2000 stop CZUBUTHAN 5 year old correct very good far better than Bakhtiari unknown doctor White further available immediately five chestnut mares BABOLNA OLCHA RYBITWA SEPJA UGRA supposed average price dollars 1300 stop All prices franco pier Gdynia shipment possible September hope obtain export permit

Dzieduszycki

General Dickinson's friend Dr. George Ransom White, M.D., D.V.M., of Nashville visited Travelers Rest in August 1937 following the May arrival of the Polish mares. White, recently returned from Poland, regaled Dickinson with his enthusiastic praise of Poland, its people, and horses, prompting Dickinson to inquire of Polish breeders about the possibility of acquiring more horses, including a stallion. White considered two Polish stallions the best he had seen in the world, Kaszmir, the exceptional racer, and Ofir, so Dickinson tactfully inquired as to their availability. Count Alexander Dzieduszycki, president of the Arab Horse Breeding Society of Poland, replied first by telegram, offering terms on two Kaszmir daughters, the stallion Czubuthan, and several other mares.

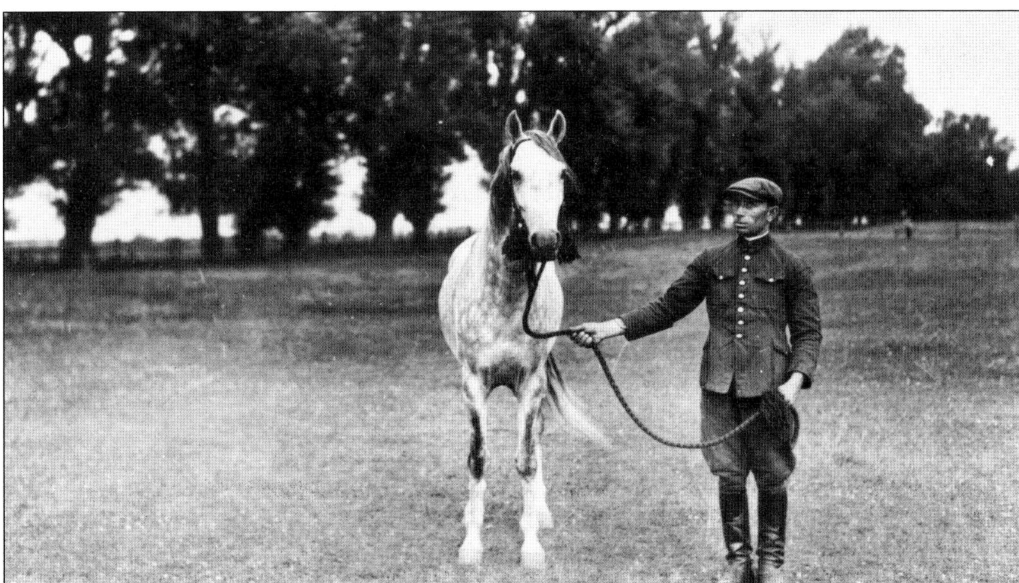

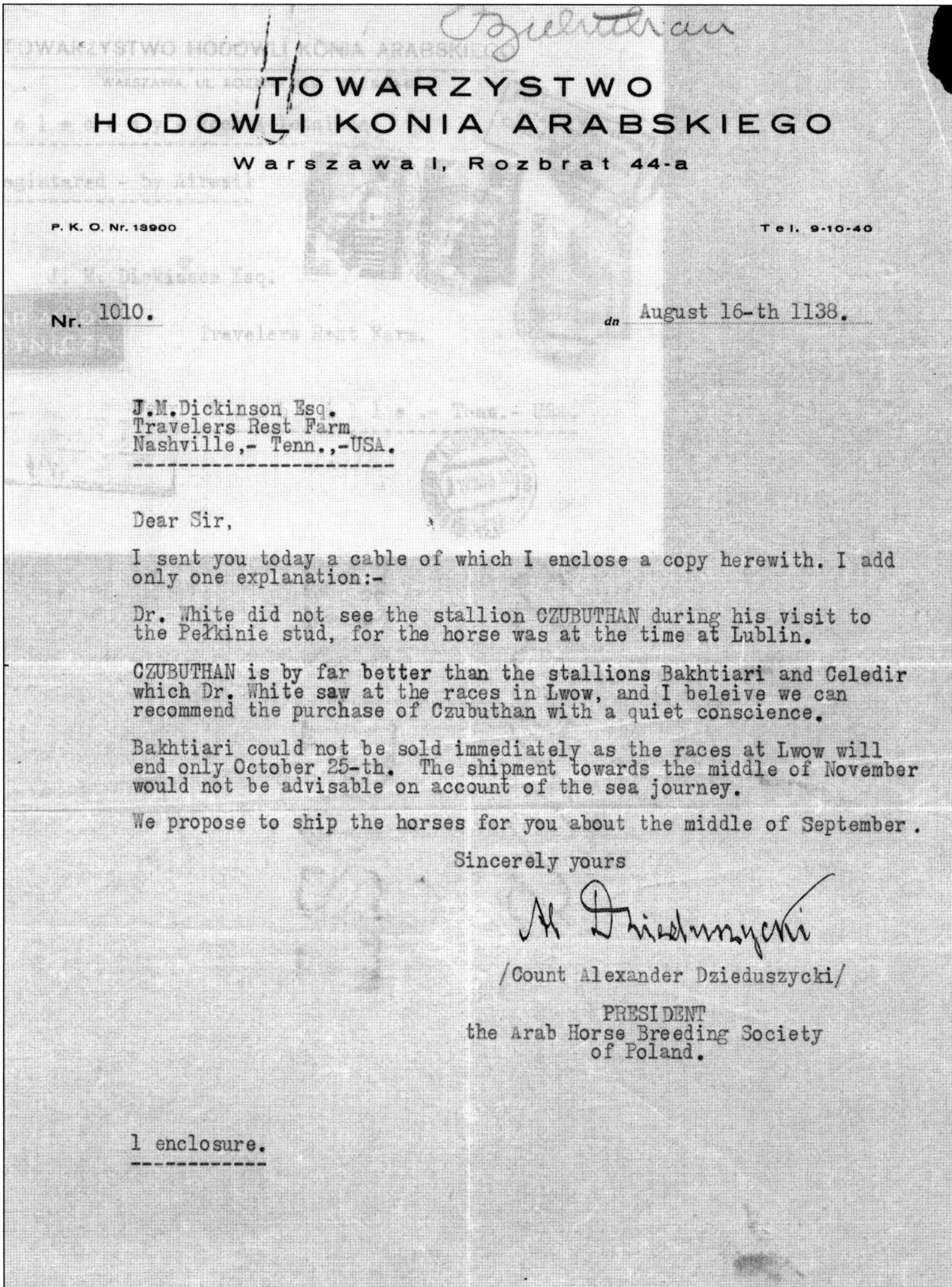

Bzubuthan

TOWARZYSTWO HODOWLI KONIA ARABSKIEGO

Warszawa I, Rozbrat 44-a

P. K. O. Nr. 13900 Tel. 9-10-40

Nr. 1010. dn August 16-th 1138.

J.M.Dickinson Esq.
Travelers Rest Farm
Nashville,- Tenn.,-USA.

Dear Sir,

I sent you today a cable of which I enclose a copy herewith. I add only one explanation:-

Dr. White did not see the stallion CZUBUTHAN during his visit to the Pełkinie stud, for the horse was at the time at Lublin.

CZUBUTHAN is by far better than the stallions Bakhtiari and Celedir which Dr. White saw at the races in Lwow, and I beleive we can recommend the purchase of Czubuthan with a quiet conscience.

Bakhtiari could not be sold immediately as the races at Lwow will end only October 25-th. The shipment towards the middle of November would not be advisable on account of the sea journey.

We propose to ship the horses for you about the middle of September.

Sincerely yours

Al Dzieduszycki

/Count Alexander Dzieduszycki/

PRESIDENT
the Arab Horse Breeding Society
of Poland.

1 enclosure.

Dzieduszycki followed the telegram with a letter, explaining in greater detail that Dr. White had seen two other, lesser-known stallions while at the racetrack at Lwow, but that Czubuthan was a better horse.

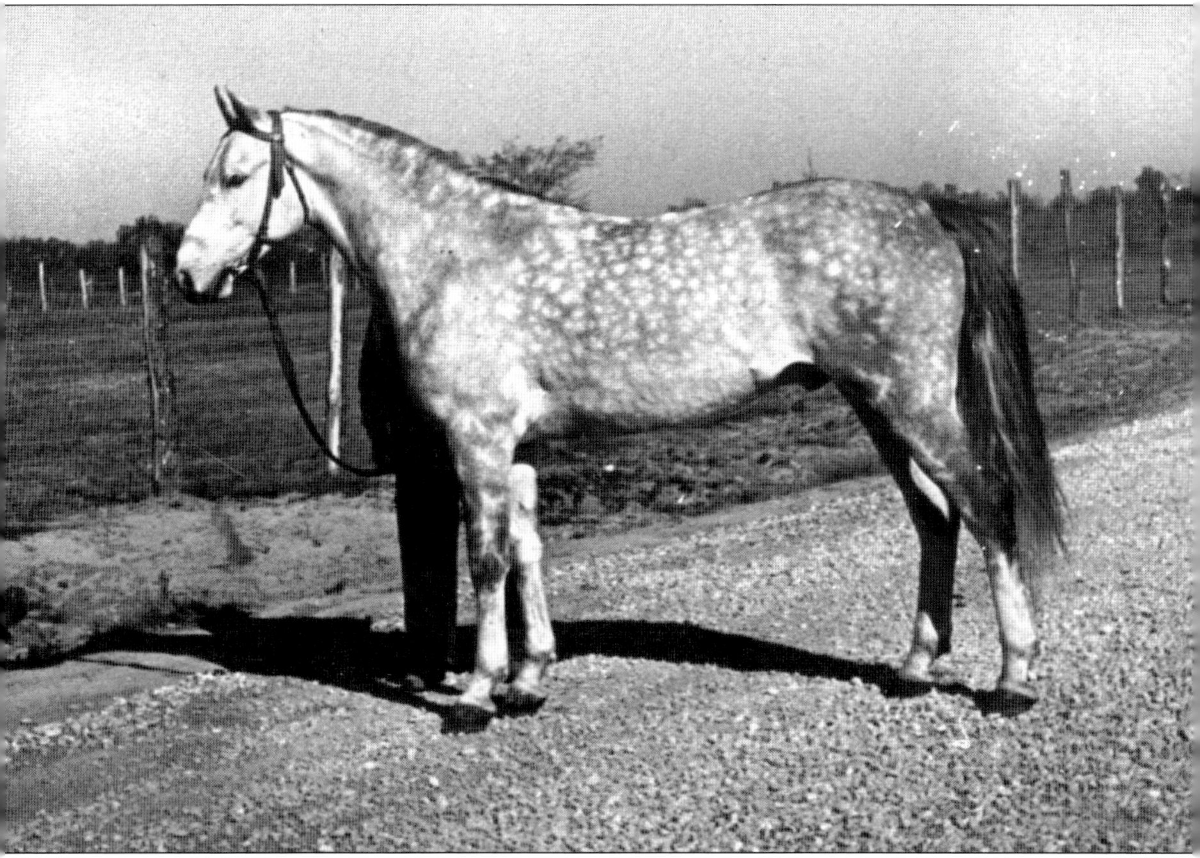

Dzieduszycki recommended the dapple-grey stallion for purchase. (An offer of $10,000 from Dickinson could not buy the esteemed Kaszmir.) Czubuthan, owned by Prince Witold Czartoryski, was currently enjoying his second successful racing season in Poland but could be ready for shipment to the United States within a month. In total, Czubuthan raced 17 times and was always in the money. In 1937, he was the second leading money winner in Poland, even racing against Anglo-Arabs (half-Thoroughbred crosses).

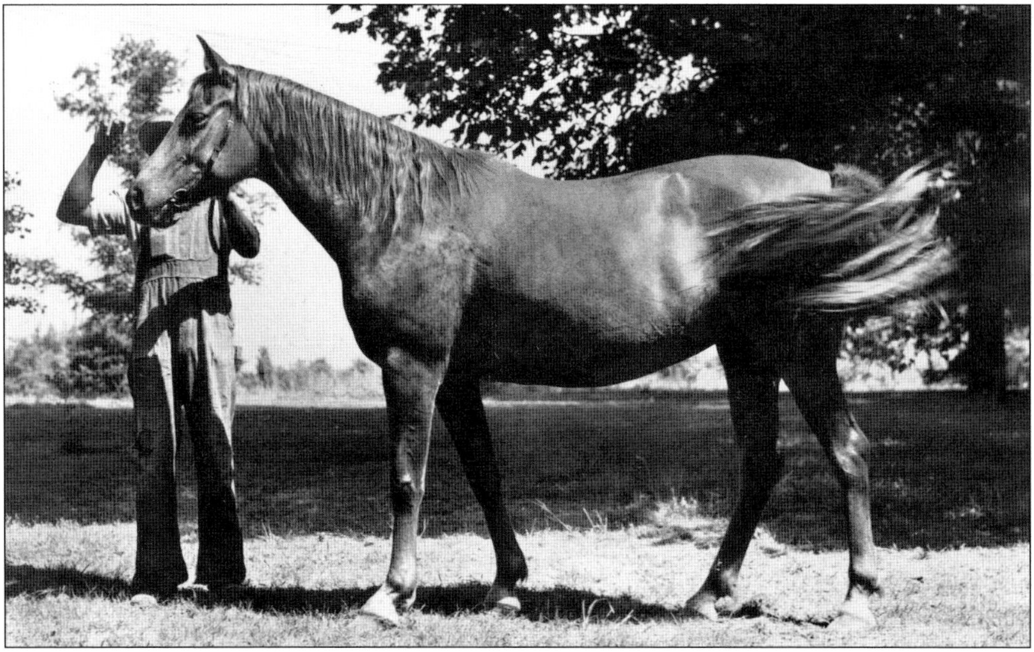

Dickinson's second importation from Poland also included several mares: Ba-Ida, Aeniza, Ugra, and Babolna. The group left Poland on October 15, 1938, arrived at New York City docks on October 23, and was loaded for rail transport to Nashville following a veterinary inspection. Dickinson immediately informed Dzieduszycki of their safe arrival at Travelers Rest, commenting on each horse. *Ba-Ida endured the arduous trip without duress, earning praise from her new owner. *Aeniza was of classic Arabian beauty, though Dickinson critiqued her legs as a touch too fine. He rather did not like *Babolna's head, but found her a tough, well-built mare.

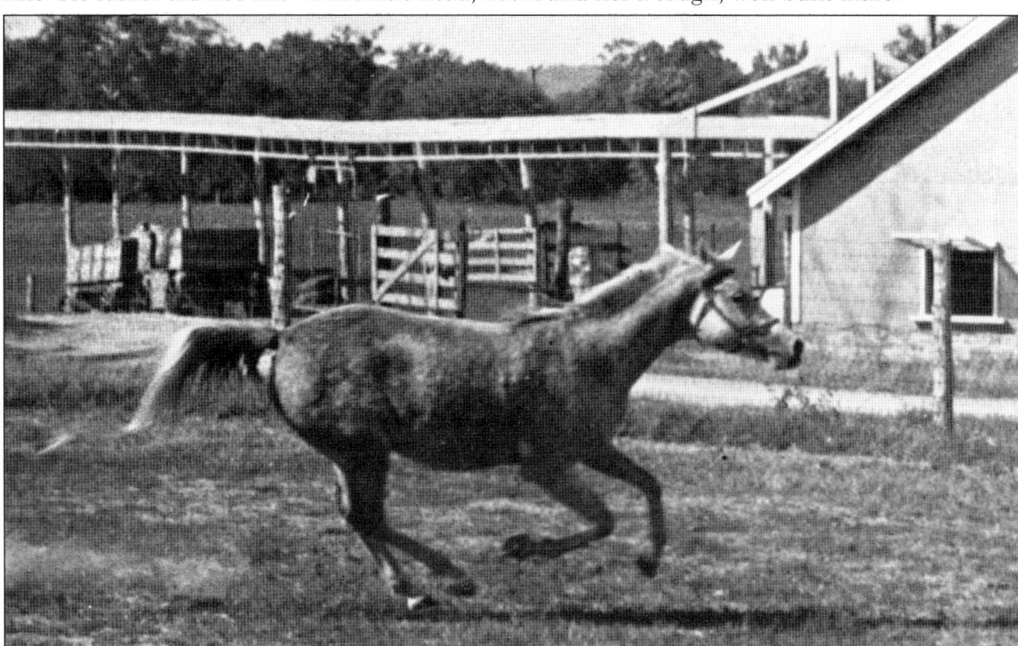

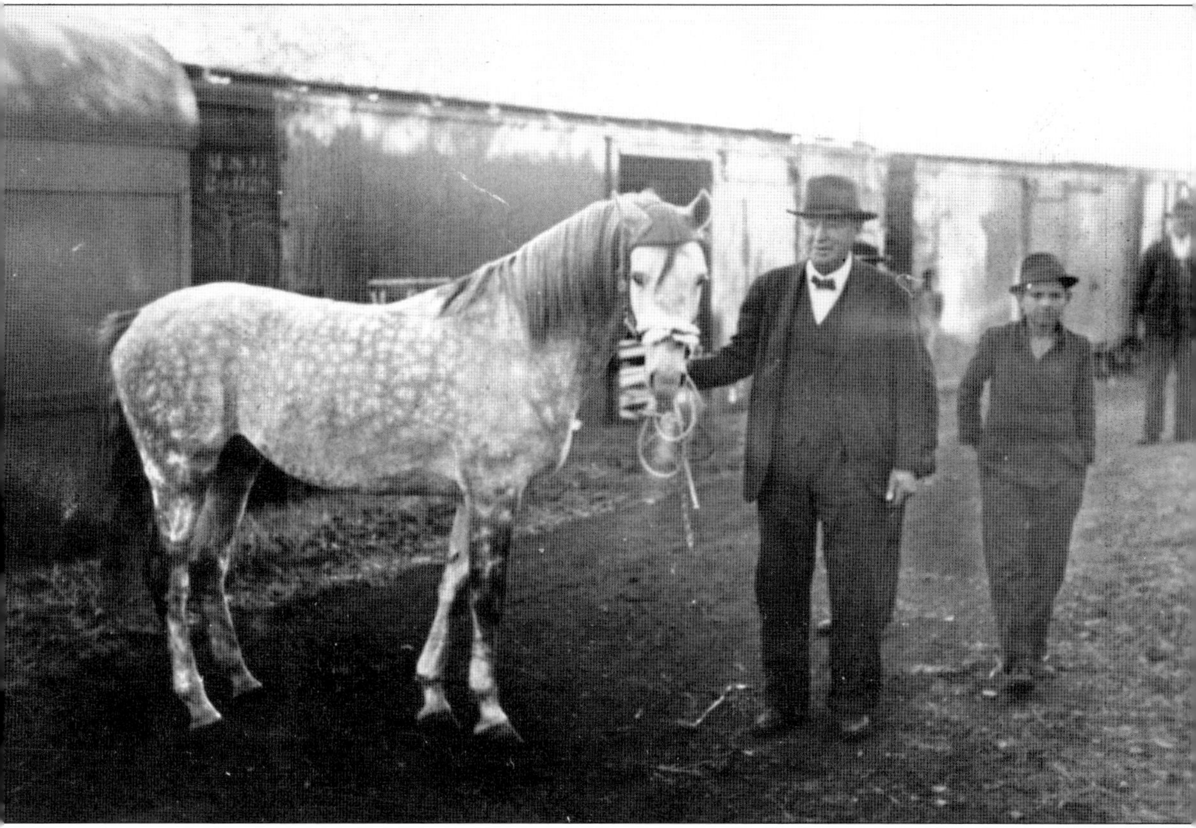

Dr. White apparently arrived at the Nashville Fairgrounds to greet the arrivals. White, a worldly traveler and observer of Arabian horses in five continents, was something of an authority on the breed in the United States. Following his trip to Poland, he had written essays proclaiming the superiority of the Polish Arabian horses even to those raised in native Middle Eastern environs. His opinion was that the temperate Polish climate produced ample feed to raise sturdy, substantial horses. White's first-hand knowledge influenced Dickinson, encouraging this second importation. Having not seen *Czubuthan while visiting Poland, White was likely eager to lay eyes upon the stallion in Nashville.

TRAVELERS REST
ARABIAN HORSES

PEDIGREE OF
THE REGISTERED ARABIAN HORSE

*CZUBUTHAN

	Sire / Dam	Grandparents	Great-grandparents
*CZUBUTHAN AHC. PASB.	DZINGISHAN III, PASB.	HERMIT, DB. PASB.	
		OAZA, PASB.	EL-KEBIR I, PASB.
			GAZELLA III, PASB.
	RYFKA, PASB.	MAZEPA, I, PASB.	MAZEPA, PASB.
			LANIA, PASB.
		FRYGA, PASB.	KOHEJLAN, PASB.
			OAZA, PASB.

*—Imported. DB—bred in the desert of Arabia; ASB—American Stud Book (Jockey Club); GSB—General Stud Book (Weatherby's); FrSB—French Stud Book; E—bred in Egypt; SBRg—Brazil; SBA—Argentine; PASB—Polish Arabian Stud Book; AHC—Arabian Horse Club of America; TRF—Travelers Rest Foal.

7th. Dam: GAZELLA, a desert bred Kehilet Ajuz, imported to Poland in 1845 by Count Julius Dzieduszycki.

Bred at the Pelkinie Stud of Prince Witold Czartoryski, Jaroslaw, Poland.

Description from PASB. "dark grey- apple - both hind legs with tuft, in front dark strips, 150 centimeters high.

A successful race horse in Poland; out of 17 starts he won 6, was second 8 times, third 3 times, never unplaced. In his final season he was the second largest Arab winner in Poland and in his last race won the Minister of Agriculture Stake at 3,200 meters, substantially 2 miles, defeating the holder of the Polish Arab Derby record.

Imported to USA. in 1938 by J.M.Dickinson.

Sold 5/12/49 to
Ejercito de Cuba

J. M. Dickinson

J. M. DICKINSON
DEL RIO PIKE
FRANKLIN, TENN.

*Czubuthan's pedigree would today be called "Old Polish." His sire and dam are not commonly seen today, as they did not produce a great many offspring, and war took its toll on the Polish people, land, and animals soon after *Czubuthan left there.

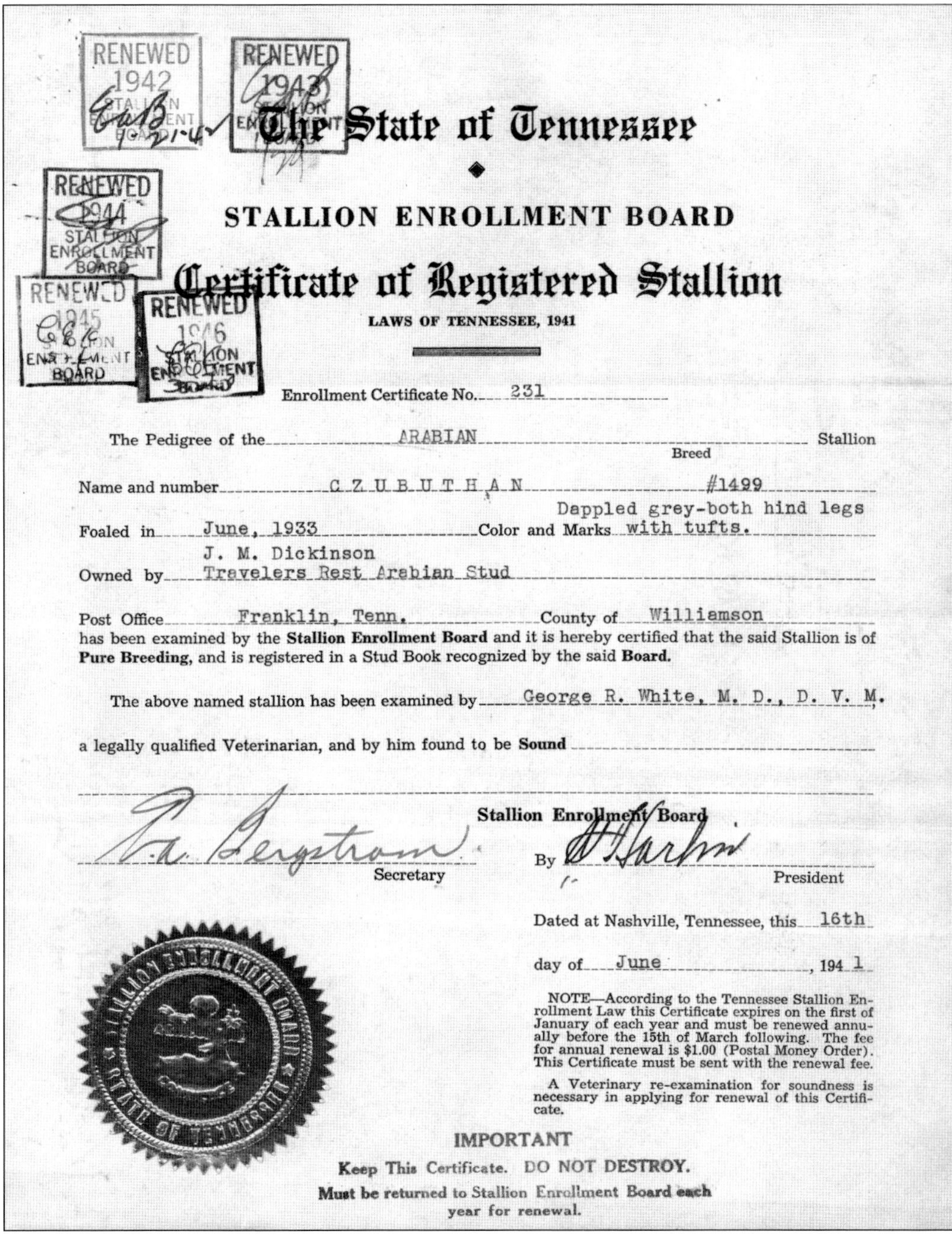

RENEWED 1942 STALLION ENROLLMENT BOARD

RENEWED 1943 STALLION ENROLLMENT BOARD

RENEWED 1944 STALLION ENROLLMENT BOARD

RENEWED 1945 STALLION ENROLLMENT BOARD

RENEWED 1946 STALLION ENROLLMENT BOARD

The State of Tennessee

◆

STALLION ENROLLMENT BOARD

Certificate of Registered Stallion

LAWS OF TENNESSEE, 1941

Enrollment Certificate No. 231

The Pedigree of the ARABIAN Stallion
Breed

Name and number C Z U B U T H A N #1499

Foaled in June, 1933 Color and Marks Dappled grey-both hind legs with tufts.

Owned by J. M. Dickinson Travelers Rest Arabian Stud

Post Office Franklin, Tenn. County of Williamson
has been examined by the **Stallion Enrollment Board** and it is hereby certified that the said Stallion is of **Pure Breeding,** and is registered in a Stud Book recognized by the said **Board.**

The above named stallion has been examined by George R. White, M. D., D. V. M.

a legally qualified Veterinarian, and by him found to be **Sound**

Secretary

Stallion Enrollment Board

By President

Dated at Nashville, Tennessee, this 16th

day of June, 1941

NOTE—According to the Tennessee Stallion Enrollment Law this Certificate expires on the first of January of each year and must be renewed annually before the 15th of March following. The fee for annual renewal is $1.00 (Postal Money Order). This Certificate must be sent with the renewal fee.

A Veterinary re-examination for soundness is necessary in applying for renewal of this Certificate.

IMPORTANT

Keep This Certificate. DO NOT DESTROY.

Must be returned to Stallion Enrollment Board each year for renewal.

Dickinson was most pleased with his new stallion, expecting *Czubuthan to make a lasting impact on American breeding of Arabian horses. In a period when the horse-breeding industry was influenced by the federal government's desire to help improve the equine gene pool, each stallion owner had to enroll his breeding horse in the Stallion Enrollment Program.

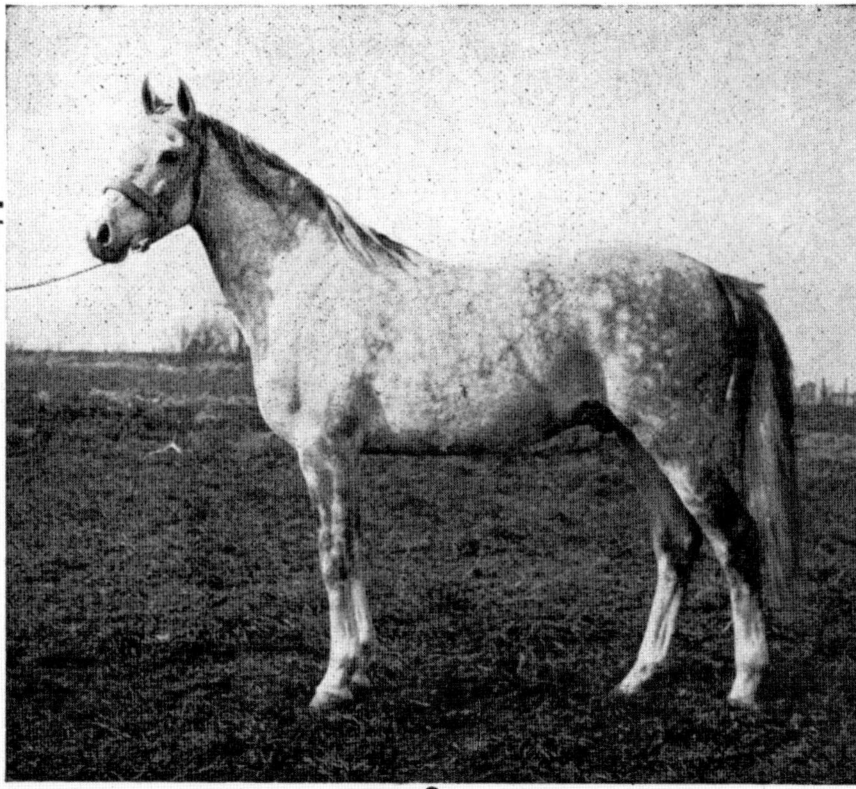

Imported CZUBUTHAN from Poland

Travelers Rest Arabian Stud consists of approximately fifty Arabs bred in the United States, Argentina, Brazil, Egypt, England, France and Poland. The Stud produces registered, pure bred Arabs for sale as colts and fillies, and does not engage in buying or selling horses on commission or for the profit in the turnover. Horses from this Stud have gone to forty states and territories and to a dozen foreign countries.

The stallion pictured is one of the thirty imported Arabs of the Stud. Bred at the celebrated Pelkinie Stud of Prince Witold Czartoryski, he was the principal long distance Arab race horse when imported from Poland. He won the two-mile Minister of Agriculture Stake, defeating the Arab Derby record holder. *Czubuthan is by disposition, quality and soundness, the embodiment of the most noted characteristics of the Arab horse developed to a very high degree.

Travelers Rest Arabian Stud

Del Rio Pike Franklin, Tennessee

*Czubuthan likely surpassed Dickinson's expectations, becoming the most prolific Arabian sire in the country for the 10 years following his importation to Tennessee. In total, he sired 98 purebred Arabian horses for Travelers Rest. His influence on the breed extends into the 21st century.

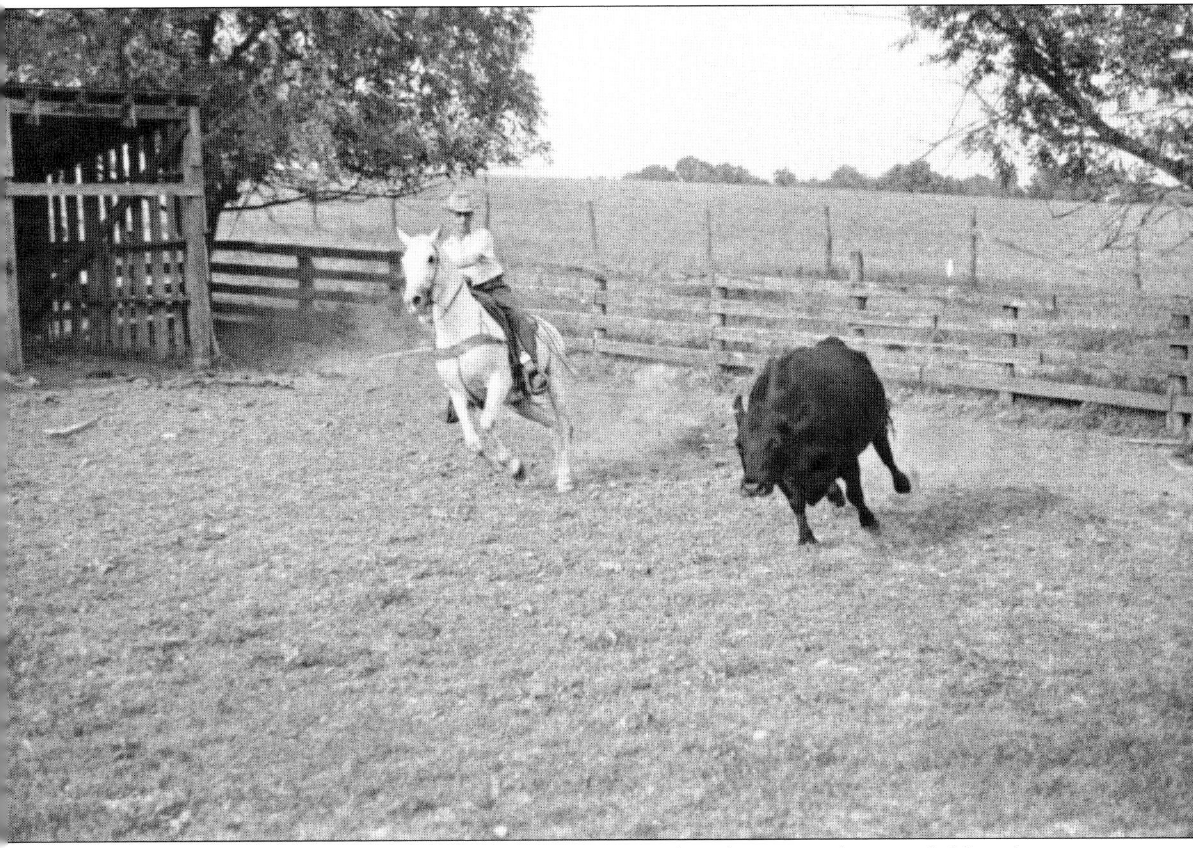

Travelers Rest (TR) horses distinguished themselves as show horses, endurance field trial mounts, army horses, coastal patrol mounts, working ranch horses, jumpers, and pleasure horses for amateur and youth riders. Dickinson kept notes on the horses he sold, as new owners sent him messages of praise for their Arabians' beauty and versatility. Pictured here is Faza, son of *Czubuthan. Some years after Dickinson disbanded the TR herd, his daughter Peggy recovered some of the horses and continued breeding of the historic bloodlines. Faza was bred to a *Nasr daughter to produce Nickajack, Peggy's primary breeding stallion at her Travelers Rest, Columbia (Tennessee), farm. Nickajack sired TR Tlingit, who represented Travelers Rest heritage in official Arabian horse races during the 1970s, running at several tracks in Michigan.

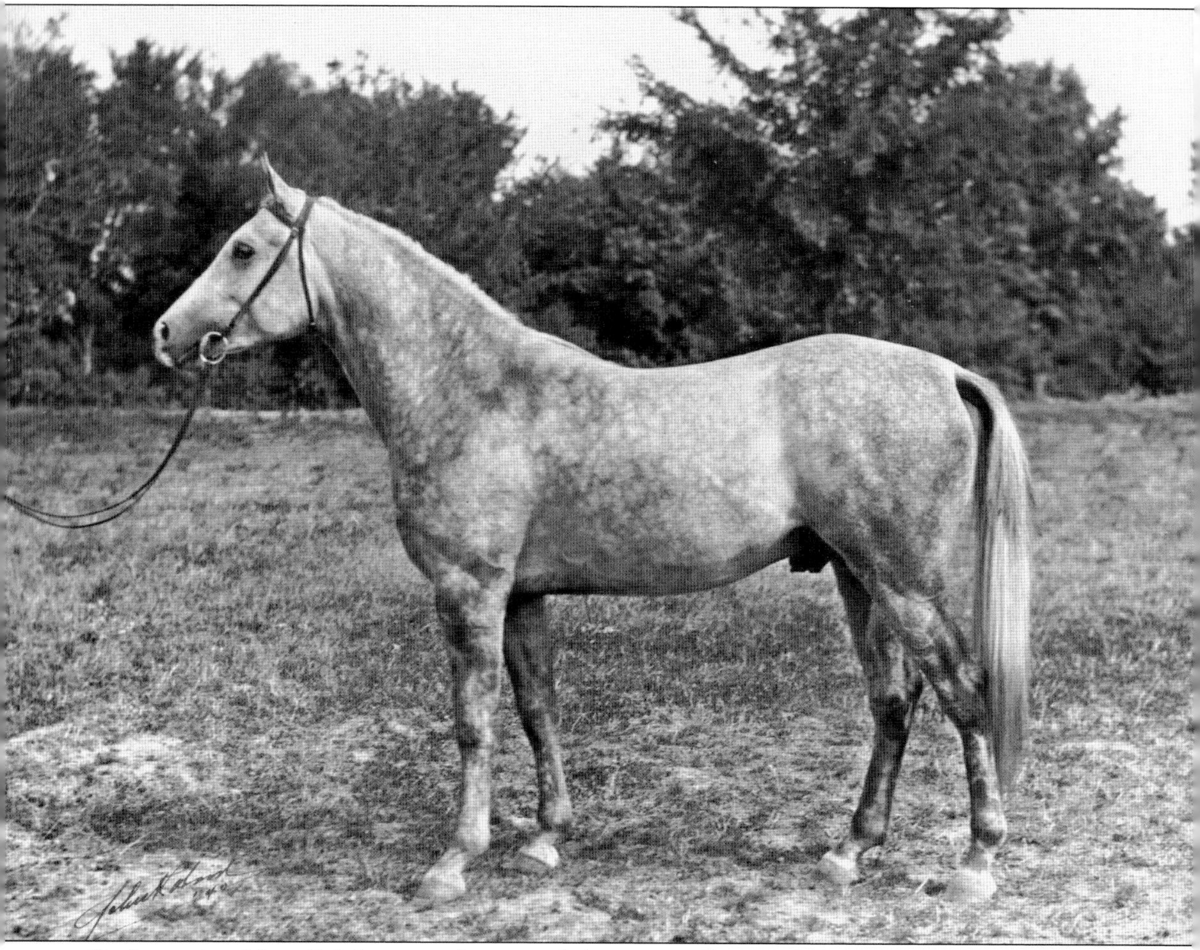

Rodasr was sold to California and was used for mounted coastal patrol during World War II. Some 3,000 horses were employed thusly. During the war, Arabian horse owners donated select horses to the U.S. Remount Service. This agency oversaw the training of cavalry horses and leased out stallions to civilian agents as part of the government's effort to make quality horses available to working ranchers and pleasure horsemen alike. The system upgraded the national equine population, created a market for horse breeders, and made quality horses available for purchase for remount use.

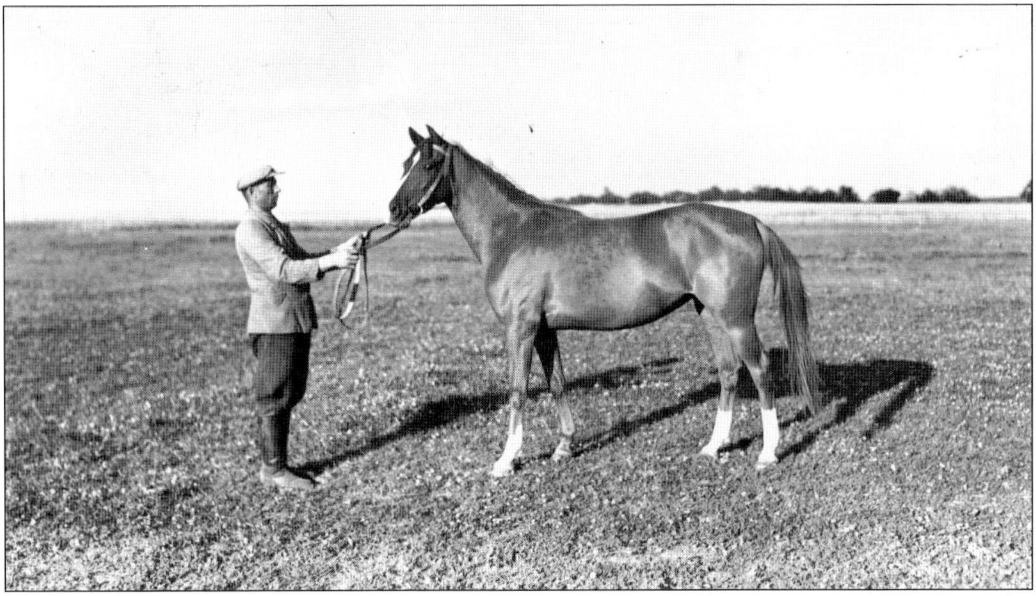

Dickinson donated the imported Polish mare *Babolna to the U.S. Remount Service. He also donated Mazeppa, a son of *Babolna. Both horses can be found in the pedigrees of early American Arabian racehorses. Later Dickinson also donated Bataan, a horse bred from crossing two imported Polish horses, *Czubuthan and *Ba-Ida. Bataan also contributed to early racing through his son Halali Phoenix, whose dam was Serdecka, a Travelers Rest mare (see above under *Nora). The army's Arabian horses were consolidated at the Pomona, California, remount depot, at the site of Will Kellogg's former ranch, consisting of the horses, land, and facilities Kellogg had gifted to the state.

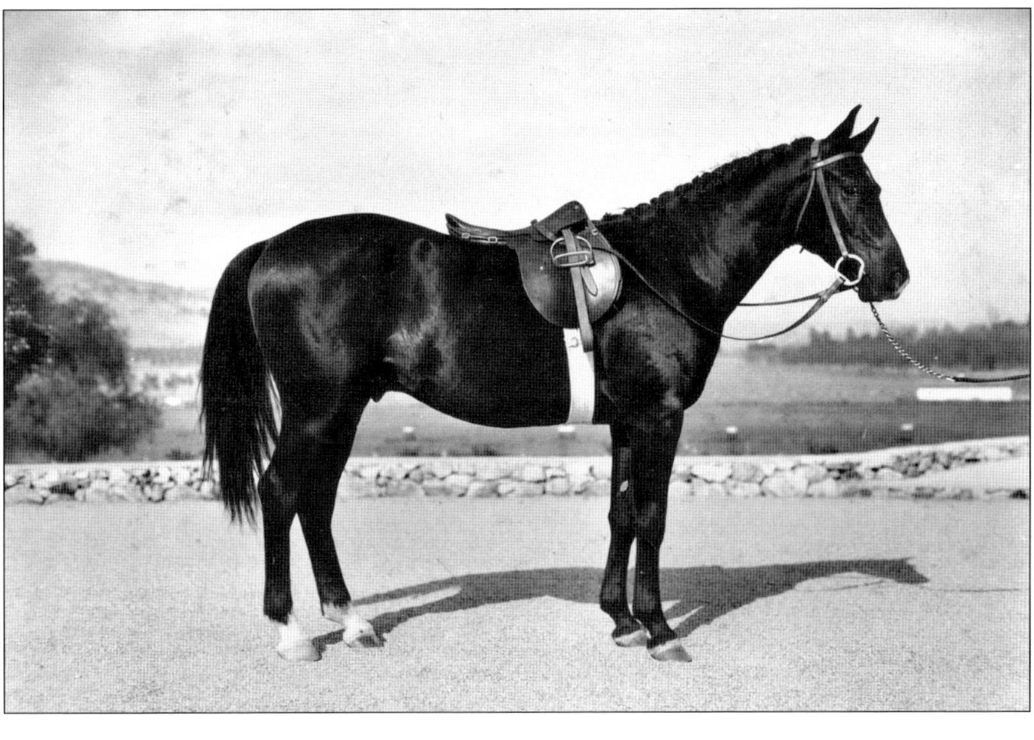

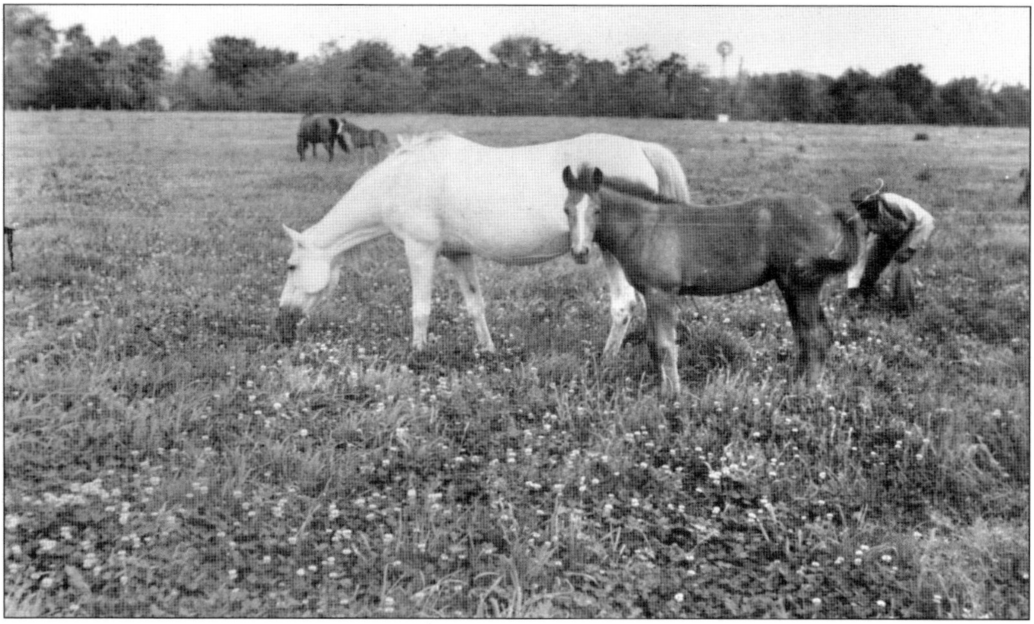

The chestnut filly Rose of Luzon was sold as a weanling in 1942. Later she figured in the first official Arabian horse race held in 1959 in Maryland: her son Al-Marah Ibn Indraff finished fourth in that race (see next chapter). The owner of Al-Marah Arabian horse farm, Mrs. Bazy Tankersley, helped organize the race as a means to showcase the breed as the amateur's racehorse.

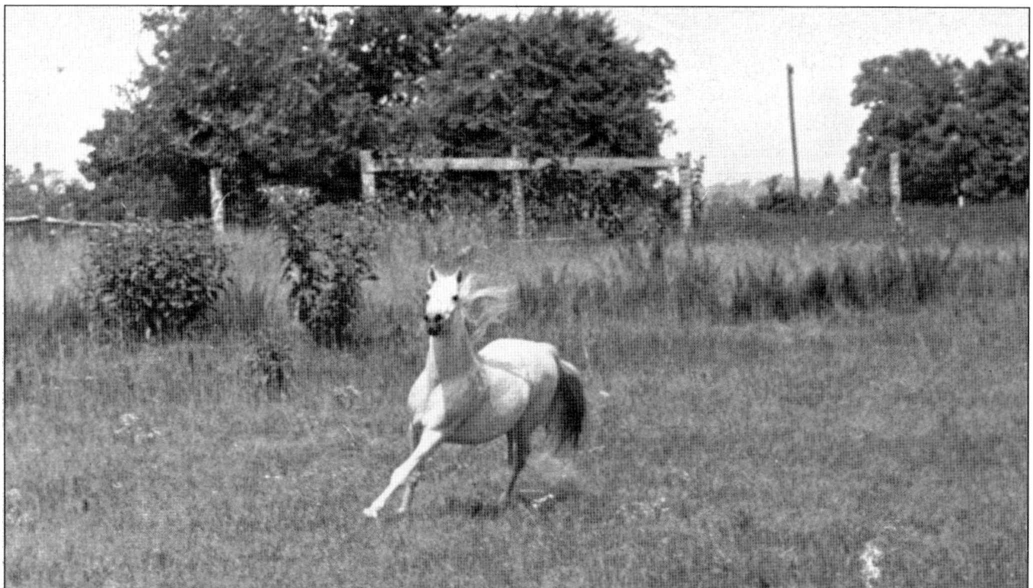

The World Arabian Horse Organization determined in 2003 that 25 percent of all registered American Arabian horses trace in at least one line to *Czubuthan. This statistic is a testament to Dickinson's goal of dispersing his horses to middle-class owners. *Czubuthan's name recently resurfaced prominently in contemporary Arabian horse racing circles, specifically through the successful race sire KA Czubuthan, who carries two lines to his namesake great-grandsire from Poland.

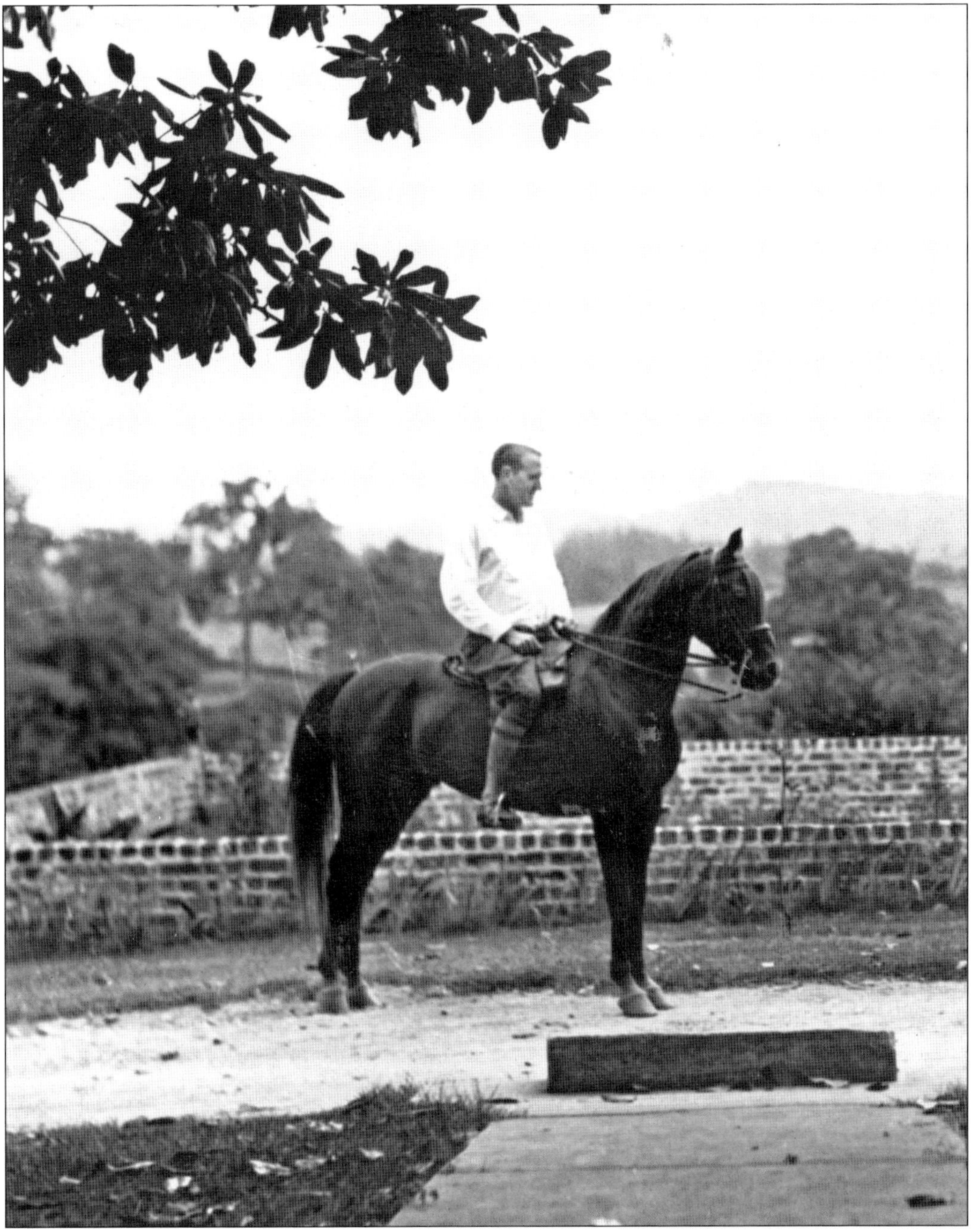

Gen. Jacob McGavock Dickinson's influence was vast. In maintaining affordable prices, he offered quality horses to new, middle-class owners. His correspondence with Polish horse breeders resulted in the introduction of new bloodlines in the United States, decades before importation from Poland became fashionable. Also his annual *Travelers Rest Catalog* was an invaluable resource at a time when there was little information available on the Arabian horse breed. Further, his familiarity with Polish horses and breeders became an asset following World War II. Dickinson not only assisted several Polish friends to relocate relatives in the war's aftermath, he assisted the U.S. Army in processing the so-called prizes-of-war Polish Arabian horses taken from German possession.

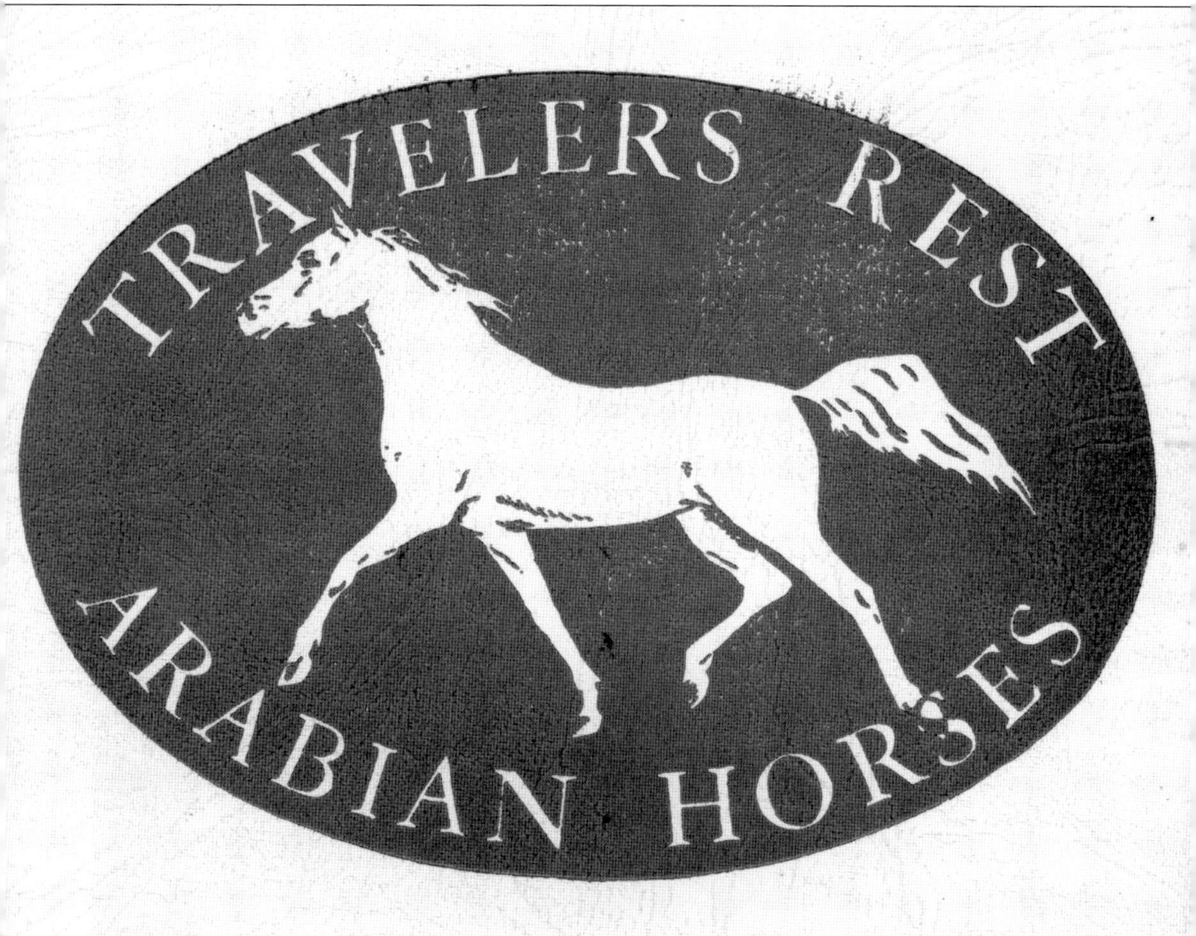

The Travelers Rest Arabian Horse Stud logo featured a depiction of the Egyptian stallion *Nasr, taken from a photograph of him at liberty, trotting boldly through his pasture at the farm. The logo was used on signs, in magazine advertisements, and on the cover of the annual Travelers Rest catalogs that became informative resources for Arabian horse owners in America. The image is still recognized today as representing the influential Arabian horse breeding operation that J. M. Dickinson established in Middle Tennessee.

Two

BRICK AND MORTAR

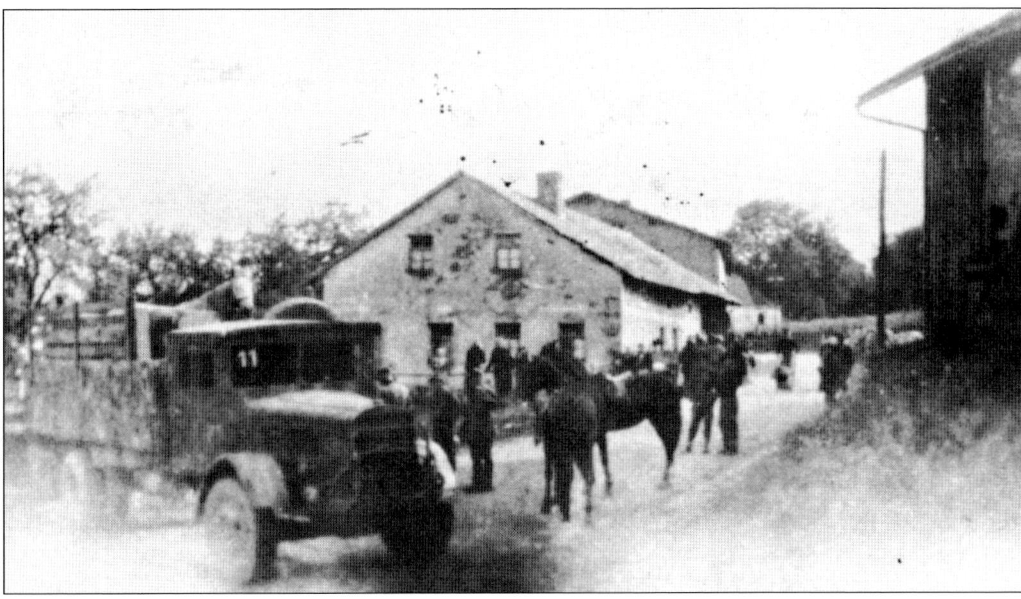

In April 1945, at the end of World War II, the 2nd Armored American Cavalry discovered a German horse-breeding operation in Czechoslovakia. Polish Arabians, Austrian Lipizzaners, Hungarian Shagyas, and French Thoroughbreds represented Europe's finest horses, taken from their native lands for the purpose of breeding "superhorses" for the German war machine. Gen. George S. Patton of the Third Army gave Col. Charles H. Reed orders to secure the compound, which included 400 Allied prisoners of war. Capt. Thomas M. Stewart, a knowledgeable horseman as well as an associate of J. M. Dickinson from Tennessee, was fluent in German and negotiated the surrender. Sensing imminent defeat, the German officers surrendered, preferring to relinquish the prized horses to the Americans than to the advancing Russians. Patton gave road clearance to the 2nd Cavalry to move the horses from Hostau, Czechoslovakia, to safer territory, Bavaria. Mares with foals were loaded on available trucks; most of the horses were moved on foot, herded by mounted officers and vehicles. (U.S. Army photograph.)

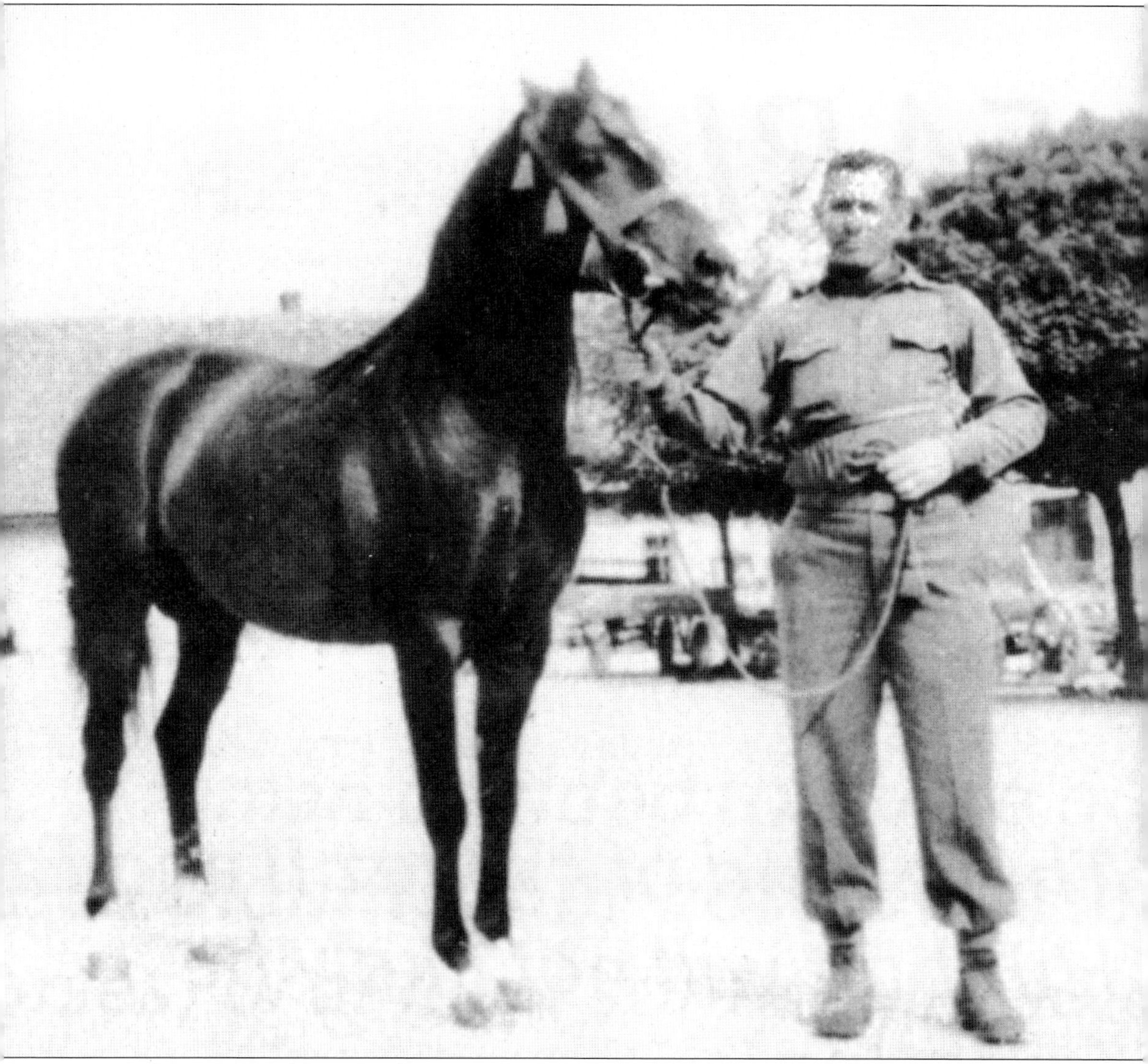

Some horses were then moved to Monsbach, Germany, after others returned to their country of origin, such as the Lipizzaners to neutral Austria. From more than 1,000 horses discovered in Czechoslovakia, the U.S. Army handpicked approximately 150 horses as prizes of war. Col. Fred L. Hamilton, remount chief, flew from Washington to assess them. The bay stallion Witez II, here posing with a Captain White at Hostau, was among the 18 Polish Arabian horses selected for shipment to the United States. His name translates as "Prince." (U.S. Army photograph.)

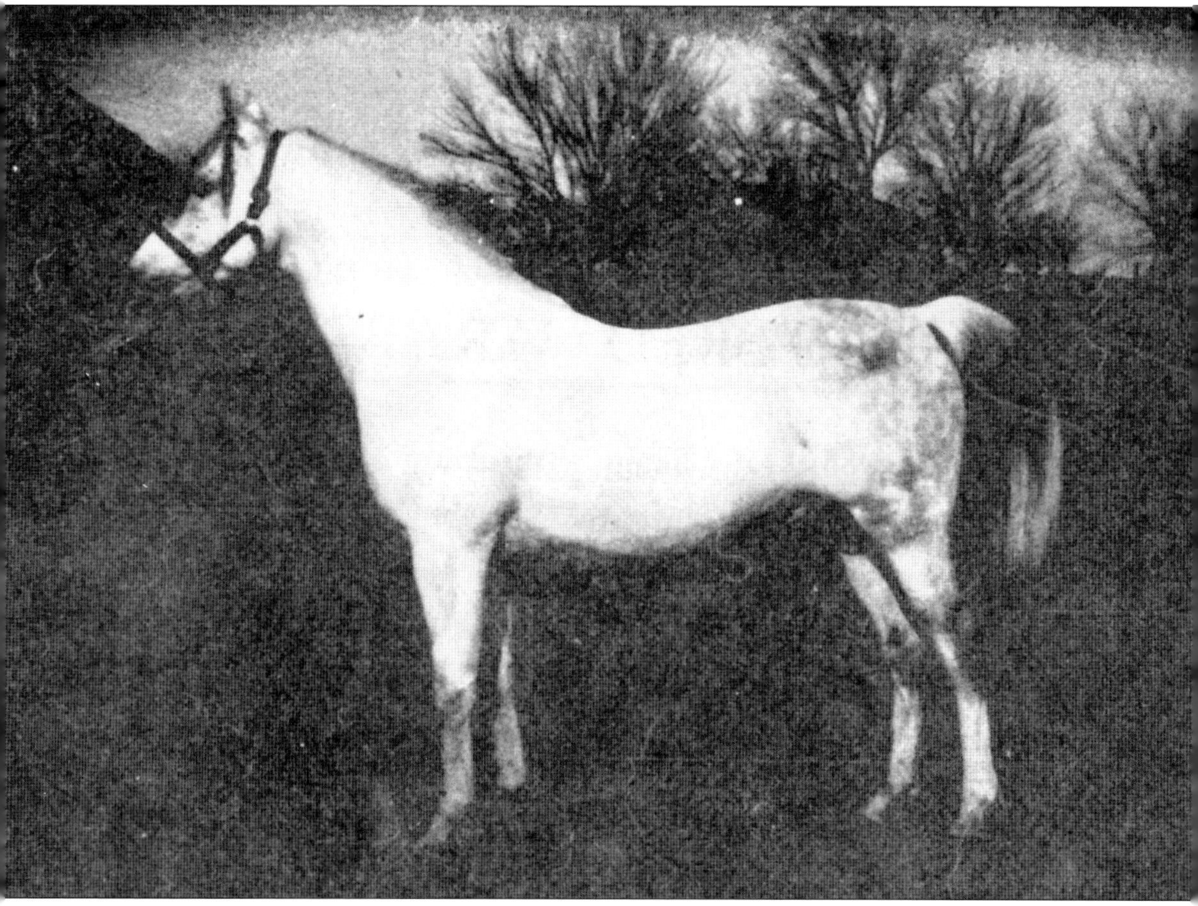

Another Arabian stallion selected by the army was Lotnik. Bred by a private Polish breeder, Lotnik was a young horse in training at the Lwow racetrack when the Germans captured him. Lotnik, whose name translates as "Flyer," was said to be very fast, racing under German occupation, though no record is available. His son Laur, born in Poland in 1946, was a very successful racer, winning most of his races, including four stakes races. Lt. William D. Quinlivan rode the white-grey Lotnik once in the hands of the American army from Bavaria to Monsbach, Germany, with the bay Polish Arabian mare Wierna alongside. By rail, the horses then rode to the North Sea and boarded the 10,000-ton Liberty ship *Stephen Austin* for an October journey to America via the English Channel and across the Atlantic. (U.S. Army photograph.)

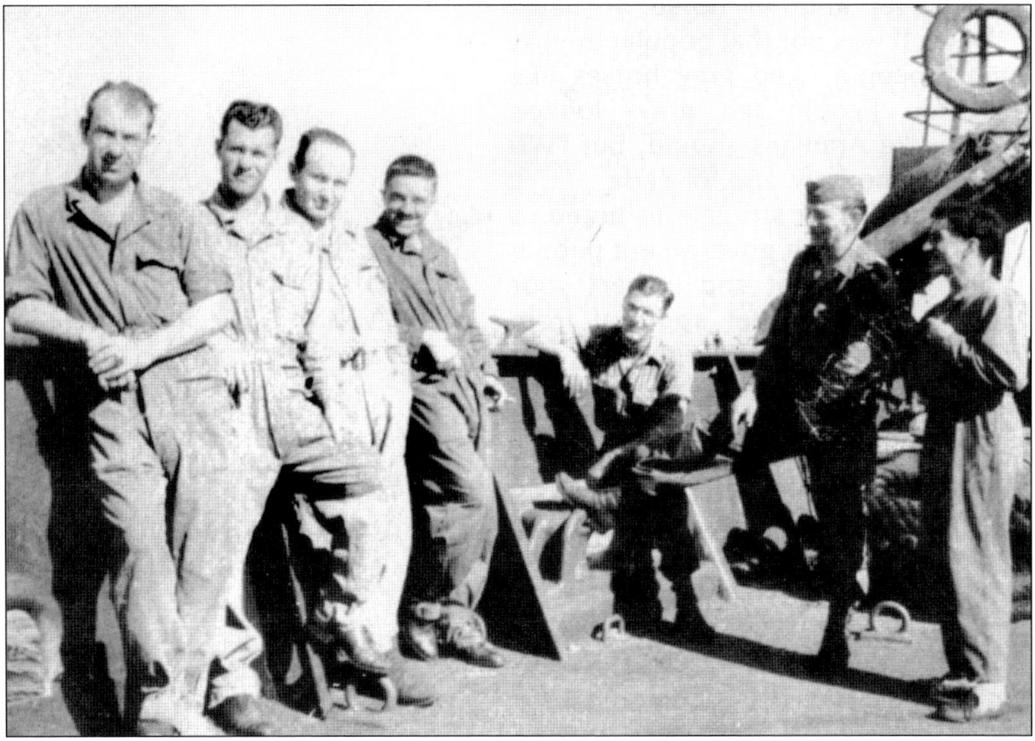

With only 800 tons of freight, the ship had a rough trip through a winter storm. Posing aboard the ship are, from left to right, Maj. ? Seibert, Lieutenant Quinlivan, Capt. ? MacLean, Maj. ? Slisher, and New Jersey Cavalry members. On October 28, 1945, the horses disembarked at Newport News, Virginia. They wintered at the Front Royal Remount Depot and were later presented to the public (pictured below). The parade included 18 Polish Arabians, 9 Lipizzaners, and 63 Thoroughbreds. The Arabian horses were transferred to the Pomona Remount Depot to join the army's herd of Arabians at the former Kellogg Ranch. J. M. Dickinson was on hand to evaluate the Arabian horses from Poland when they arrived at Pomona. He likely had more personal knowledge of Polish Arabians than any other person in America at the time, assisting in their registration. (U.S. Army photographs.)

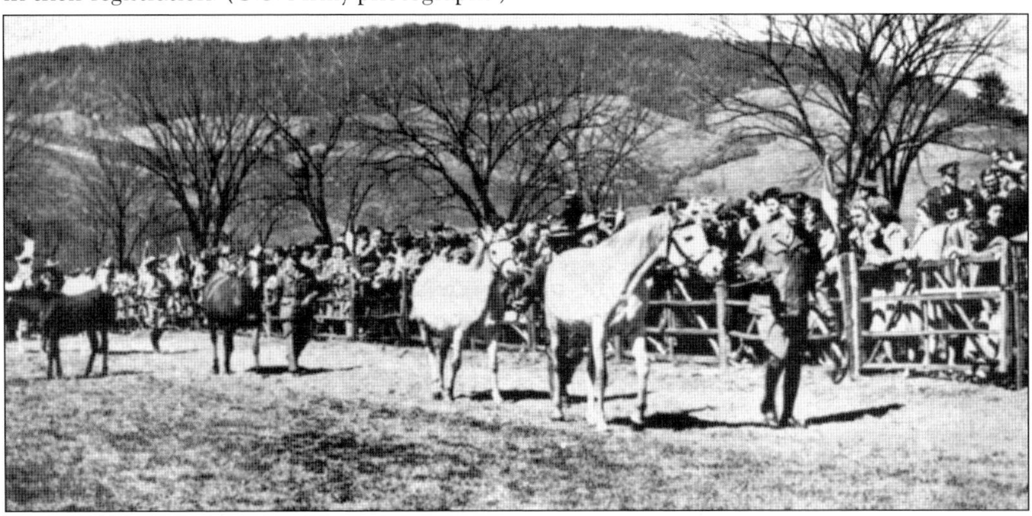

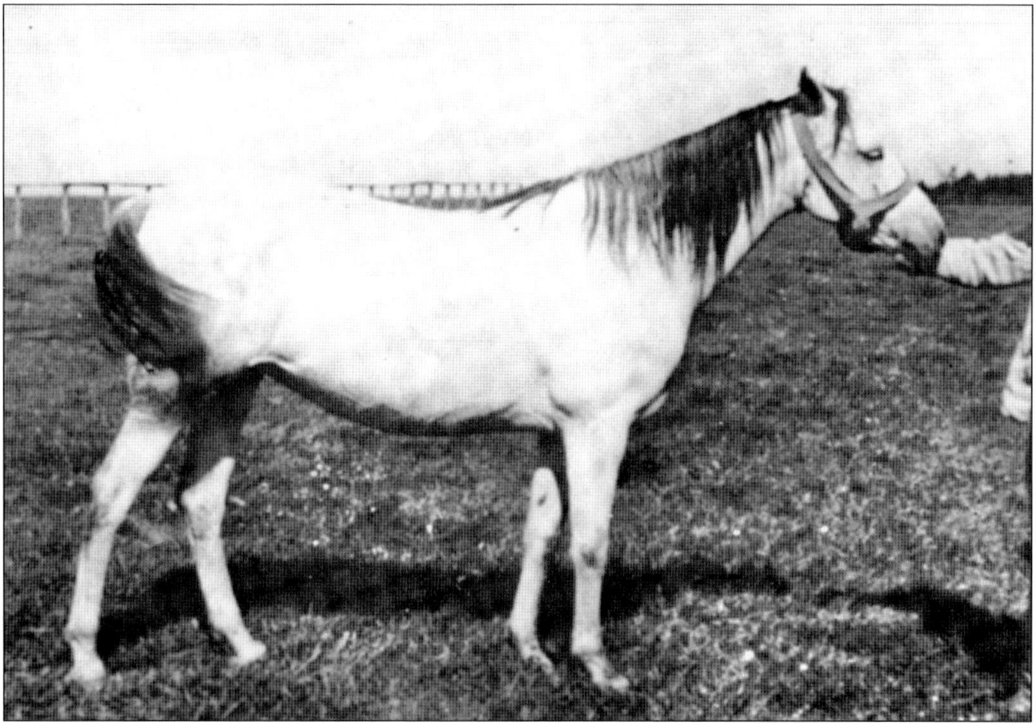

Colonel Hamilton proclaimed that the group of imported horses represented the best bloodlines in the world. *Chloe is shown here in Europe. The grey mare was originally from Janow Podlaski stud. She came in foal to *Lotnik, producing the filly *Nikole. *Chloe later produced Chloeyn, an important foundation broodmare for John Rogers, a 1960s Arabian racehorse breeder involved with the first official Arabian race in 1959 (see below). Also photographed in Europe was fellow prize-of-war mare *Iwonka III. The chestnut mare, who left a daughter in Europe, later became famous as the grandam of the celebrated American show horse *Bask, imported in the 1960s from a restored Polish state horse breeding program. (U.S. Army photographs.)

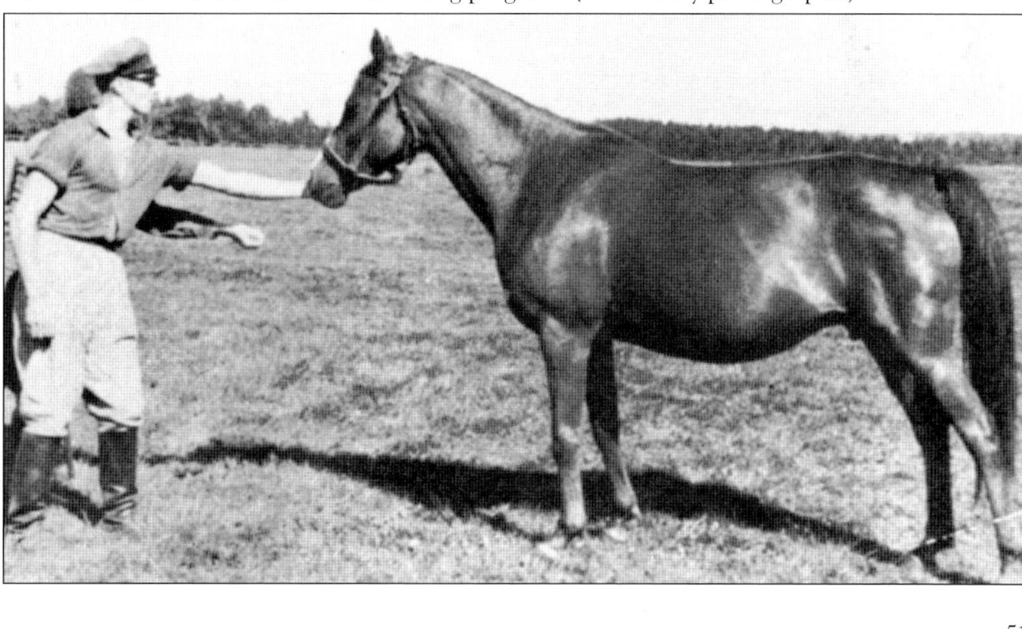

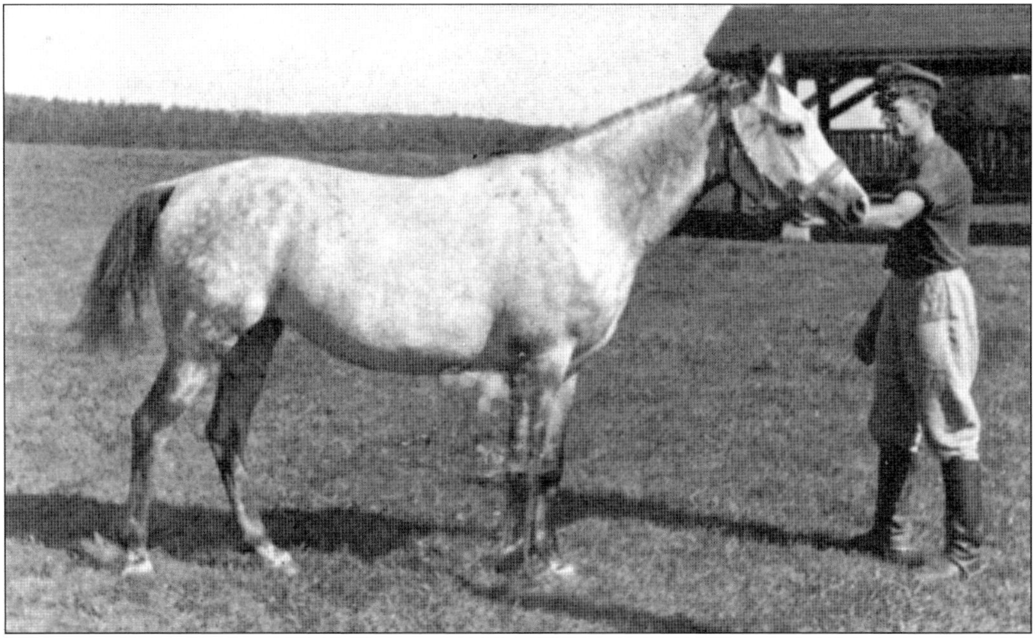

The grey mare *Tarnina, pictured in Europe, was bred at Janow Podlaski. Her sire was Lowelas (mentioned above under Dickinson's *Nora). *Tarnina's grandson Hamlet, a successful racehorse in 1969 and 1970, also traced to several of Dickinson's horses, including Antez, *Nasr, and *Przepiorka. Also pictured is the bay stallion *Wisok, a yearling son of *Witez II at the time he was selected as a prize-of-war. *Wisok's dam was a daughter of the revered Polish racer Hardy, sire of Dickinson's *Nora. Unfortunately *Wisok injured a rear leg while lying down to rest during the trip from Virginia to California. His impressive disposition and conformation saved him from being euthanized. Though his injury prevented him from demonstrating his racing heritage, he was placed with a civilian agent whose family enjoyed him as a pleasure horse.

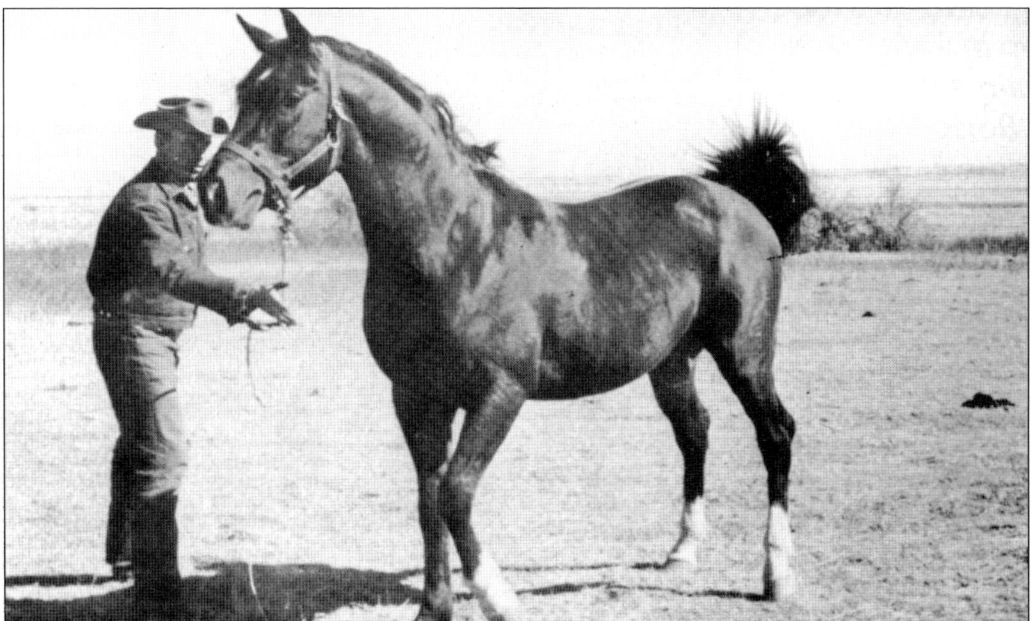

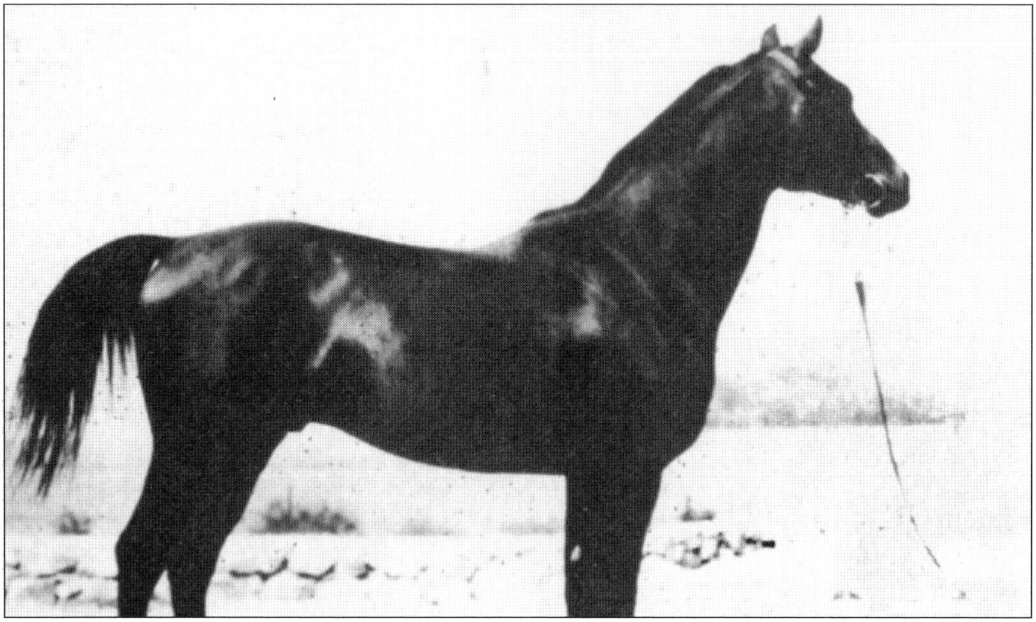

The stallion *Witez II (above) and the mare *Wierna (below), pictured after their arrival at Pomona, figured prominently in the breeding of early Arabian racehorses, especially in combination with Dickinson Arabians. *Witez II was bred to a daughter of *Wierna's, producing Ofir, winner of the first official Arabian race. The *Witez II son Witraff was acquired by Chuck Tolbert, a cornerstone in the development of Arabian horse racing in the West. Tolbert crossed Witraff, a racer himself, on the mare Gemma, whose sire was *Wisok and whose dam was three-quarters Dickinson breeding by pedigree. The offspring of Witraff and Gemma, such as Gemimah (1969), Witema (1973), and Witachi (1974), were all early racers. A third example of *Witez II racing offspring was Janow Witez, out of the mare Serdecka, of Dickinson breeding (see *Nora above). (U.S. Army photographs.)

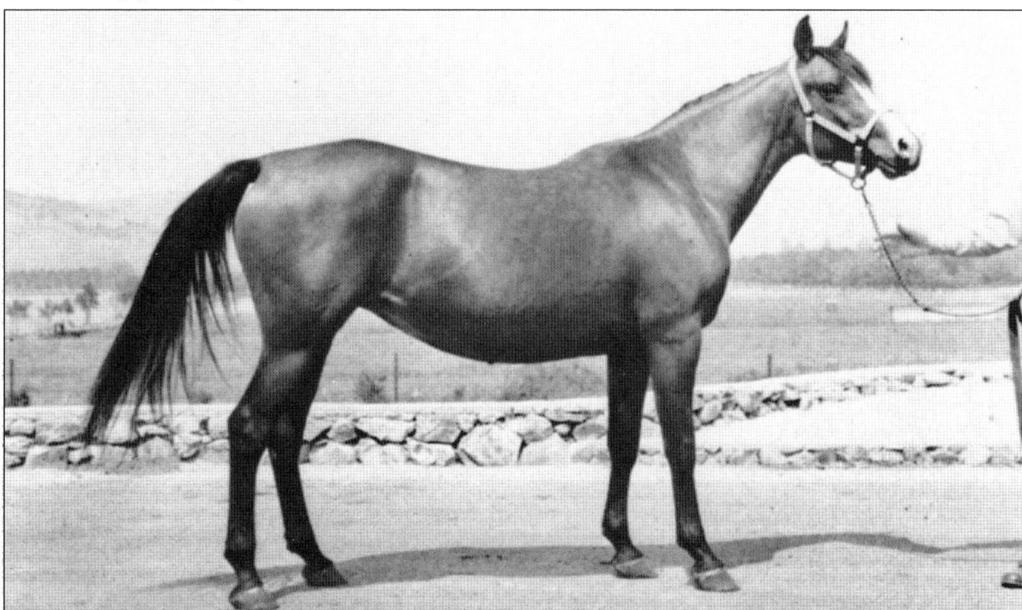

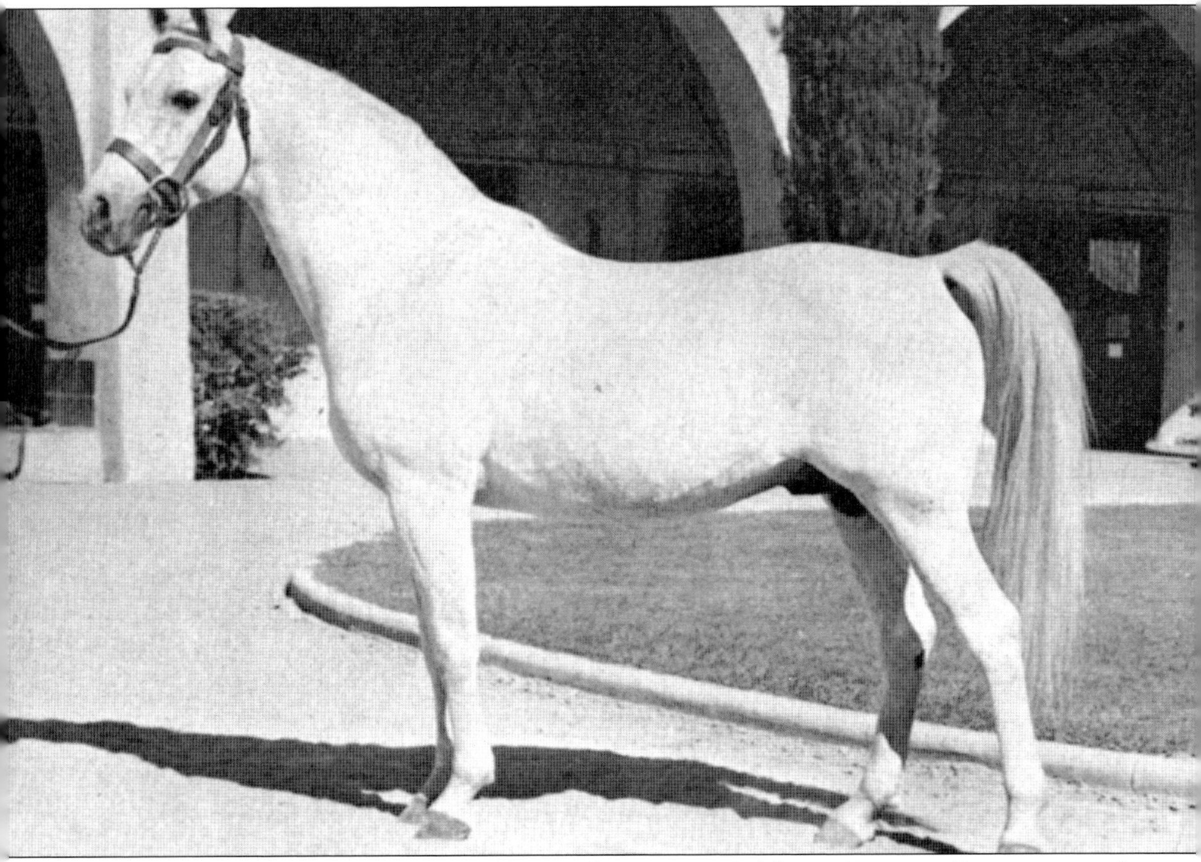

Col. Fred W. Koester, commanding officer at the Pomona, California, Remount Depot, reported that equine authorities described *Lotnik as one of the finest imported stallions available. Remount chief Fred Hamilton concurred, calling the Arabian stallion one of the best in the world. However, the U.S. Horse Cavalry was on the wane. By 1948, the remount closed, and the horses were sold at auction. At the time, *Lotnik was sold to Julius Kahn Jr. of Canoga Park, California. Kahn placed the stallion with friends when he moved east, with the condition that the horse never be sold. Unfortunately, this stipulation caused trouble for *Lotnik when the couple divorced; the horse, unable to be sold, was boarded out and fell into obscurity. Colonel Koester rediscovered the aged stallion working on a ranch and helped arrange for his sale to a new, appreciative owner. (Photograph as it appeared in a 1951 advertisement by owner Julius Kahn Jr.)

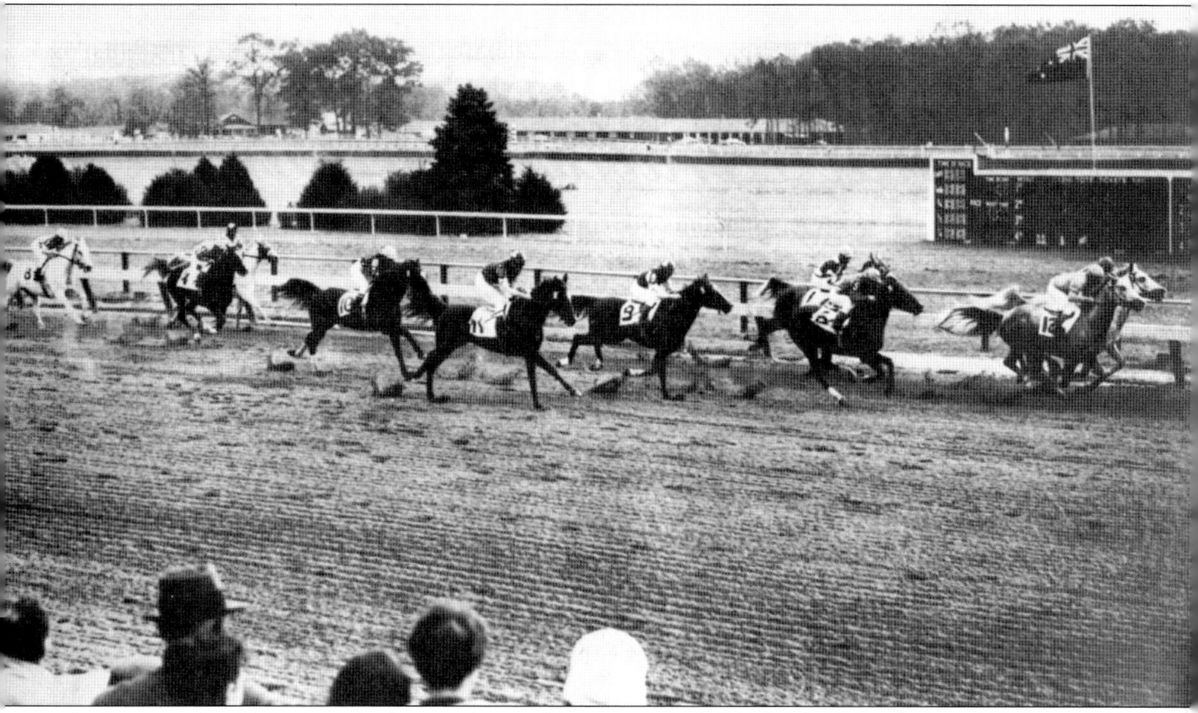

Following the U.S. Army's dispersal at public auction of surplus horses, the Arabian Horse Owners Foundation (AHOF) was founded. AHOF promoted the breed as "the amateur's race horse" at the first Arabian competition in the United States at a regulation track. Member Bazy Tankersley, owner of Al-Marah Arabians of Washington, D.C., convinced Laurel racetrack in Maryland to include a 2.5-mile exhibition (non-wagered) Arabian horse race in its schedule on November 11, 1959. Participants included Tish Hewitt (Illinois), Max Culpepper (Florida), John Rogers (California), and Gina Manion (Indiana). John Rogers, who became the first president of Arabian Horse Racing Association of America, and his wife, Gladys, entered the horse Ankthor, a grandson of J. M. Dickinson's world-traveled Antez. Norman Reed's Ibn Lwow, Number 12, was a son of Lwow, bred by Dickinson from his 1937 Polish imports. Tish Hewitt's Al-Marah Ibn Indraff, number 11, was out of the mare Rose of Luzon, bred by Dickinson. (Photograph originally from Gladys Brown Edwards's *The Arabian: War Horse to Show Horse.*)

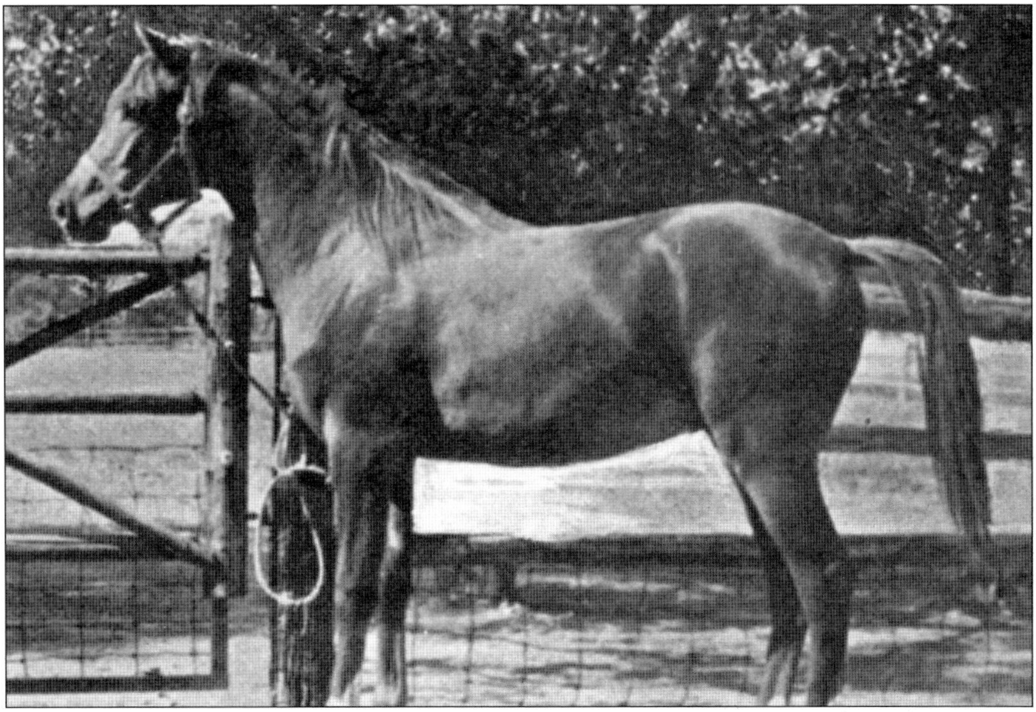

Tish Hewitt's Ofir, number 9, was the victor of the Laurel race, the first in a series of similar non-wagered, exhibition races of the same distance. Ofir also won the second race, held at Pimlico track in Baltimore on Thanksgiving Day, 1959; Al-Marah Ibn Indraff was second. Ofir took second to Max Culpepper's Michael on January 15, 1960, at Tropical Park in Florida. On February 25, 1960, Ofir won again at the Hialeah track in Florida, while Michael won the second annual Arabian race at Laurel later that year. Ofir was by the Polish, prize-of-war stallion *Witez II and out of Tiara, a daughter of the Polish, prize-of-war mare *Wierna. Ofir is here depicted as a young colt in a painting in an advertisement for the Arabian Horse Racing Association of America.

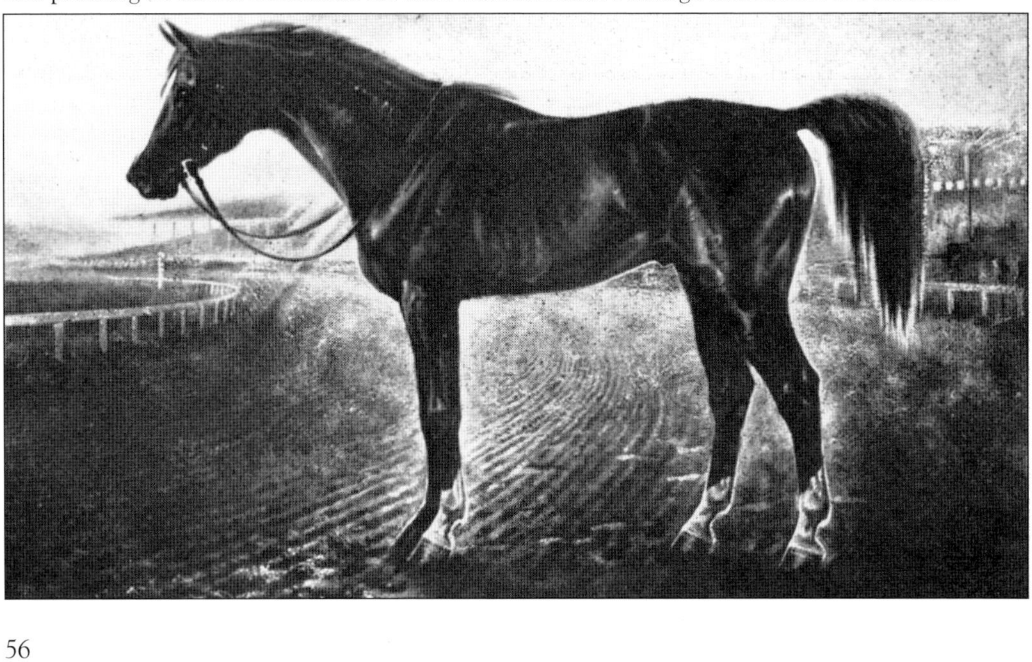

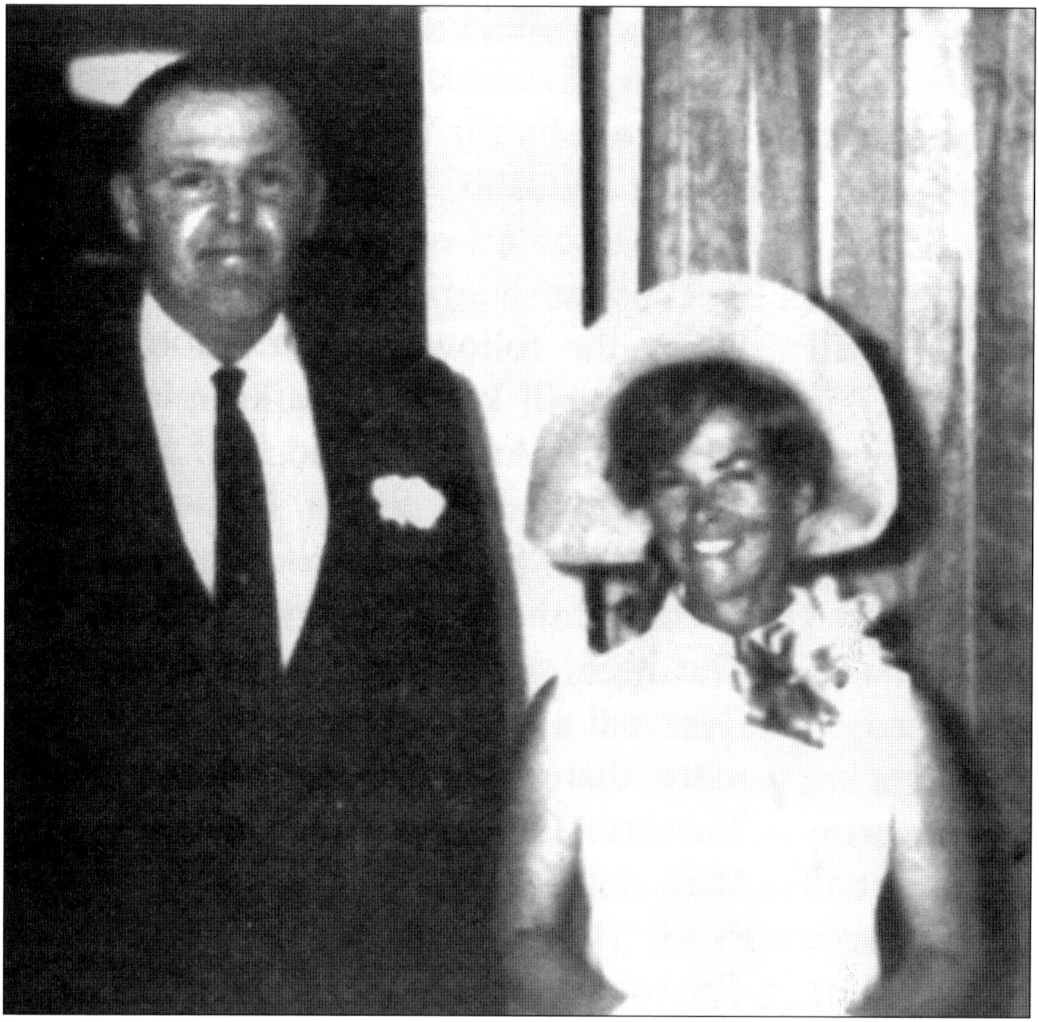

Altogether Arabian horse racing enthusiasts held two races in 1959, five races in 1960, and six races in 1961. During the 1960s, racing gained ground mainly in the western United States. Dominating these races were horses from the Lucas Arabian Stud (LAS), owned by Austin and Hazel Lucas, pictured here. To a large degree, this trend reflects the influence of Travelers Rest and Kellogg Ranch/U.S. Remount Arabian horses. Their availability was concentrated from California eastward to the Midwest region, given the Pomona Remount's location and Dickinson's sales of Traveler's Rest Arabians to Western ranches. J. M. Dickinson's influence is also evident through the pedigrees of several early racehorses, whether through their Travelers Rest ancestors or Dickinson's assistance in registering the army's Polish imports. In 1955, newlyweds Hazel and Austin "Luke" Lucas purchased the first Arabian horses that would help them build a racing legacy: their stallion Nusik descended from Kellogg/Remount stock, and their mare Nevada Star was a daughter of the Polish *Lotnik. (Courtesy of Tracy Singley.)

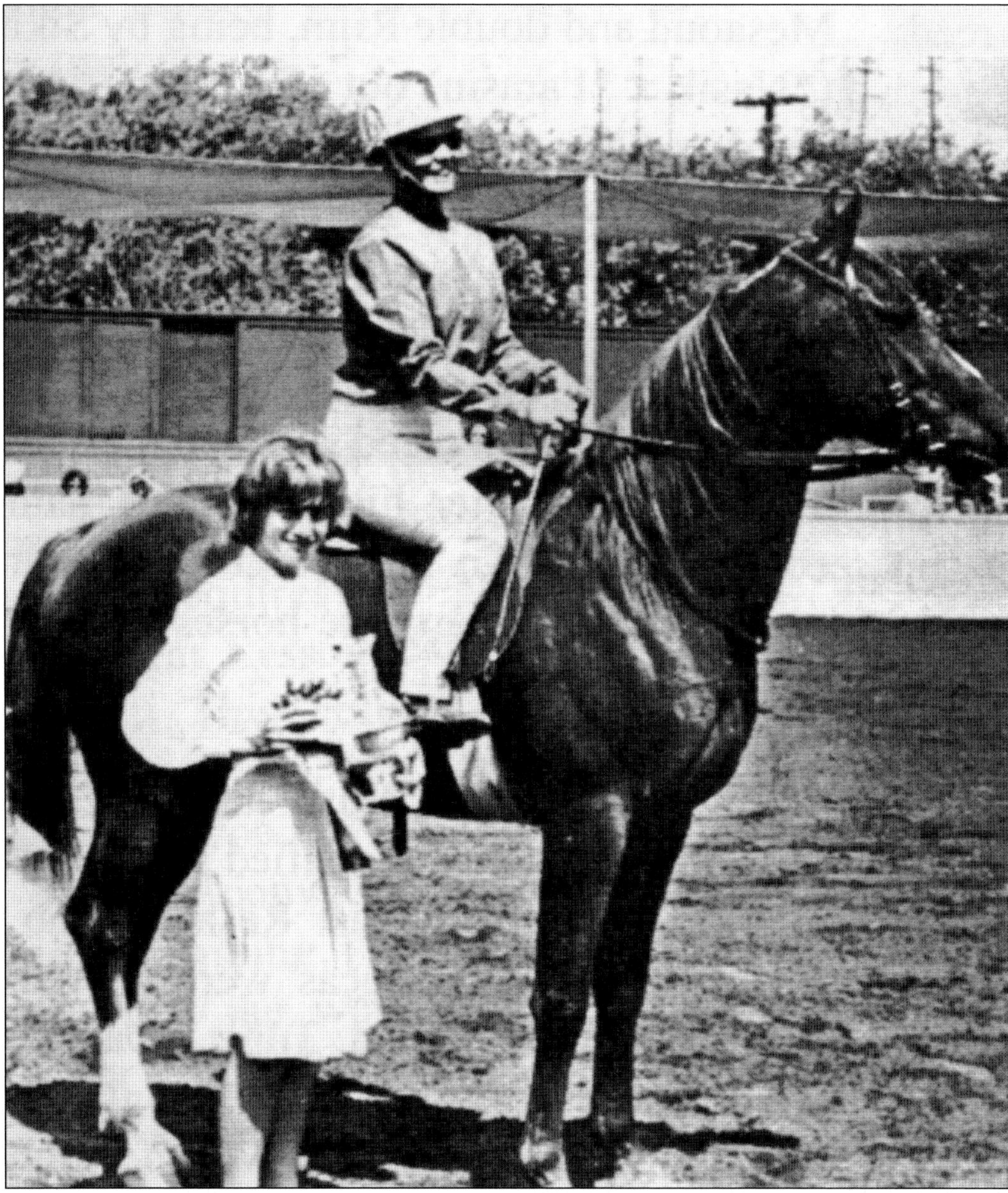

The Nusik son Beau Reshan was born in 1960; in 1961, Nusik sired Nusabre out of the mare Nevada Star. In 1963, the Lucases settled their Lucas Arabian Stud in Fernley, Nevada, and these were foundation horses of the LAS racing herd. Robert "Bob" Raine, a Thoroughbred racehorse trainer, assisted them in conditioning their Arabian horses for racing. The partners began contacting Arabian horse shows held at fairgrounds with racetracks in Nevada, Idaho, and California, asking management to include a race event on the program. From the two 1930s "National" Arabian horse shows organized by Dickinson in Nashville, Tennessee, Arabian horse shows had grown dramatically as postwar, middle-class recreation. In 1966, Beau Reshan won the Mile Race held at the National Championship Arabian horse show in Springfield, Illinois. Hazel Lucas was her own jockey. One of Beau Reshan's toughest competitors was the *Witez II son Witraff, a contemporary of this early period in the sport's history. (Courtesy of Tracy Singley.)

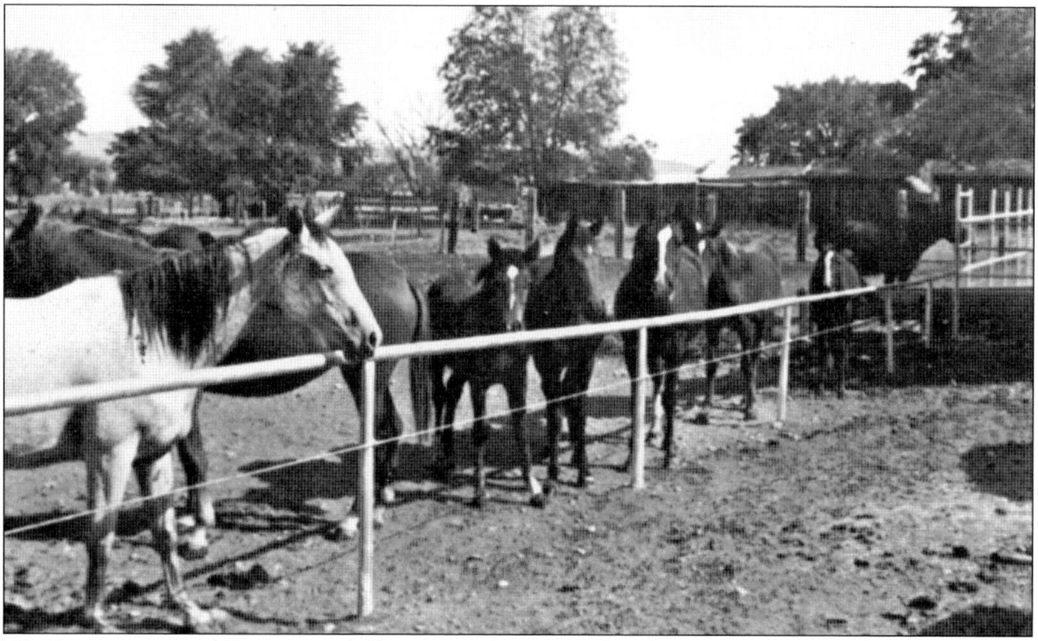

The Lucases personally managed all aspects of training their horses, including conditioning them at home on a dirt road alongside an irrigation canal that provided a flat, maintained surface for miles. The LAS horses lived outdoors in the natural environment of the West, not in extravagant stables. Pictured here are mares and youngsters in a dry lot. During the 1960s, Bob Raines and Hazel hauled horses around the western United States to compete in races at Del Mar and Santa Rosa, California; Fallon and Elko, Nevada; Klamath Falls and Salem, Oregon; and Calgary, Canada. Hazel referred to Luke as the one who made it all possible, as he remained at home to take care of the ranch while she traveled to shows, races, conventions, and meetings that would help build Arabian horse racing and showcase their horses. As a team, they were determined to keep the amateur sport alive and growing. (Courtesy of Tracy Singley.)

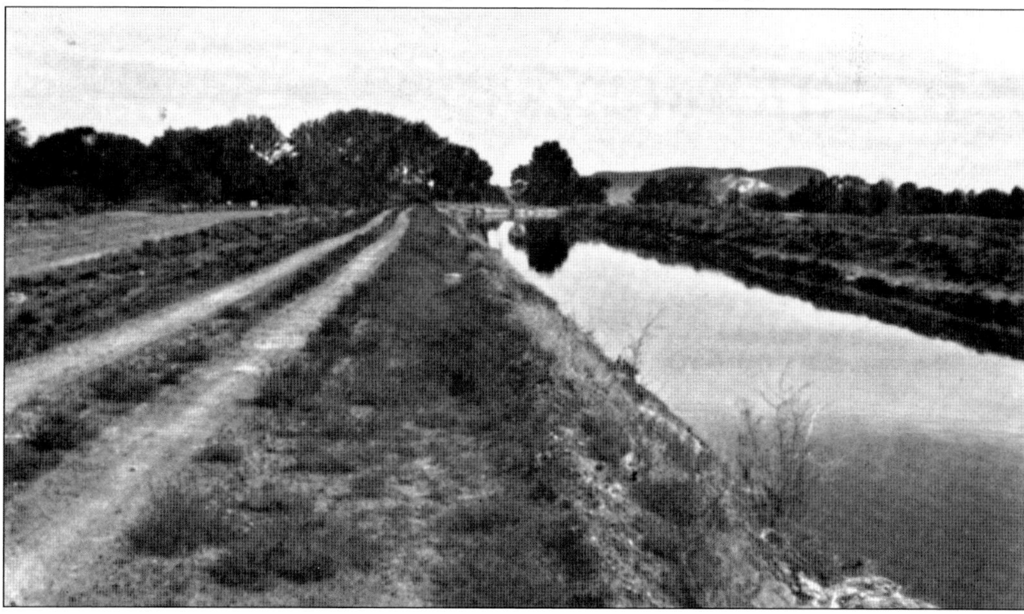

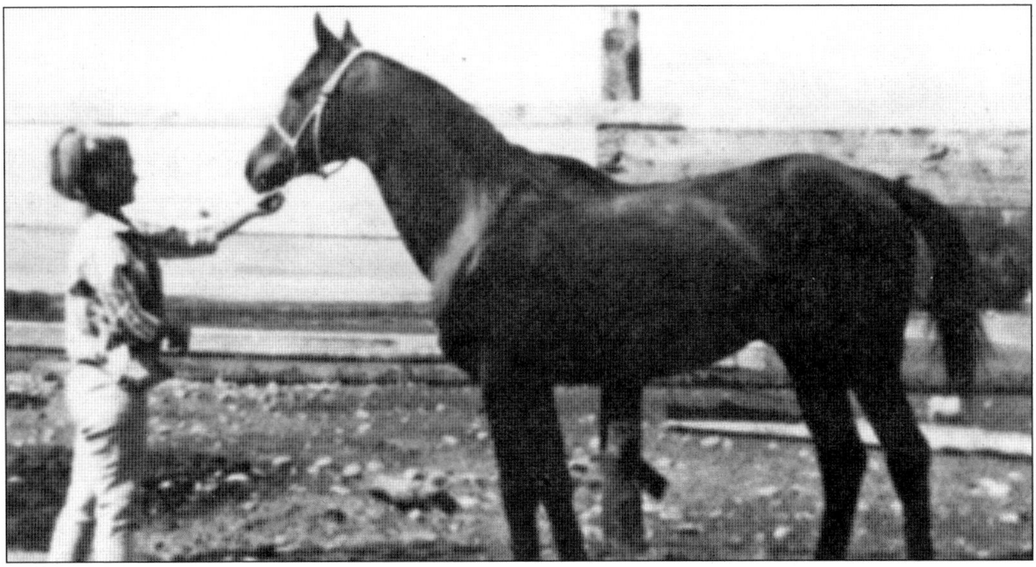

In 1963, Nevada Star made her debut in a race at Boise, Idaho, with the Lucases' daughter Tracy as rider. Shortly thereafter, the mare was retired from competition and became the cornerstone of the LAS breeding program. Nevada Star appears in most of the LAS horses' pedigrees, and sometimes twice, most often through her son Nusabre, born 1961. Through the 1960s and into the 1970s, Nusabre racked up an impressive record: running six years in 33 races, he won 10 times, placed second 3 times, and finished third 8 times (written 6/33 [10-3-8]). Nusabre's career spanned from the days of "show races" at fairgrounds to the earliest pari-mutuel (wagered) races for Arabian horses, held at regulation Thoroughbred racetracks. Nusabre can still be found today in Arabian racehorse pedigrees, including through two impressive daughters, LAS Tigre Lil and LAS Hilare. These three horses and Lucas herself were inducted into the Arabian Horse Trust Racing Hall of Fame. (Courtesy of Tracy Singley.)

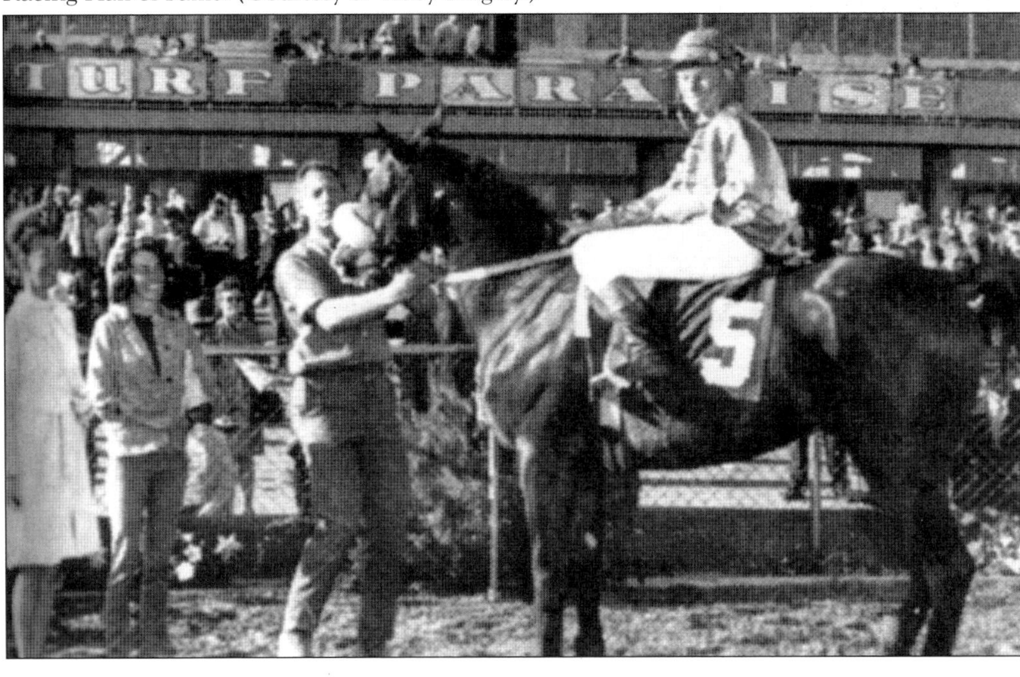

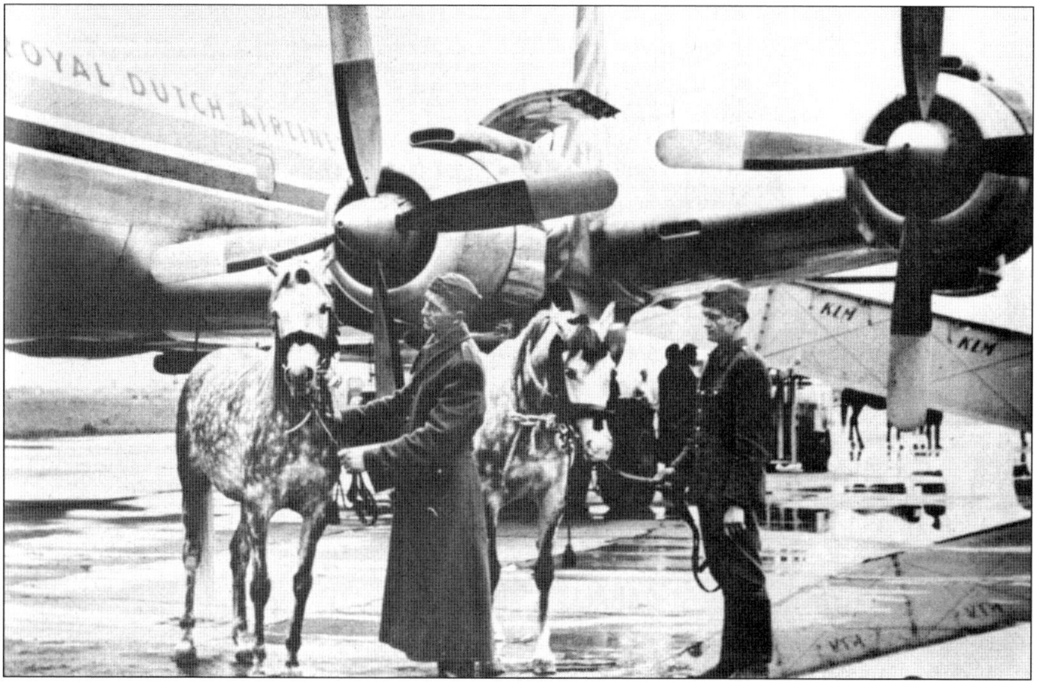

Dickinson's 1930s importations from Poland, and the army's prizes-of-war importation, were dormant trends that germinated during the 1960s. Ed Tweed, an architect in the 1920s, a soda-shop restaurateur during Depression years, then a general manager for Dole Refrigeration Manufacturing Company, built a home in Scottsdale, Arizona, where he kept Arabian horses for riding. Tweed discovered the history of Polish Arabians and in 1963 imported several mares, shown here at Warsaw.

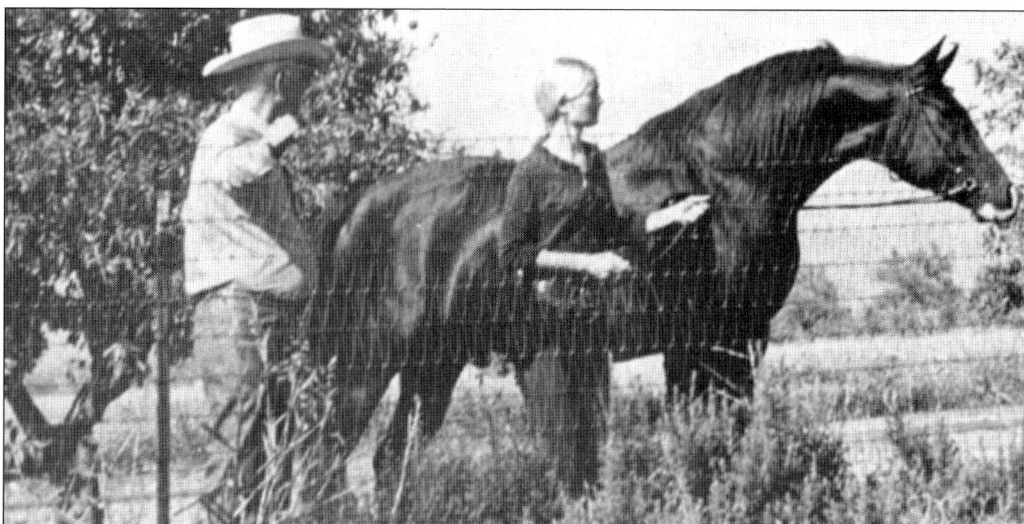

In 1967, Tweed imported two stallions from Poland that became extremely influential in Arabian horse racing, *Orzel and *Zbrucz. Shown here is *Orzel with Tweed and his granddaughter, Shelley Groom. *Orzel, whose name translates as "Eagle," had a good race record in Poland, 1/7 (2-3-1). In the United States, he won four of his five races, coming in second place one time. *Orzel was named National Champion Arabian Racehorse in 1967.

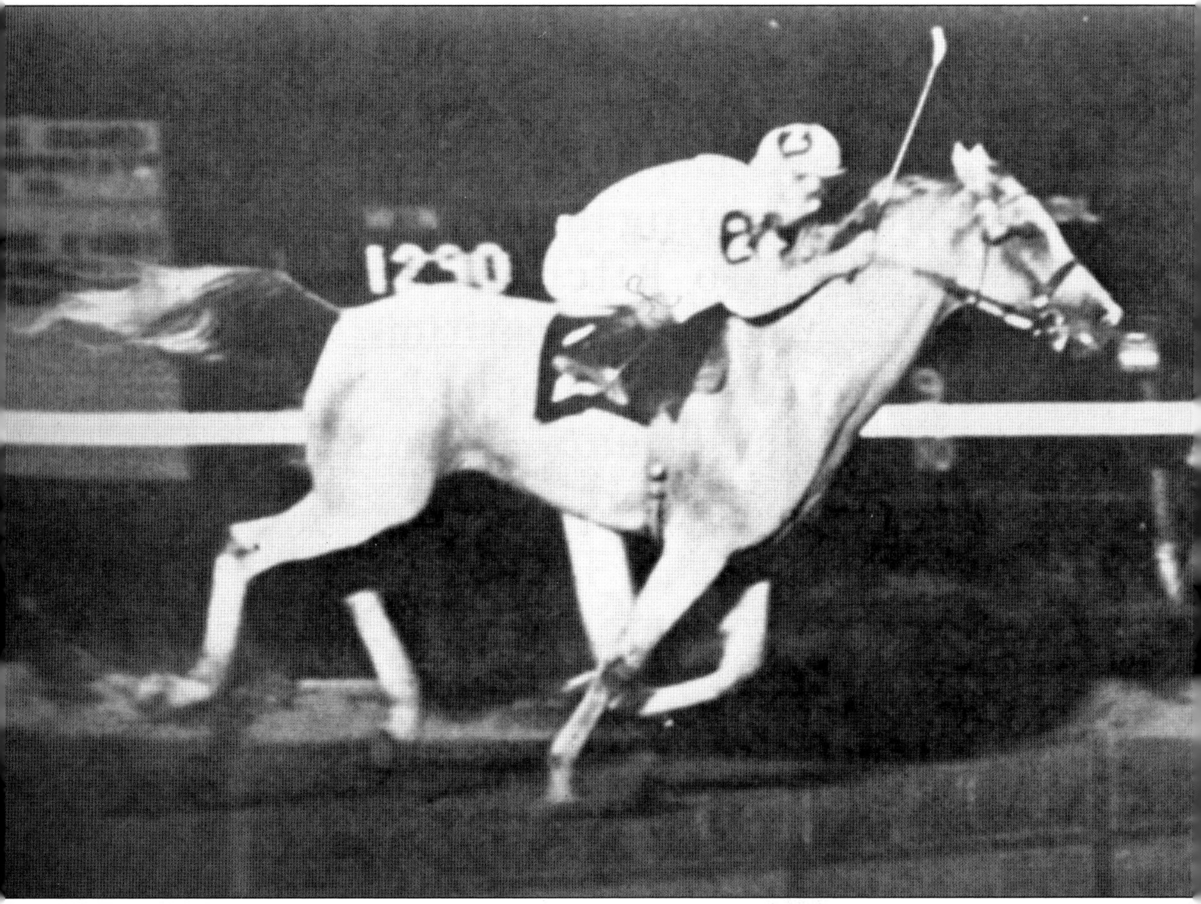

The only horse ever to beat *Orzel on American soil was the grey El Gohari, in the first Arabian race ever held at Turf Paradise in Phoenix, Arizona, on November 19, 1967. (The third-place horse in that race was the 16-year-old Al-Marah Ibn Indraff, veteran of the first exhibition Arabian race at Laurel track in 1959.) El Gohari was fresh from his victory in the first pari-mutuel Arabian race ever held in the United States, the Invitational Arabian Handicap at Evangeline Downs in Lafayette, Louisiana, September 2, 1967. (Hazel Lucas's Nusabre was second in that race.) The race marked a new beginning for Arabian horse racing, as more and more pari-mutuel races were available for the breed. El Gohari also won the 1968 Evangeline Downs Arabian Classic, pictured here. The grey gelding continued successfully at Colorado and New Mexico races, too. He proved the Arabian breed's durability, running 41 races over seven years.

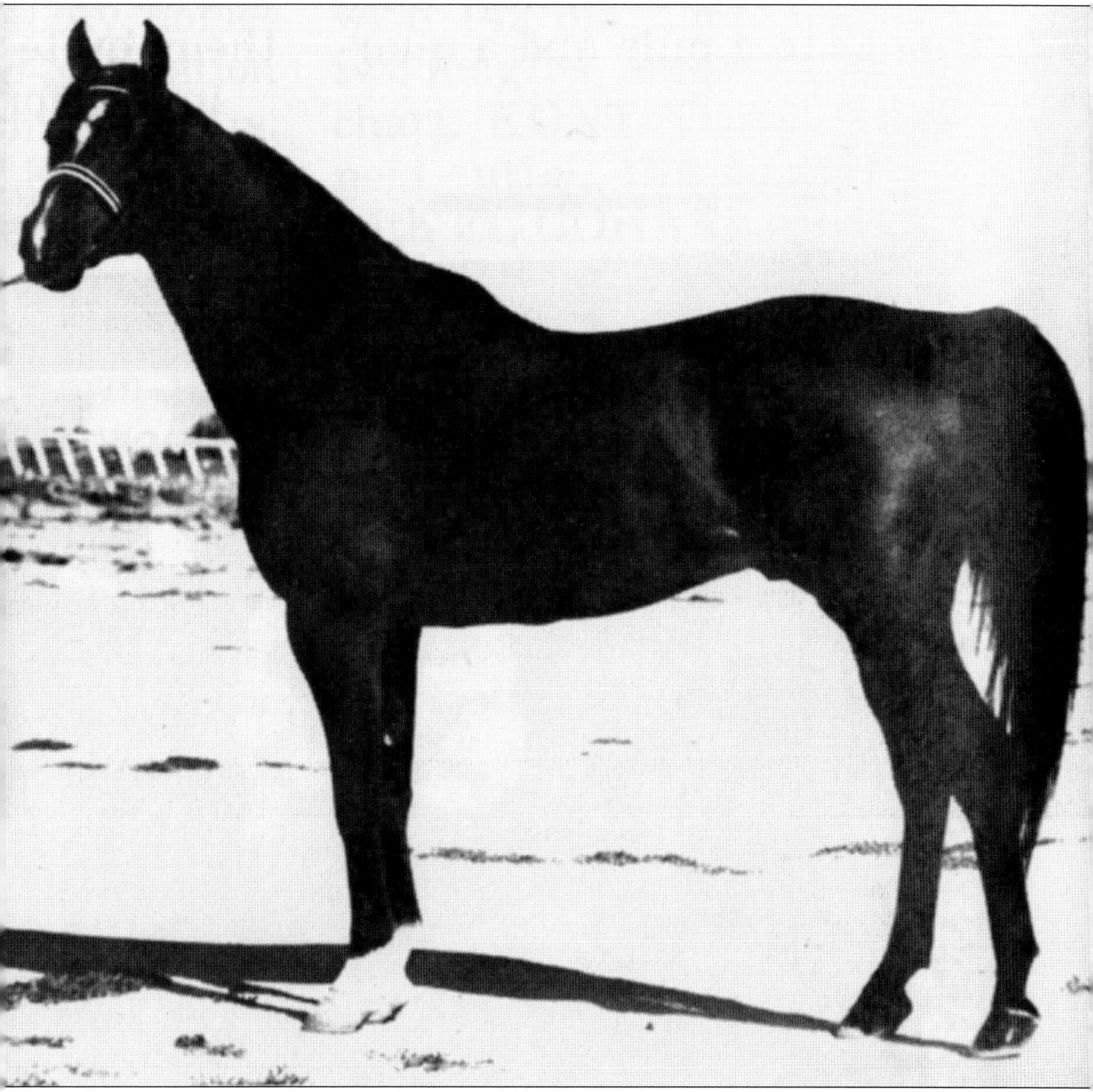

*Allahabad, shown here, was another imported Polish stallion that achieved National Champion Arabian Racehorse status in the United States. In two years, he ran nine times, winning eight of the races. His only loss was to Hazel Lucas's LAS Ferseyk. The trend of successful Polish racers was no surprise, as these were horses tested for athletic performance in their native country. Certain Polish bloodlines evidenced themselves as the cream of the crop. *Allahabad shares a common grandsire with *Orzel, as does another National Champion originating from Poland, *Algorab.

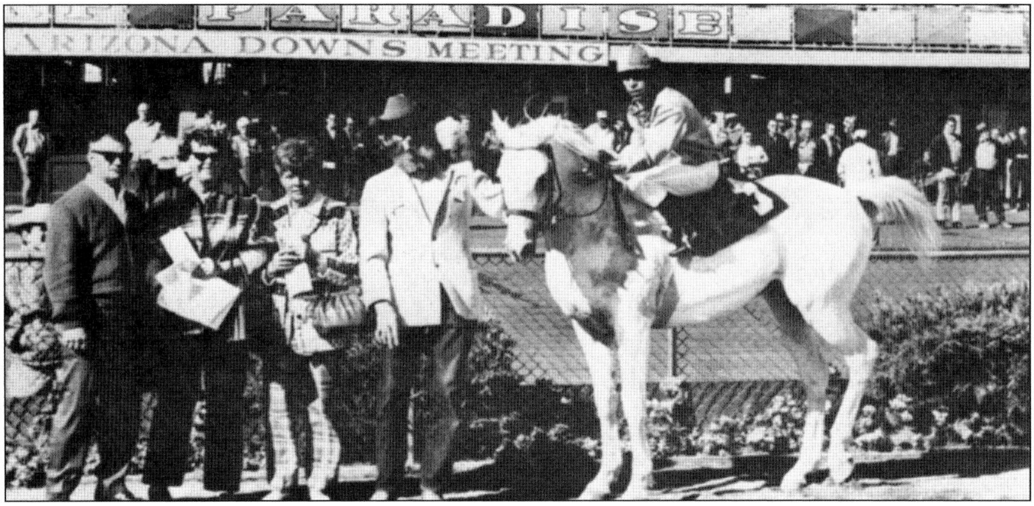

During the early 1970s, Polish-bred horses didn't corner the market on trips to the winner's circle at the racetracks. The pedigree of the great Kontiki (above) exemplifies domestic Arabian horse breeding of the period, even incorporating a few of Dickinson's famous Travelers Rest horses, Antez, *Nasr, and *Przepiorka. Kontiki's near-perfect record was marred only by one loss to *Orzel. The two met at Turf Paradise in a 1.5-mile race with a field of eight runners. Handicap weights were assigned to the horses based on their racing records, with *Orzel carrying 142 pounds and Kontiki, 140 pounds, indicating that they were the favorites. *Orzel won by one length over Kontiki, while Nusabre, carrying 113 pounds, finished third. Kontiki went on to win the National Championship title in 1971, after winning a two-mile stakes race held at Sunland Park, New Mexico (pictured below). Owned by Stanley and Robbie Kubela, the grey stallion set an Arabian racing record at Phoenix for 6.5 furlongs in 1971, also pictured. Today Kontiki's name is still revered in the pedigree of contemporary Arabian racehorses.

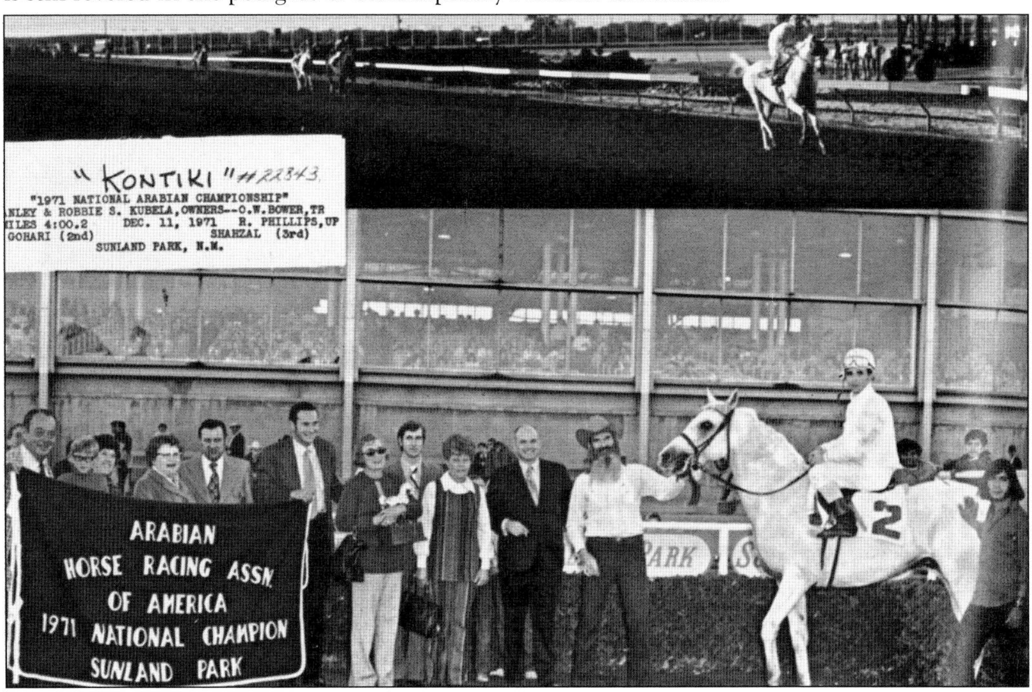

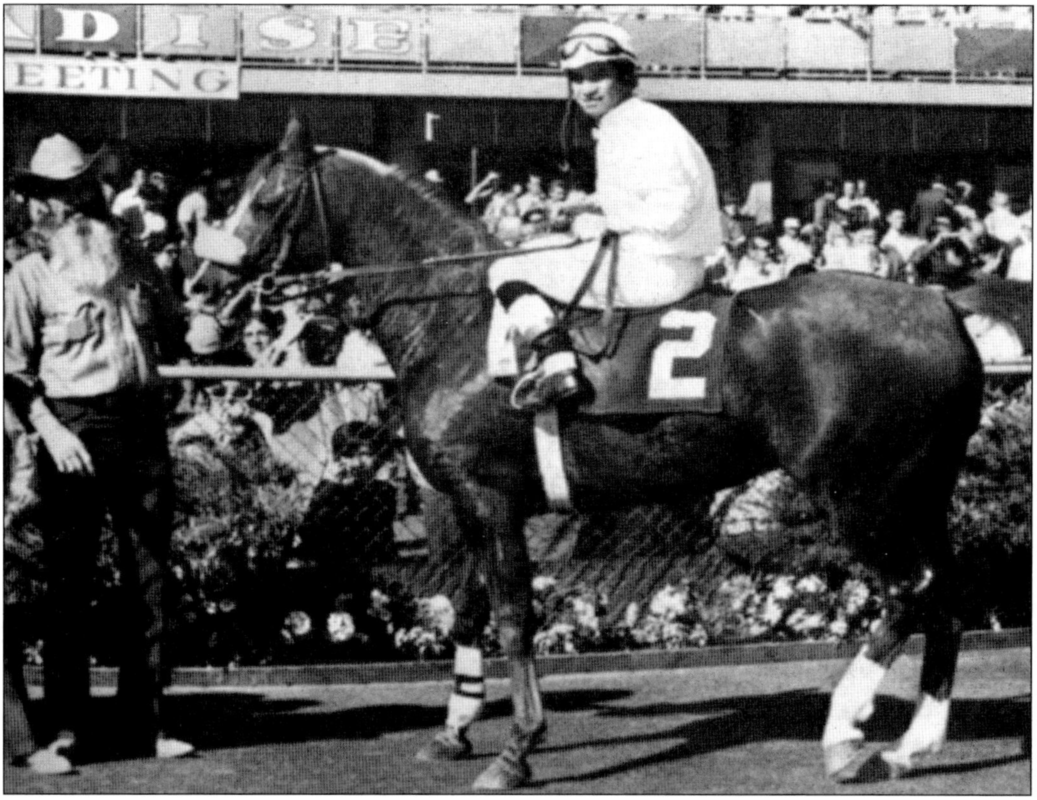

Like *Lotnik, *Witez II continued the legacy of the army's Polish imports in Arabian horse racing. Here are pictured two grandsons: Kemah's Polka, a son of Ofir, winner of the 1959 inaugural race at Laurel, and Afatez, by the *Witez II son Bolero. Pictured above, Kemah's Polka is winner of a mile race at Turf Paradise on March 3, 1971. He set a record for Arabians, clocking in at 1:46.3. At right is Afatez, winner of a mile race in 1:49.4 at Phoenix in 1972. *Witez II descendants are still valued today for their athleticism, though more for endurance racing distances (25–100 mile rides) than at the track.

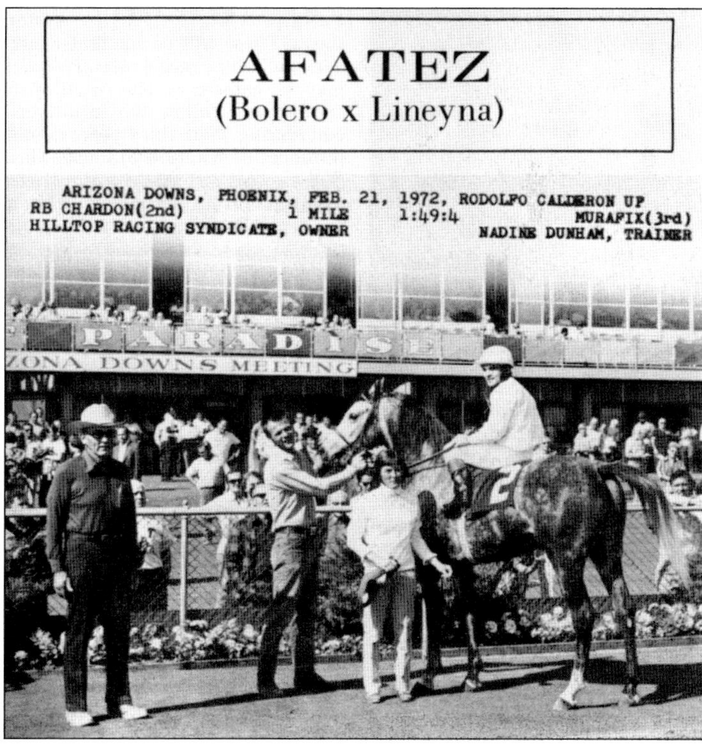

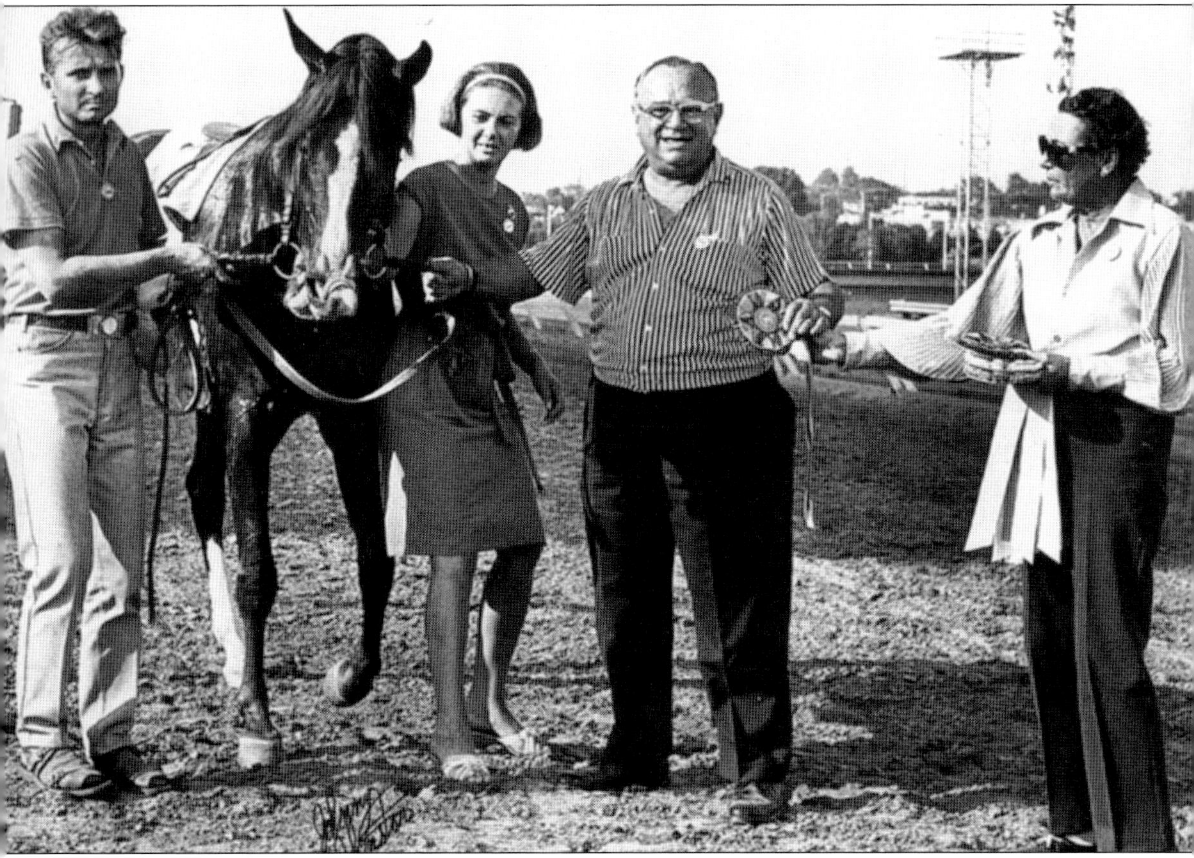

The chestnut stallion Sambor was born in Poland in 1965; his parents were the best racers in post–World War II Poland. American horse breeder Leon Rubin of Sir William Farm in New York was in Poland in 1968, when Sambor began his racing career. Rubin offered a job to Zenon Lipowicz, a young racehorse trainer, asking him to pick a couple of racing prospects for him to purchase. Sambor and Algorab, already mentioned, left Poland with Zenon and his wife, Jolanta. Once arrived, *Sambor was delivered to Turf Paradise but didn't take immediately to the track, despite his impressive racing record in his native country, 1/8 (3-2-1). With patience and attention from the Lipowicz couple, including regular sugar cubes, *Sambor blossomed. After some wins in Arizona, he was shipped to Oklahoma City to win the Arabian National Championship race. *Sambor was retired to stud in 1970. His legacy took shape the next year, when his first foals hit the ground.

Three

Structure

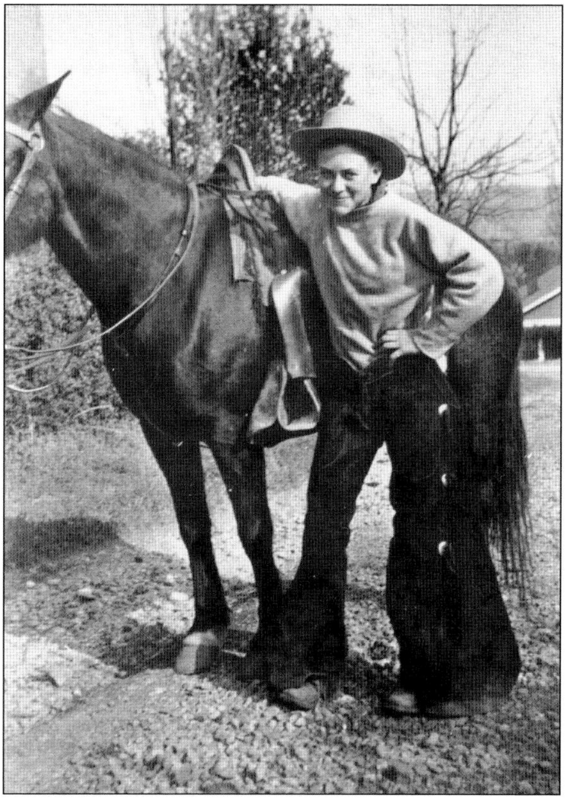

Sam Harrison grew up with horses, getting his first pony at age five. He progressed through various horses until entering medical school, and only after beginning medical practice in Loudon, Tennessee, did he ride his first Arabian horse. Little did he know that he would become an indelible name in the history of Arabian horse racing, travel the world to promote the sport, and create an enduring legacy of programs and bloodlines that still drive the sport today.

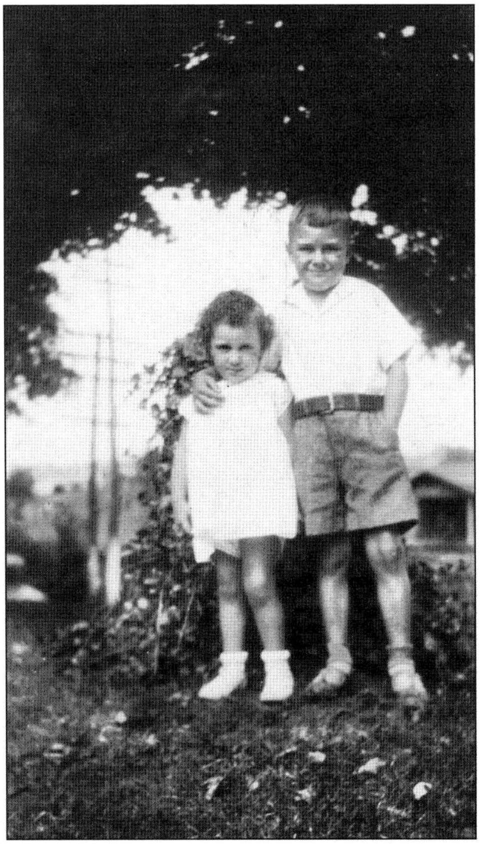

Samuel Arthur Harrison was born February 23, 1925. He came from a line of country doctors who made house calls on horseback. Both his father, Arthur, and his grandfather, William, practiced medicine in Loudon, a small town along the Tennessee River in East Tennessee. The Harrison family had originally arrived to the area by riverboat around 1812, settling on land that is still known today as Harrison Bend (pictured below). Sam is pictured here at age seven with his sister, Ruth, born in 1927.

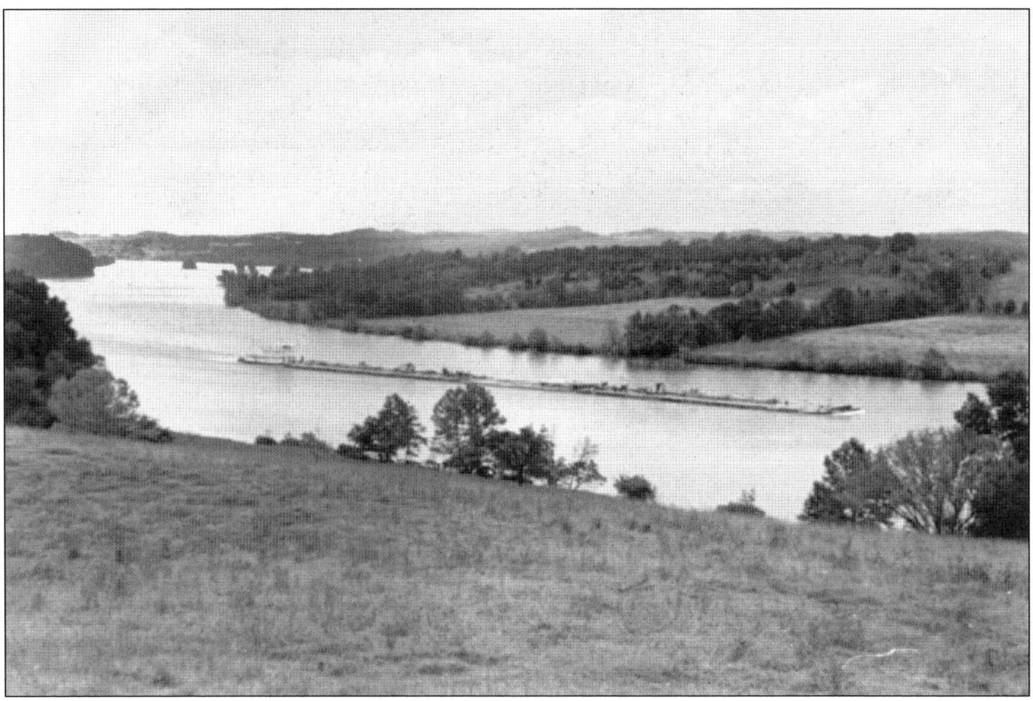

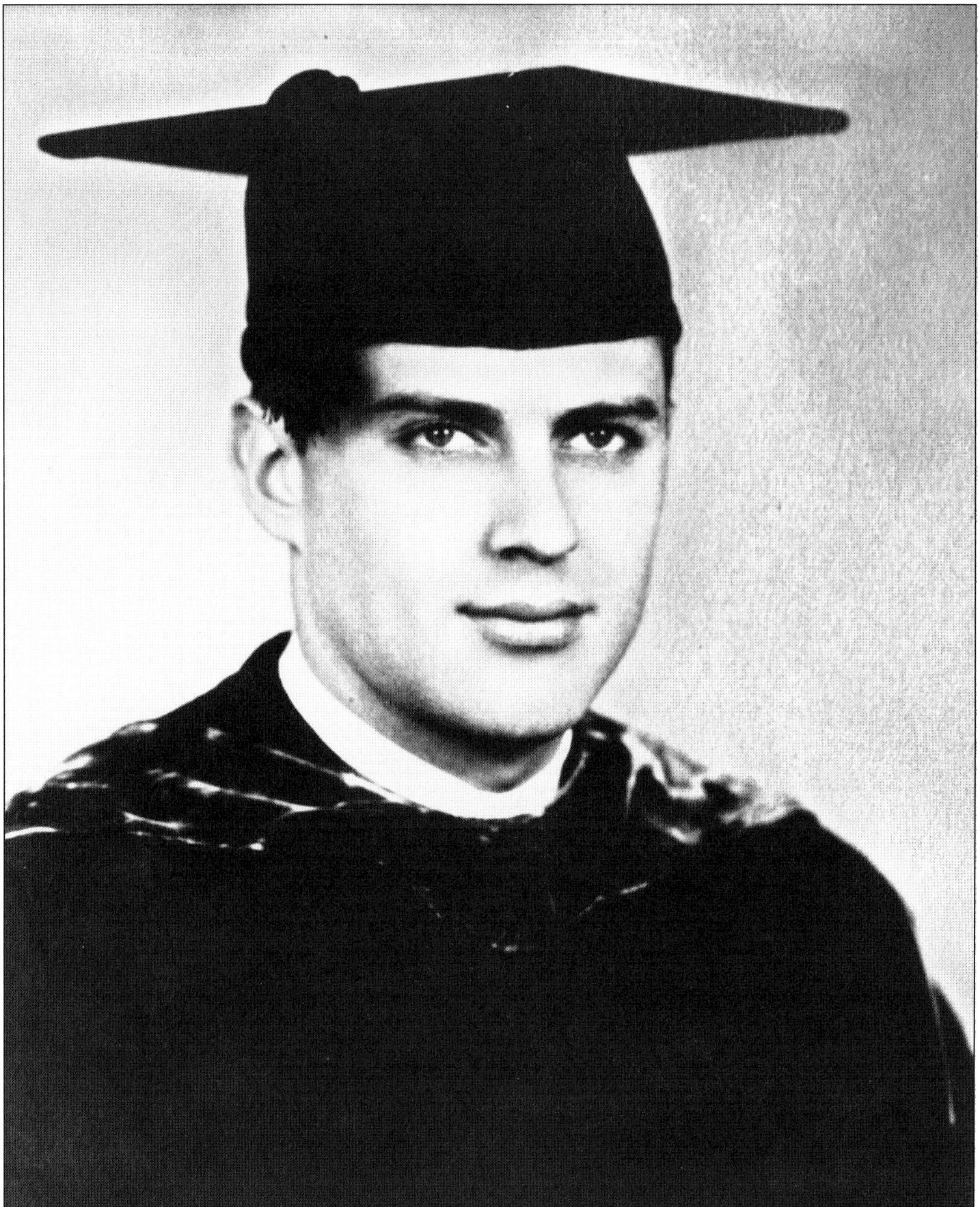

Harrison attended Emory University in Atlanta and served in the army for two years during World War II. Harrison went to medical school in Memphis, where he met and on June 18, 1946, married Bettye Louise Whitsitt. Harrison was enrolled in his freshman year of medical school and credited Bettye with working to put him through school. Harrison graduated from medical school in 1948, and the couple returned to Loudon by 1952.

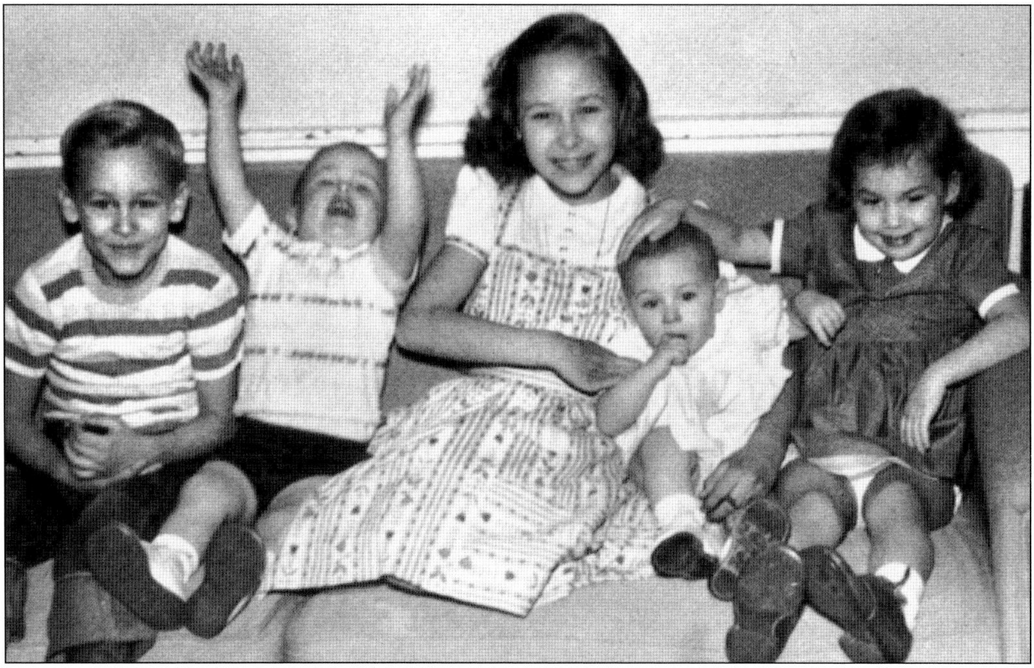

Dr. Sam and Miss Bettye had five children, shown from left to right: Scott, their second; Mark, their fourth; Whitney, the eldest; Jennifer, the youngest; and Cindy, the middle child. The children shared a pony named Dusty, and local horse shows became regular weekend events for the family.

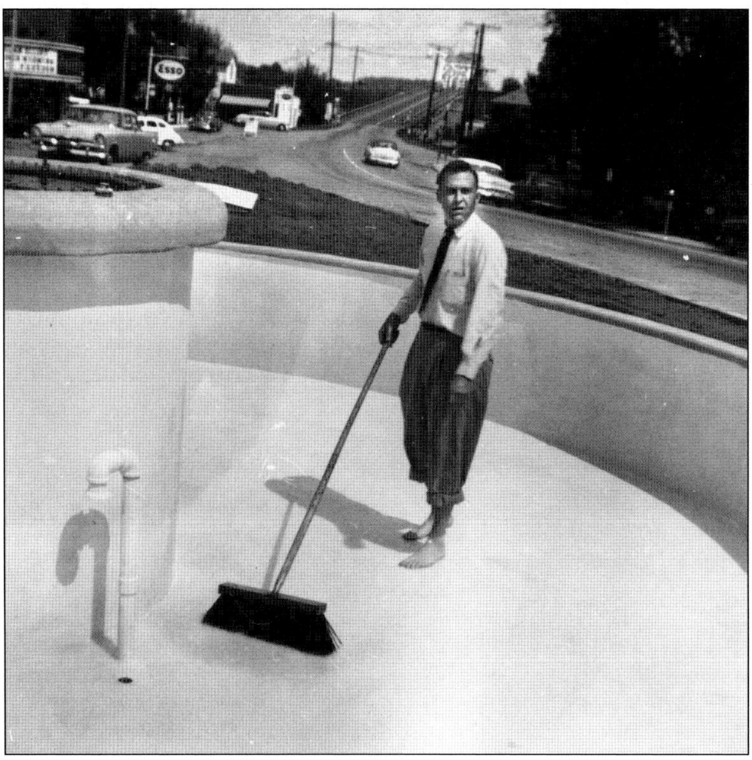

Just off the Loudon County Courthouse square is the fountain that Dr. Sam helped to encourage and build. Here he is pictured with cleaning efforts of that fountain, representative of his assertive attitude in getting an idea off the ground and a job done.

lorse Show Draws
·ood Attendance

The Philadelphia Community lub Horse Show held Tuesday ght fell somewhat short of e number of entries it had st year, but show officials y that the show was a suc- ss and that attendance and tries were higher than ex- cted.

The show was originally heduled for last Saturday, t was postponed when a orm wrecked the show area.

According to show official, . C. Anderson, 160 entries rticipated in the show, short bout 30 from last year's cord. Indications Tuesday ght showed that the club ould profit about $1,000 from e show.

Profits from the show are

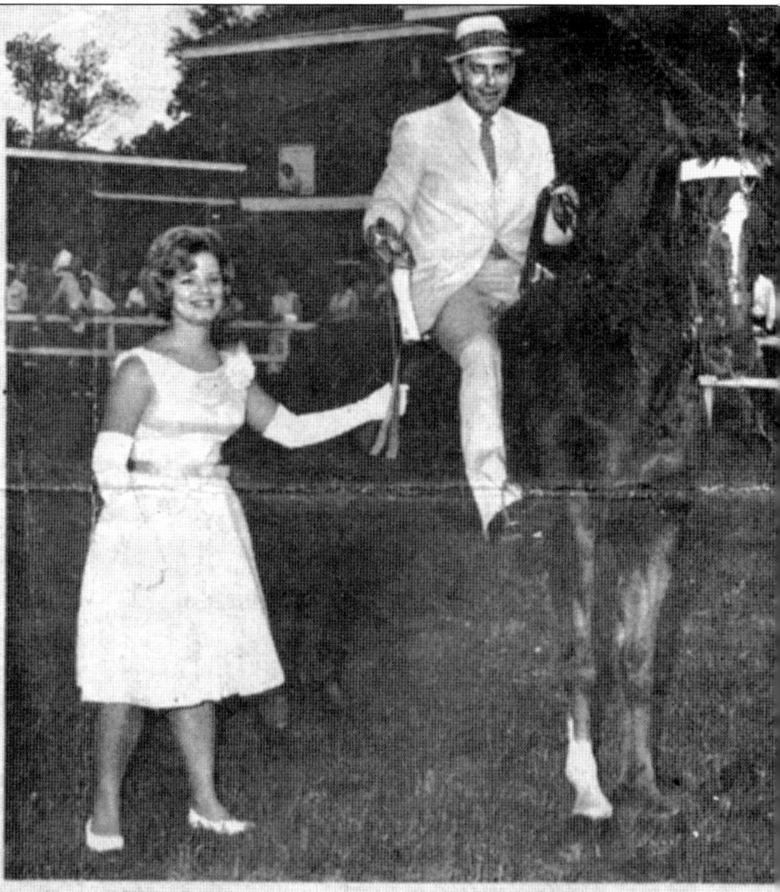

TAKES LOCAL CLASS -- Dr. Sam Harrison of Loudon shown receiving the first place ribbon in the Loudon Cou Pleasure Class at the Philadelphia Community Club Hor Show Tuesday night. His horse is Mr. Twis

Here Sam takes the blue ribbon at a horse show in nearby Philadelphia, Tennessee. The horse he rode was called Mr. Twister. Though Dr. Sam had been raised around horses, he was unfamiliar with Arabians. The first one he rode jumped out from under him several times, yet the animal's personality sold Sam on the breed. Known for their intelligence and agility as a breed, the Arabian horse seemed to catch his fancy. He first purchased the Arabian gelding Ha-jahn and next a filly named Cool Jewel, purchased from Gina Manion.

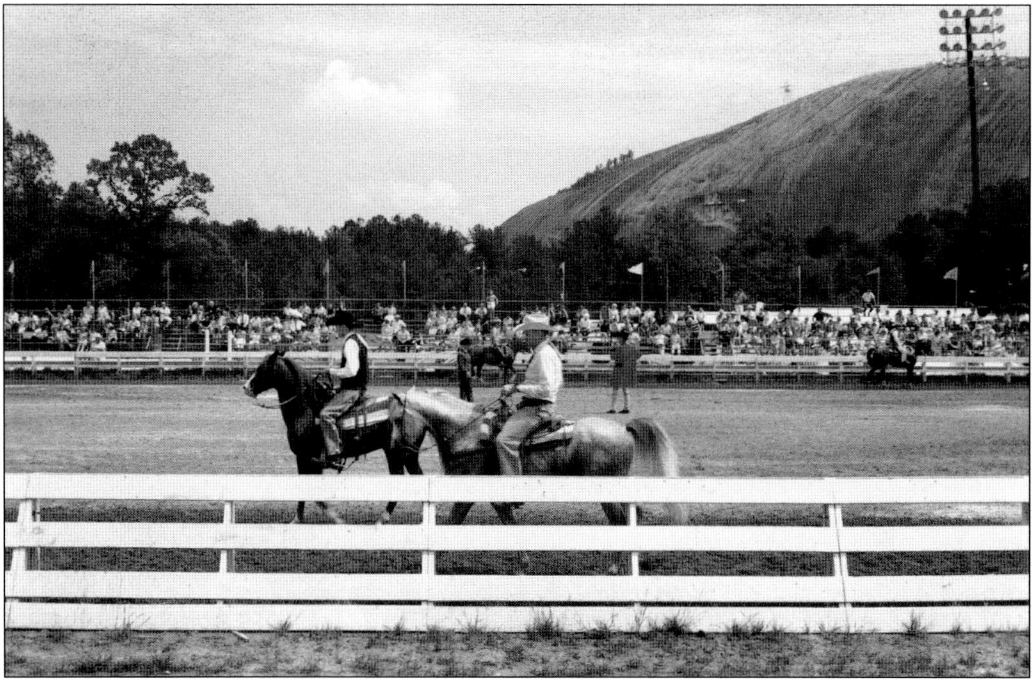

With Harrison and his five children involved in showing, he determined he needed several more Arabians. Soon he bought three more from Clarence and Gina Manion of Indiana. Here Dr. Sam competes at a show in Stone Mountain, Georgia.

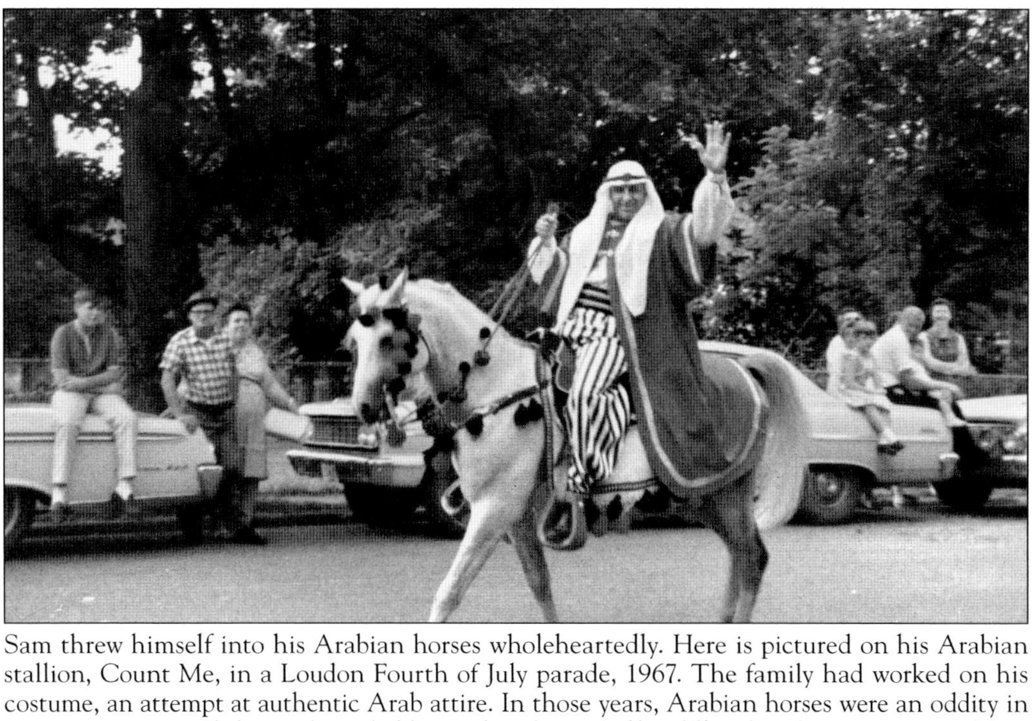

Sam threw himself into his Arabian horses wholeheartedly. Here is pictured on his Arabian stallion, Count Me, in a Loudon Fourth of July parade, 1967. The family had worked on his costume, an attempt at authentic Arab attire. In those years, Arabian horses were an oddity in East Tennessee, and the outfit probably perplexed some of his fellow Loudon County residents. One little boy was overheard to have mistaken Sam for Jesus.

FOR SALE

Phone 458-3215 Dr. Sam Harrison **Loudon, Tennessee**

1963

Mr. Twister

1963 ETHSA CHAMPION ENGLISH PLEASURE HORSE 16.2 Hands, Bay, One White Sock, White Stripe, 15 Yr. Old Registered American Saddle Horse. Formally A Parade Horse, Fully Trained, Gentle, Healthy, Just Right For 12 To 15 Yr. Old Girl Or Boy Who Wants To Show Horses And Win Some Ribbons. $500.00

Butter Scotch

Broke, 48" Hackney Mare, In Foal To Registered Arab Stud, 6 Yr. Old Bay White Star. Foal Reserved $250; Straight Sale $325.00

Sir Richard

2 Yr. Old Hackney 46" Colt Out Of Above Mare By Registered Welsh Stud, Beautiful Head, White Stripe, Gentle, Two White Stockings, Makings Of Fine Roadster Pony $175.00

Country Squire

2 Yr. Old Hackney Colt, Blaze, 4 White Stockings, Flax Mane And Tail. Gentle As A Lamb. Will Be A Wonderful Child's Pony. In The 48" Pleasure Pony Class. $150.00

Handy Dan

4 Yr. Old Gelding, White Face, 4 White Stockings, Dark Bay, One Glass Eye. 48" So Gentle Any Child Can Ride. Easy Kept, Stays Fat On Almost Nothing. $150.00

Two Horse Trailer

Single Axle, Good Shape, Lights, Paint, Canvas Top. $495.00

With Dr. Sam's new interest in Arabian horses, Mr. Twister and others found themselves advertised for sale. This sale page was also early evidence of Dr. Sam's entrepreneurialism in horse trading.

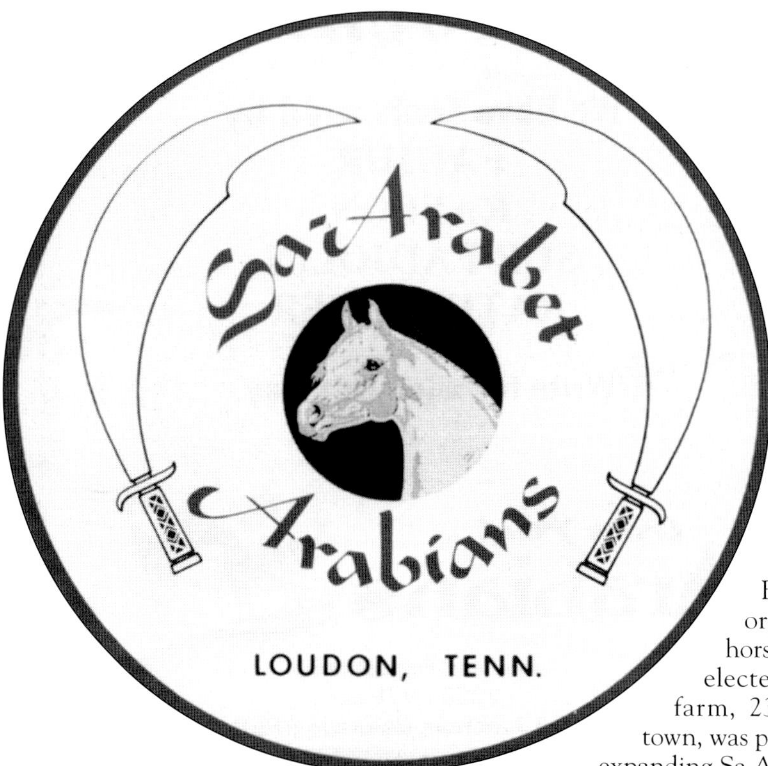

The growing Harrison herd needed a farm name and emblem. The Sa-Arabet name combined Sam, Arabian, and Bettye. By 1965, Harrison helped organize a local Arabian horse club, for which he was elected president. A second farm, 235 acres northwest of town, was purchased in 1967 for the expanding Sa-Arabet herd.

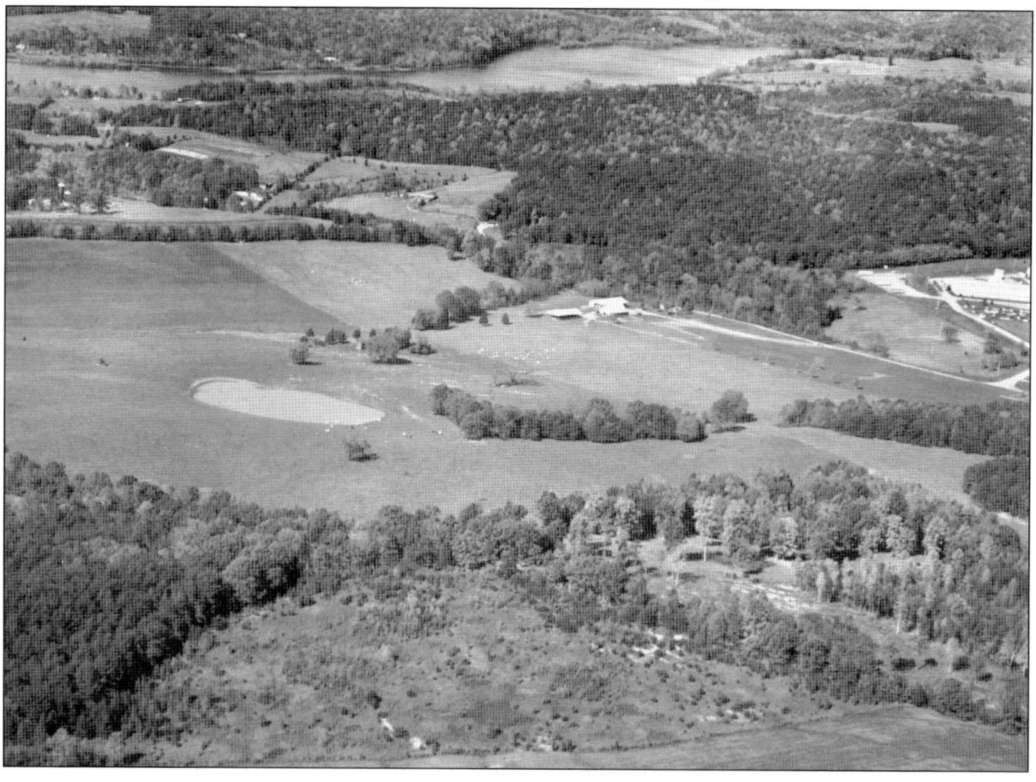

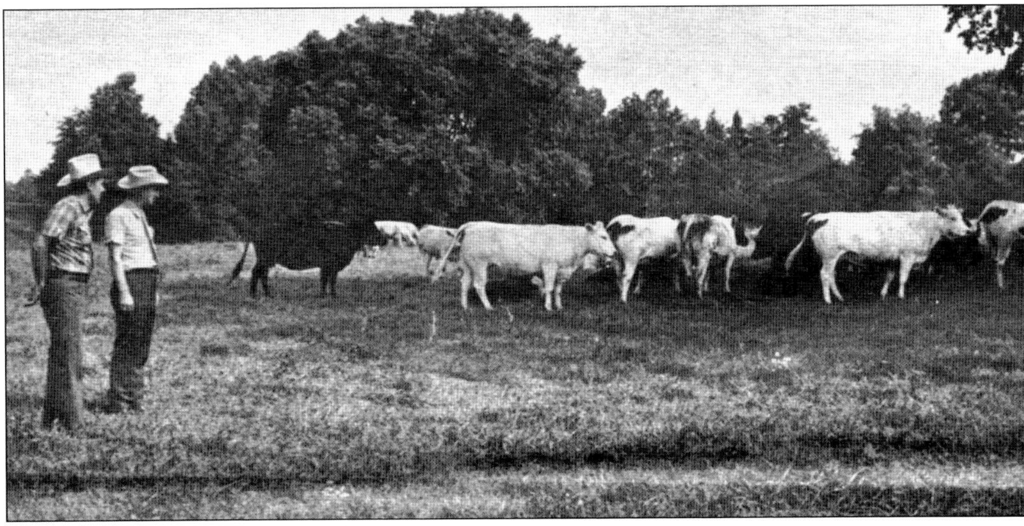

Between the farm at Harrison Bend and the Sa-Arabet farm, Harrison owned 200 head of Charolais cattle and 16 Arabian horses. The farms were models of modern agricultural management and efficiency. Limestone was added to improve the soil, and fescue and clover grasses were the forage of choice. Corn was grown for cow silage and barley for the horses and calves. Harrison used his Arabian horses around the farm, and none were pampered, living outside year-round.

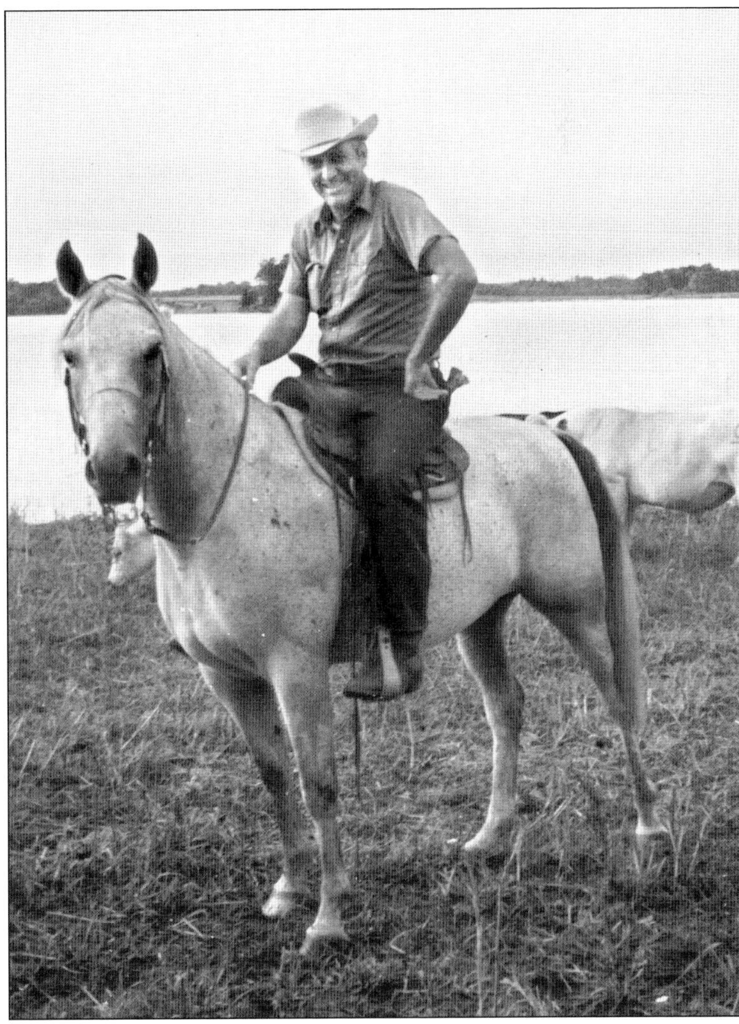

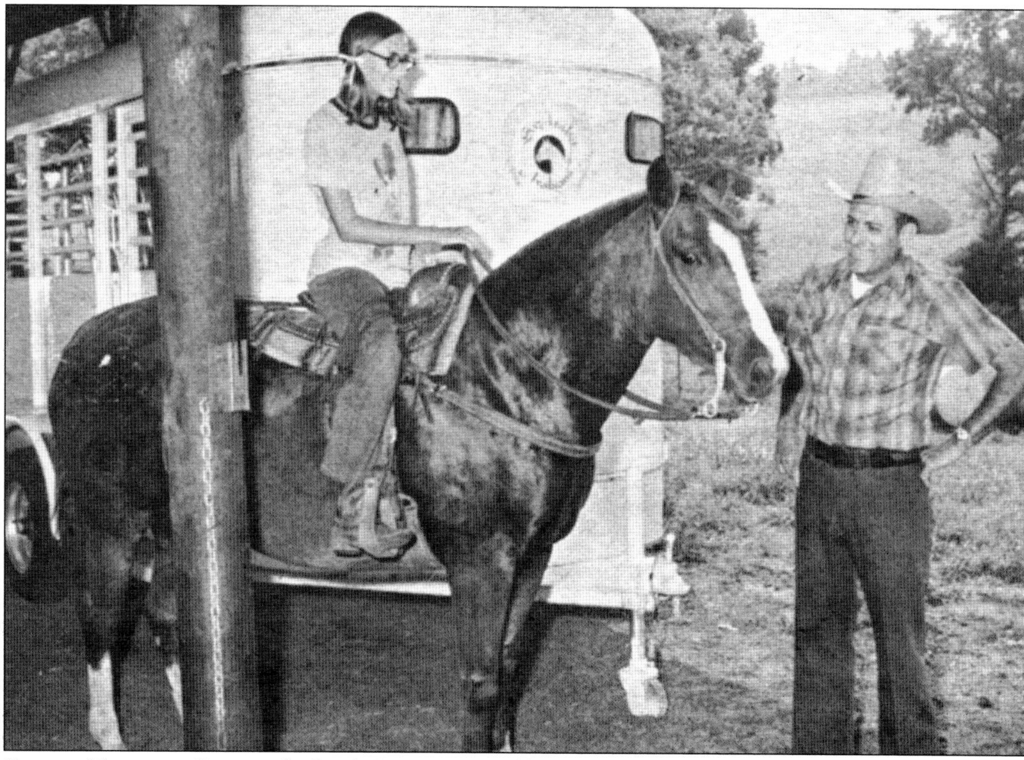

Pictured here are Sam with Cool Countis, sired by the stallion Count Me and out of the mare Cool Jewel, and daughter Jennie on a three-year-old filly. During this time, the Harrisons were learning as much as possible about the Arabian horse breed. One discouraging factor was their increasing cost, as show ring results in larger areas turned the Arabian horse into a status symbol. Also Harrison joked that as a Southerner, he resented having to go north to buy an Arabian horse. So he developed the idea of a consignment sale for middle-class buyers. His first sale was in 1970, and he continued for several more years. His partner in these annual sales was Tom Foster, a racing enthusiast.

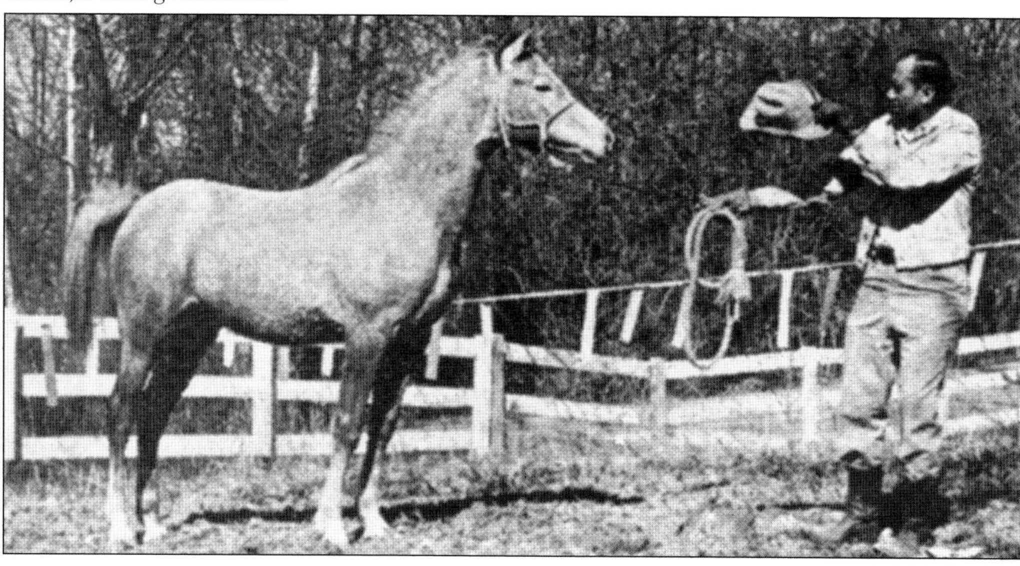

***DIMRAK**

48984

Imported Polish
Racing Stallion
Purchased April 8, 1972
at

SA-ARABET
ARABIAN FARMS
THIRD ANNUAL
CONSIGNMENT SALE
Loudon, Tennessee

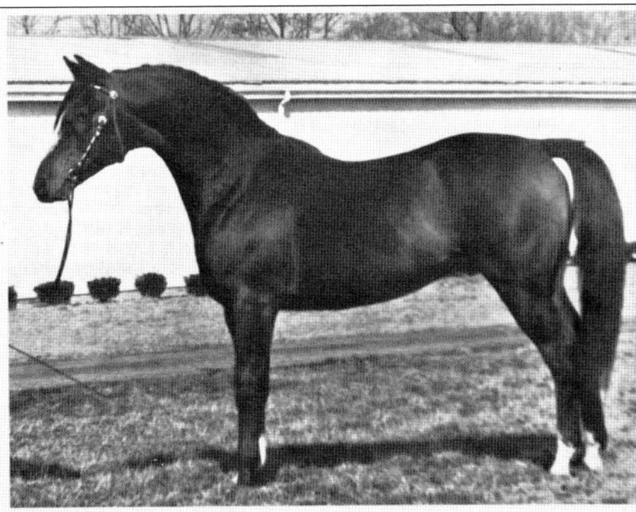

At the 1972 consignment sale, Harrison purchased a young stallion consigned by Bob and Fredericka Wagner. The Polish import *Dimrak was already racing at Sante Fe Downs in New Mexico and became Harrison's first Arabian racehorse. Paying $5,000 for a horse was unheard of at that time in Tennessee Walking horse country. By the early 1970s, Arabian horse racing had become a mix of exhibition races, pari-mutuel races, and so-called show races, which were held in conjunction with prominent Arabian horse shows. Most of the activity was in New Mexico, with smaller meets in California and Michigan. Harrison became dedicated to helping the sport grow and prosper.

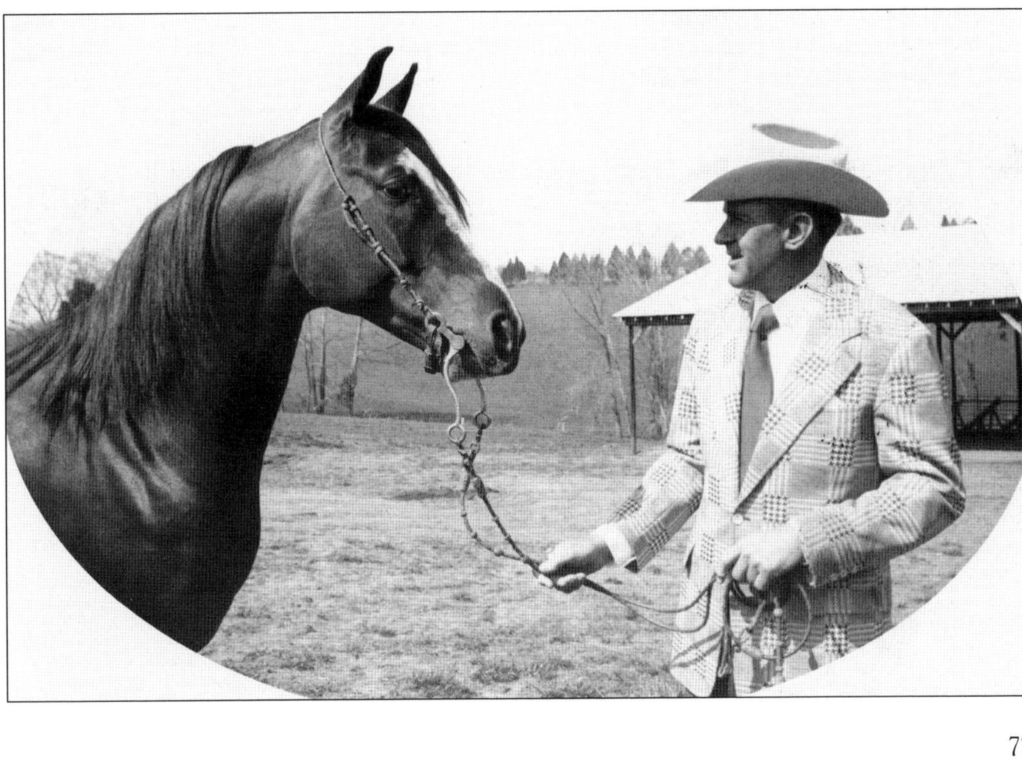

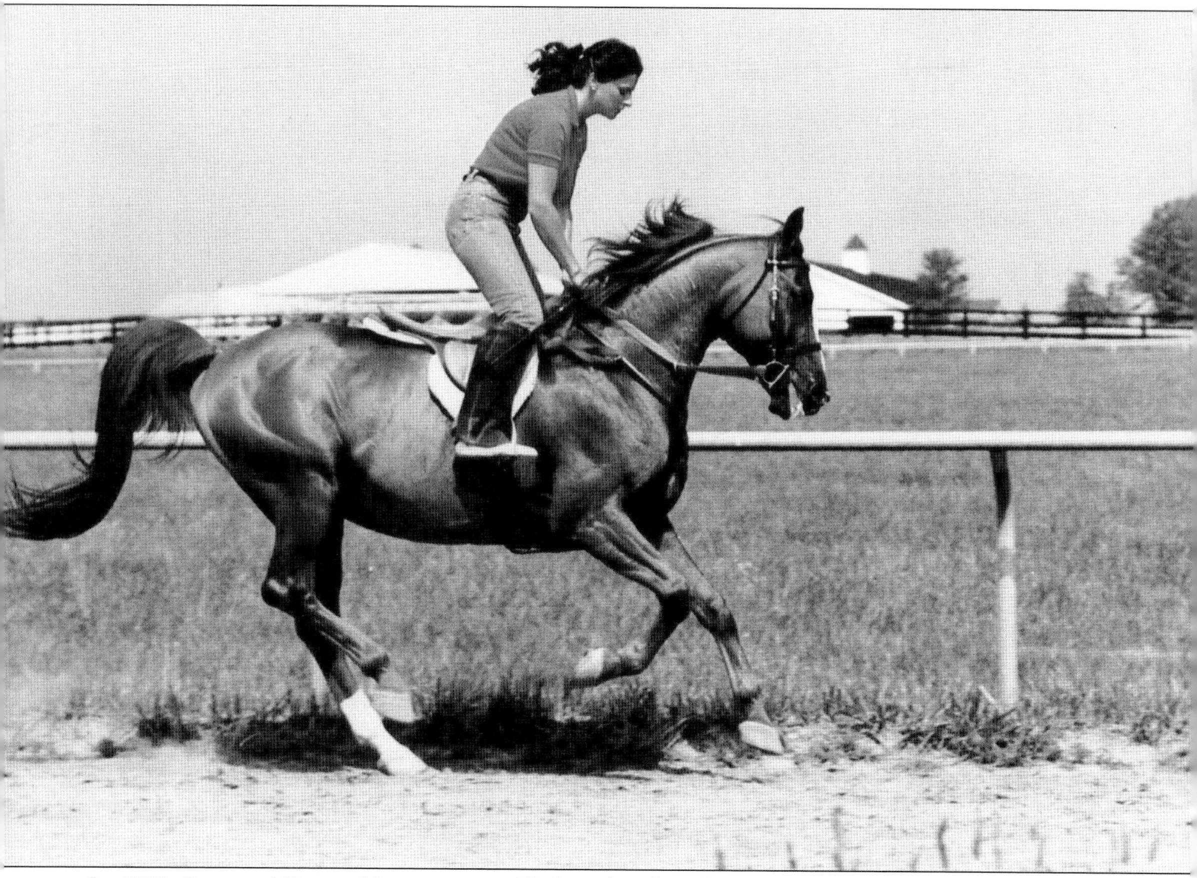

In 1972, Sam and Bettye Harrison attended a sale of Arabians at the Sir William Farm in New York. The farm was selling foals of the imported Polish stallion *Sambor, named National Champion Racehorse in 1970. Harrison and nine partners, most from Tennessee, were the successful bidders on Samtyr, a yearling colt, each contributing $440 to purchase the horse for $3,500, buy insurance, and transport him home to Loudon, Tennessee. The day was quite special for the Harrisons, as they had just received word that *Dimrak had won his first race under their ownership at Santa Fe. Samtyr spent the next two years growing up in the modest environment of Harrison's Sa-Arabet farm, as *Dimrak racked up more victories in the West. When Samtyr turned three years old, he was started under saddle. Samtyr then headed for California, where Arabian racing at the time was non-pari-mutuel.

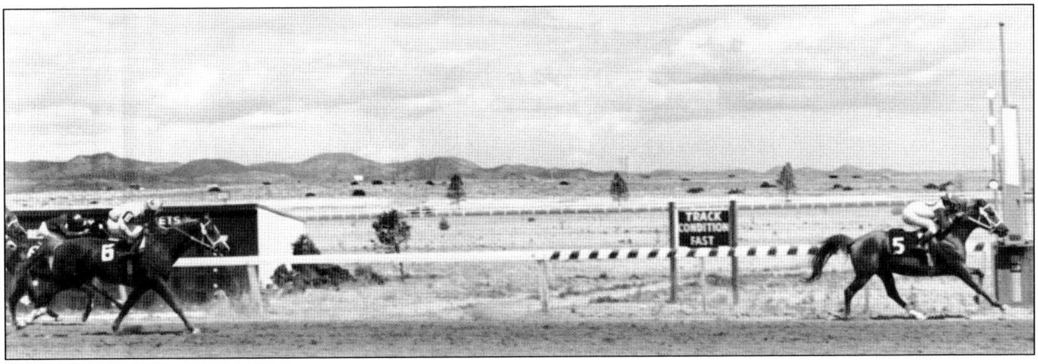

In California, Samtyr raced seven times, winning four times, placing once, and finishing in the "show," or third place, twice—written 7(4-1-2). A campaign in New Mexico, however, allowed Samtyr to earn official honors in pari-mutuel races, winning five of five, four of which set records. His lifetime race record, then, was 14(11-2-1) in two seasons. Noteworthy is the variance in distances Samtyr won, from five and one-half furlongs to the championship race distance of a mile and one half.

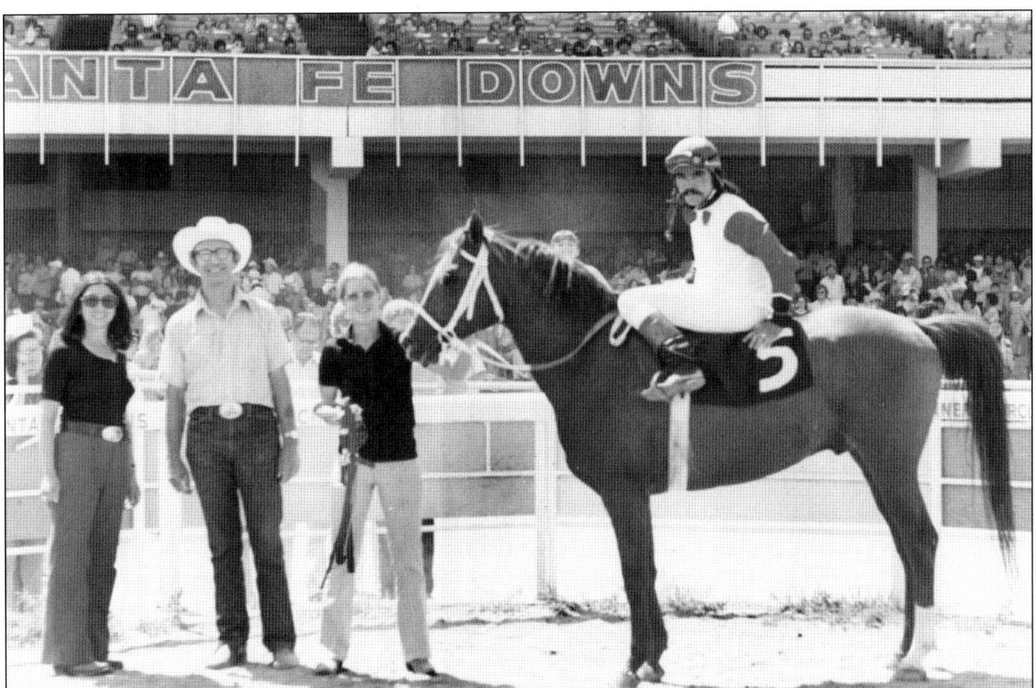

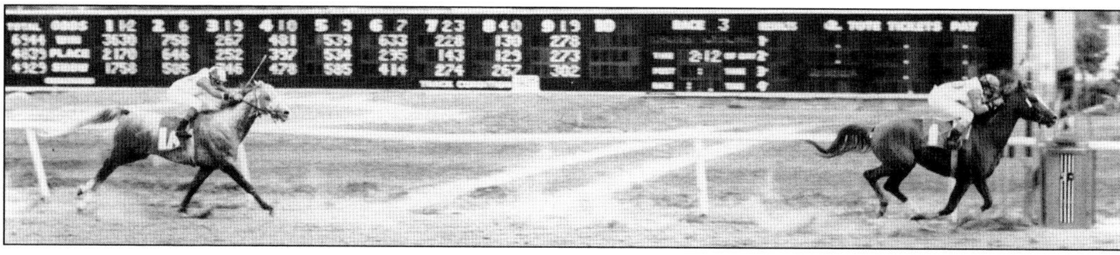

Winning the $10,000 Governor's Cup race at the Albuquerque State Fair, on September 18, 1975, Samtyr was named National Champion Racehorse. At the end of the season, he went home to Loudon to retire to stud. In the finish line photograph, another of Harrison's horses can be seen about to finish second place. LAS Nutron was from the Lucas Arabian Stud and had two lines to the prize-of-war import *Lotnik. In the winner's circle are, from left to right, the jockey's father and son, track manager Finlay MacGillivray, Tom Foster, George Whitsitt, Scott Harrison, Mark Harrison, Bettye and Sam Harrison, trainers Vic Oppegard and Nancy Kirkpatrick, Samtyr, and jockey Pat Torres.

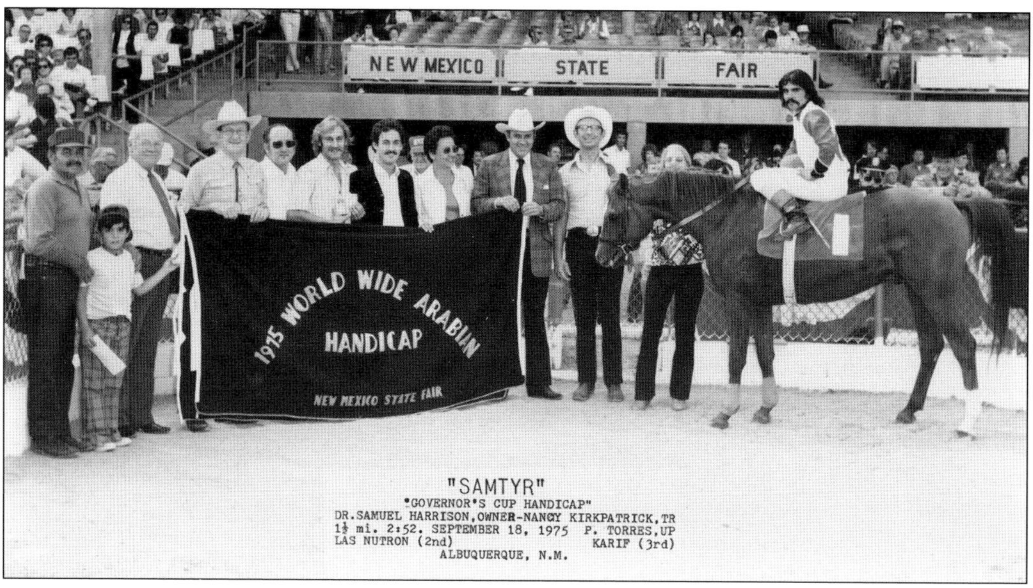

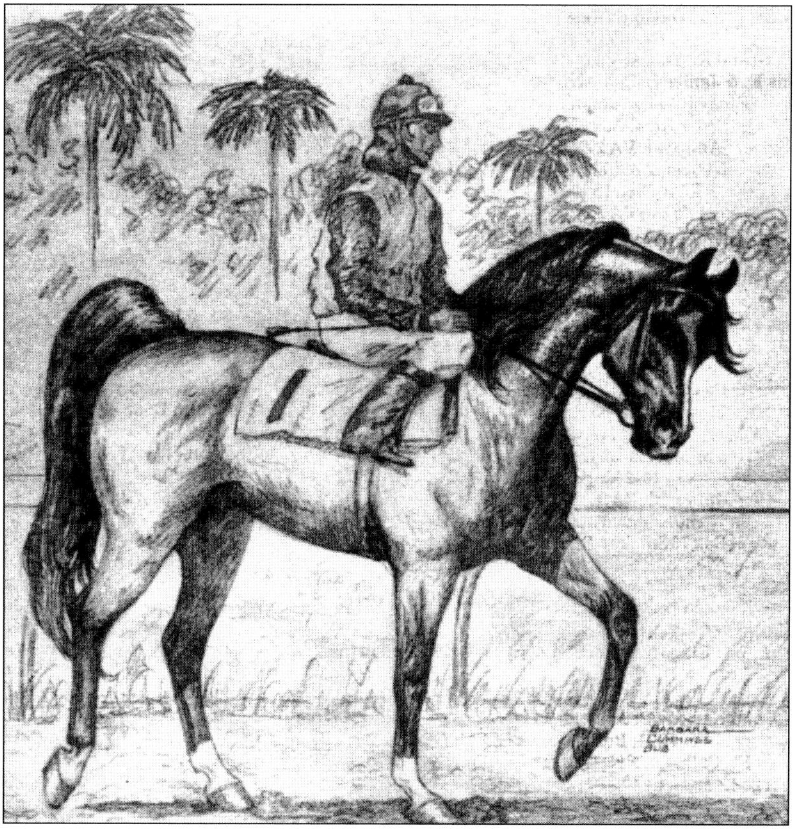

*Dimrak was a successful racer for Harrison, earning $10,000 on all kinds of tracks from New Mexico to Michigan to Ohio. Harrison occasionally held informal races in back pastures at the Sa-Arabet farm in Loudon. He later sired valuable daughters, including Dimorca, Ruraka, Tyrixa, and Dimfixa. Three of these four raced before Harrison bred them to Samtyr to produce the next generation of Sa-Arabet runners.

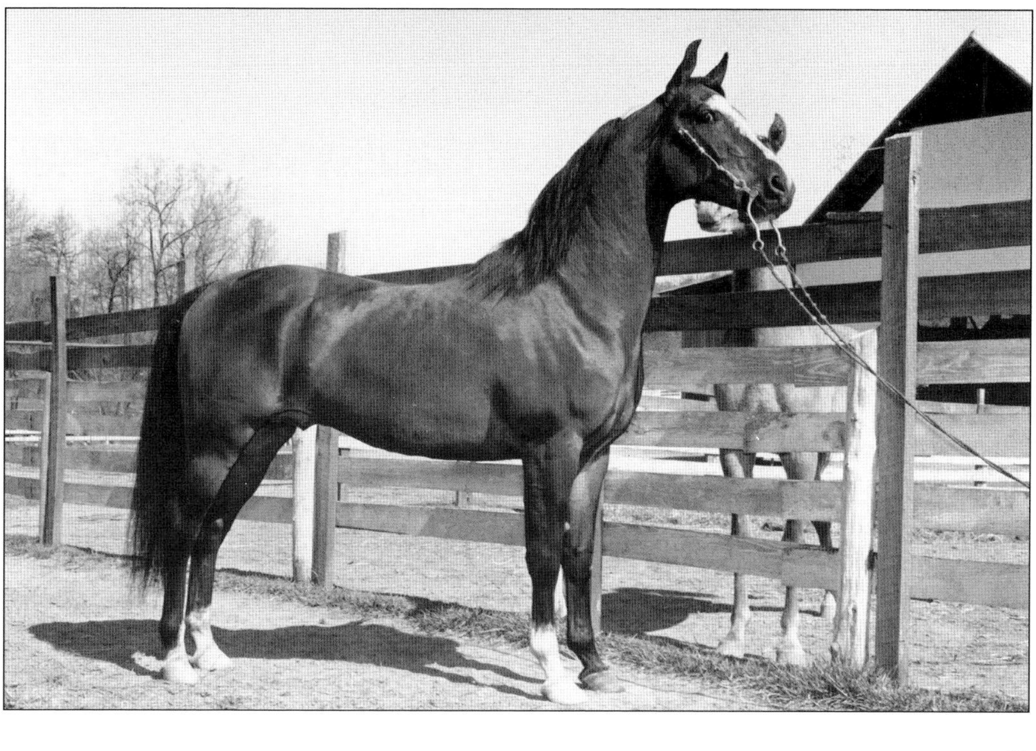

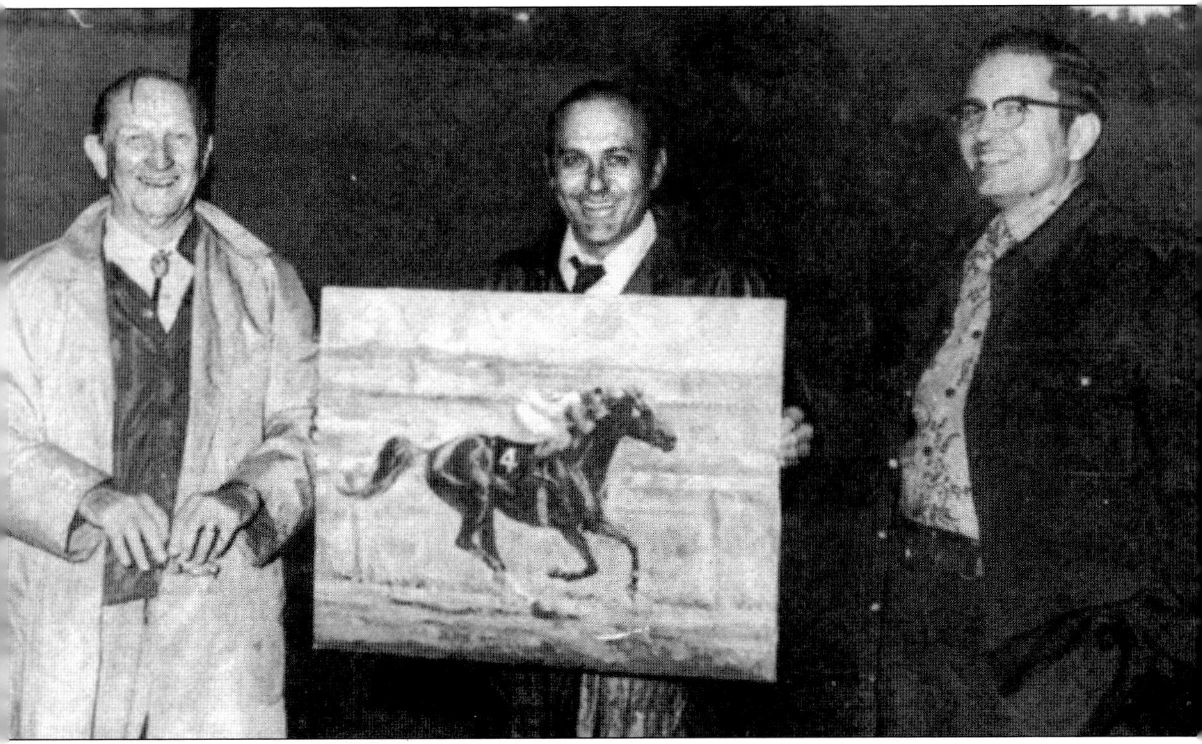

Sam Harrison holds a portrait of Samtyr, National Champion Arabian Racehorse, standing with two other owners, Col. Tom Foster (left) and Dr. Walter Shea. The painting is by Sandra Oppegard of Burbank, California.

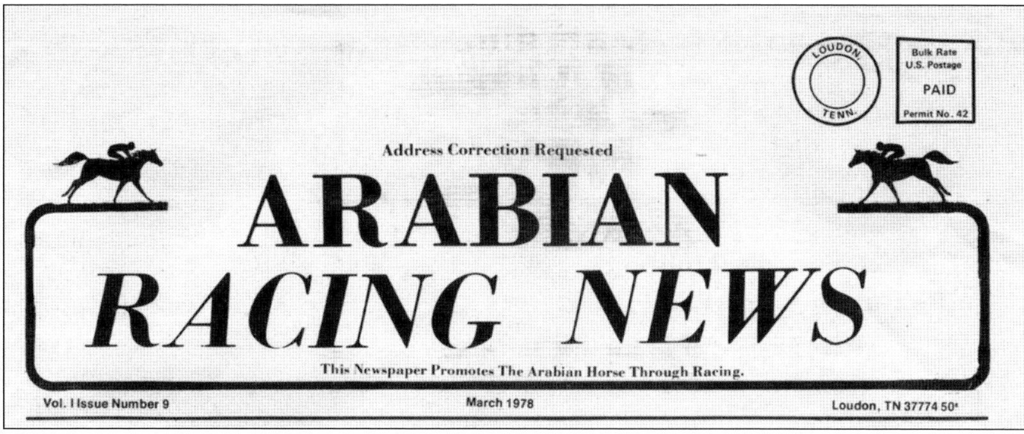

LOUDON TENN.

Bulk Rate
U.S. Postage
PAID
Permit No. 42

Address Correction Requested

ARABIAN RACING NEWS

This Newspaper Promotes The Arabian Horse Through Racing.

Vol. I Issue Number 9 | March 1978 | Loudon, TN 37774 50¢

To help promote the sport of Arabian horse racing in America, Harrison created, edited, and published the *Arabian Racing News* from 1976 through 1981 from Loudon, Tennessee. Growing from a simple four-page bulletin to a newspaper averaging 40 pages per issue, the publication reported on horses, races, and personalities in a comprehensive, entertaining style designed to attract new participants to the sport. Harrison also published *The Arabian Racing Reference, 1959–1979,* a compilation of statistics of all Arabian horse races beginning with the 1959 Laurel exhibition race. For the sport of Arabian horse racing, this book was comparable to General Dickinson's annual catalogs in collecting data and making it available to new owners.

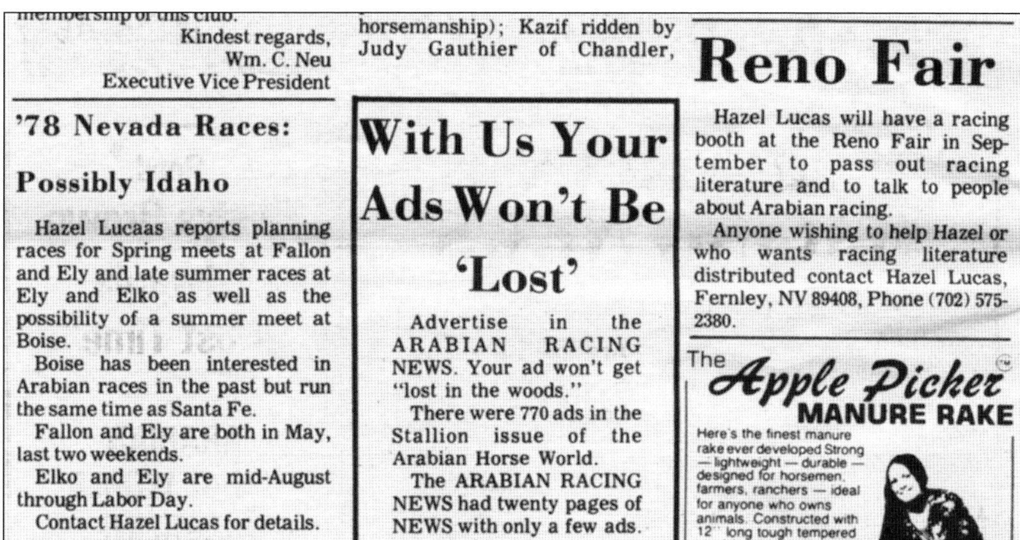

membership of this club.

Kindest regards,
Wm. C. Neu
Executive Vice President

'78 Nevada Races: Possibly Idaho

Hazel Lucaas reports planning races for Spring meets at Fallon and Ely and late summer races at Ely and Elko as well as the possibility of a summer meet at Boise.

Boise has been interested in Arabian races in the past but run the same time as Santa Fe.

Fallon and Ely are both in May, last two weekends.

Elko and Ely are mid-August through Labor Day.

Contact Hazel Lucas for details.

horsemanship); Kazif ridden by Judy Gauthier of Chandler,

With Us Your Ads Won't Be 'Lost'

Advertise in the ARABIAN RACING NEWS. Your ad won't get "lost in the woods."

There were 770 ads in the Stallion issue of the Arabian Horse World.

The ARABIAN RACING NEWS had twenty pages of NEWS with only a few ads.

The World had 1000 pages

Reno Fair

Hazel Lucas will have a racing booth at the Reno Fair in September to pass out racing literature and to talk to people about Arabian racing.

Anyone wishing to help Hazel or who wants racing literature distributed contact Hazel Lucas, Fernley, NV 89408, Phone (702) 575-2380.

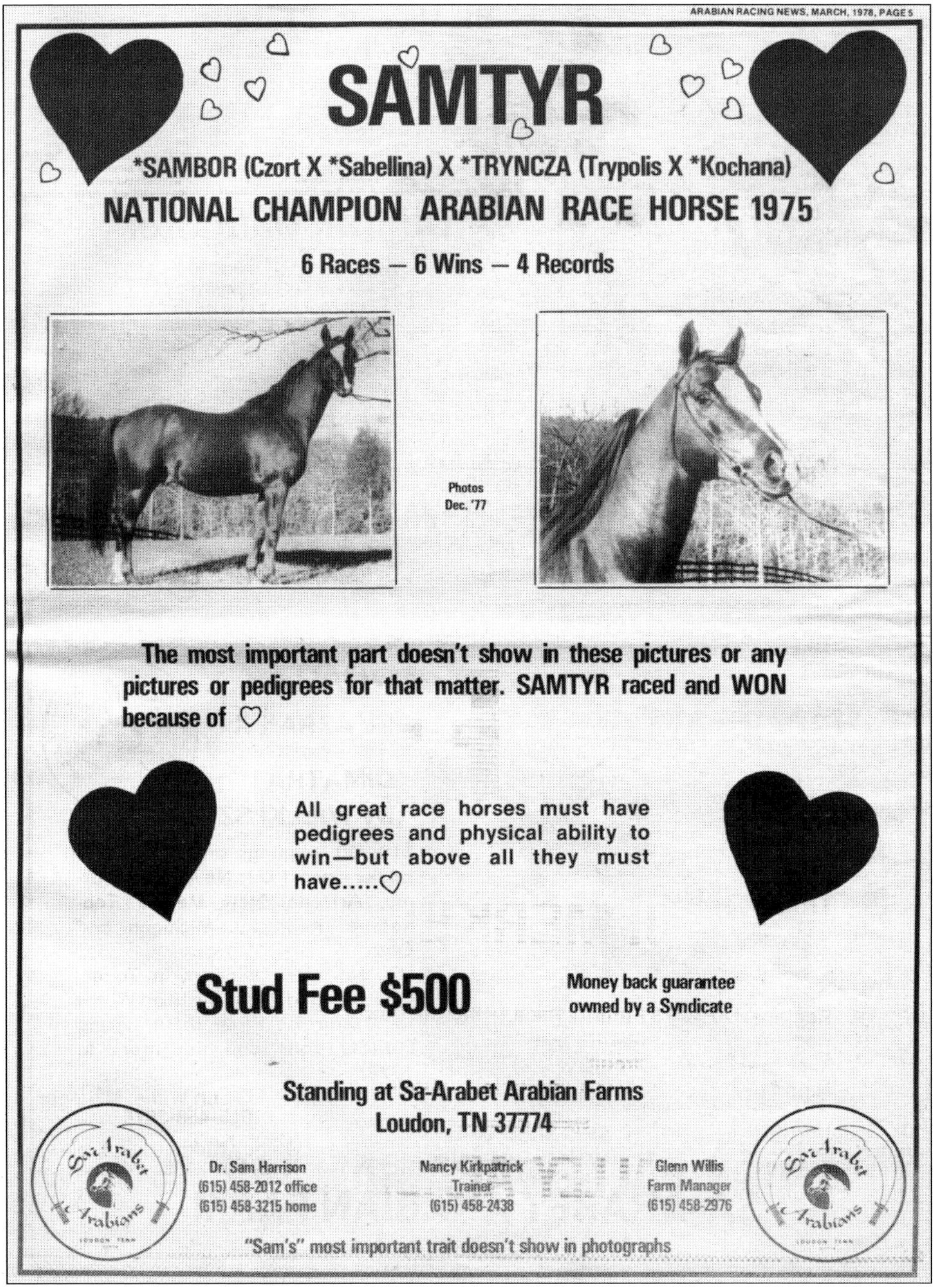

By 1978, there were 999 registered Arabian horses in the state of Tennessee, including 285 stallions, among 384 owners. Samtyr reached a national audience through Harrison's paper. The national scene for Arabian horse racing did not represent big money during the 1970s. Participants tried to attract newcomers by promoting the ability of a horse owner to do much of the preliminary training at home and the ability of a decent runner to earn his keep. However, even with pari-mutuel races, Arabian horse racing could not attract enough new horse owners to fill meets. Around 1979, an effort was made to establish a formal set of rules for racing under the auspices of the Arabian breed organization, the International Arabian Horse Association (IAHA).

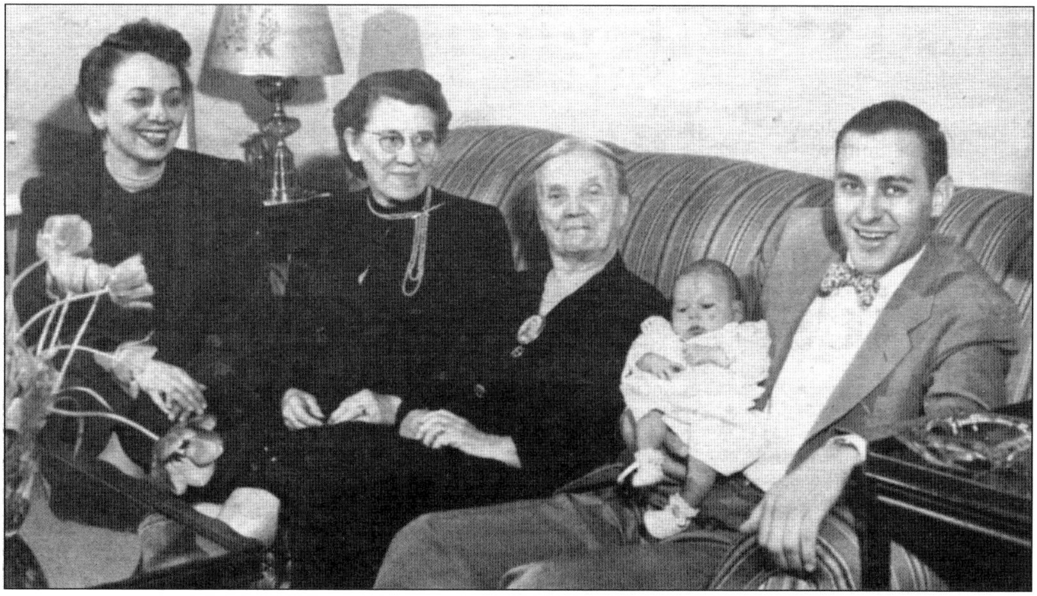

Dr. Sam unabashedly used his newspaper for a little family promotion. The two photographs, 30 years apart, show five generations of his family. From 1948 (above) are, from left to right, Mildred Welch Harrison; her mother, Effie Walker Welch; Effie's mother, Lou Ray Walker; and Sam Harrison, Mildred's son, holding his daughter Whitney. From 1978 (below) are, from left to right, Mildred Welch Harrison, Whitney Harrison Wheaton, Effie Walker Welch, and Sam Harrison holding Robin Madison Wheaton III.

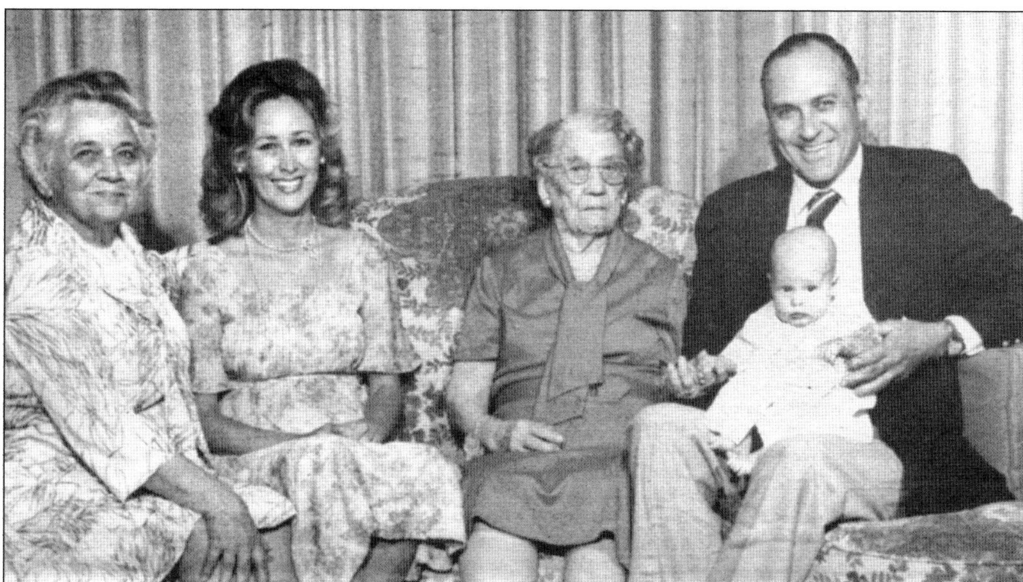

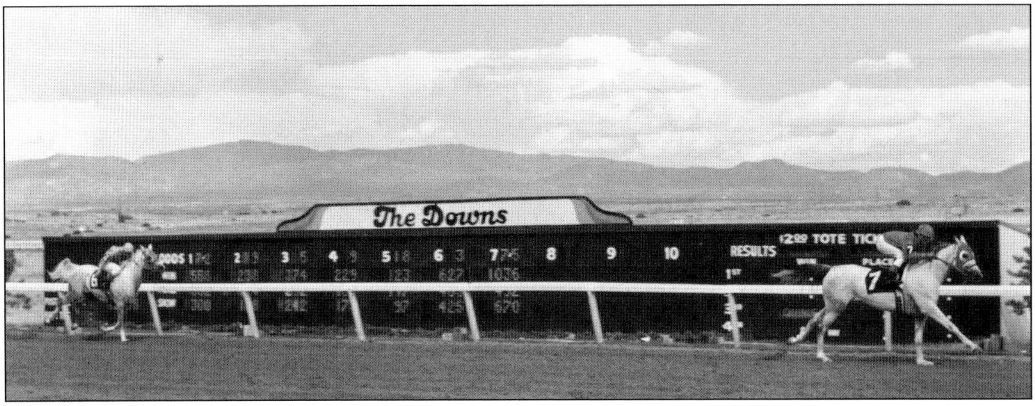

Two horses with ties to the Sa-Arabet breeding program were winners on the same day for owner Brahaim Hindi. On August 5, 1977, the mare Tikis Starlit (above) and the stallion Karif (below) found themselves in the winner's circle of the Downs at Santa Fe. Dr. Harrison later had offspring of both horses in his herd. In fact, Tikis Starla, a daughter of Tikis Starlit, was top seller in one of Dr. Sam's sales (see later in the chapter).

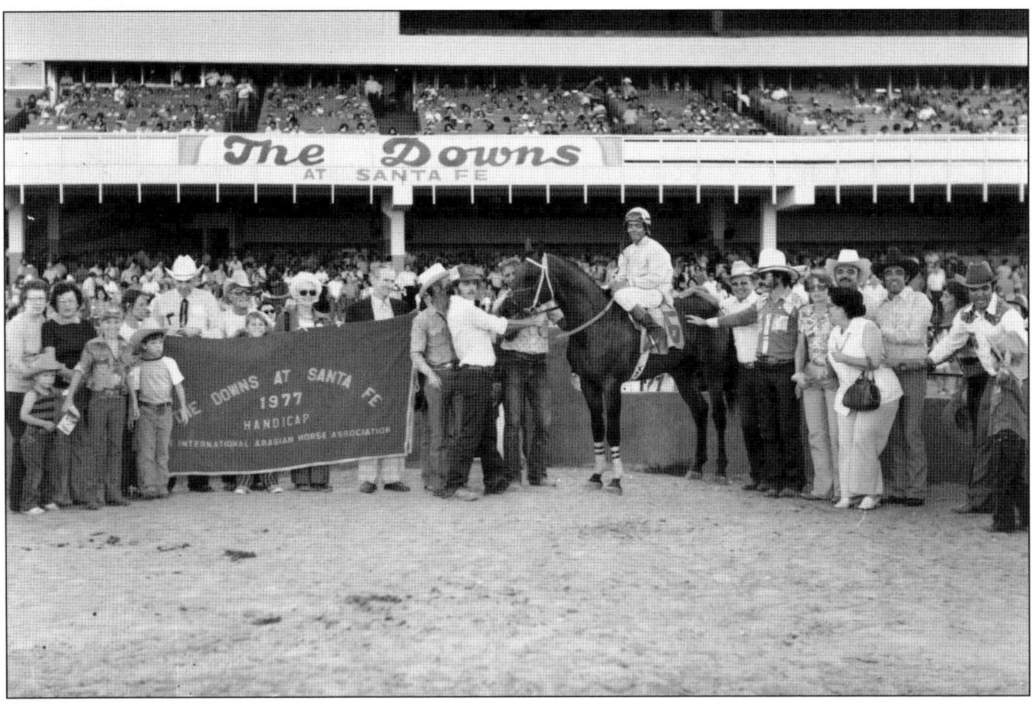

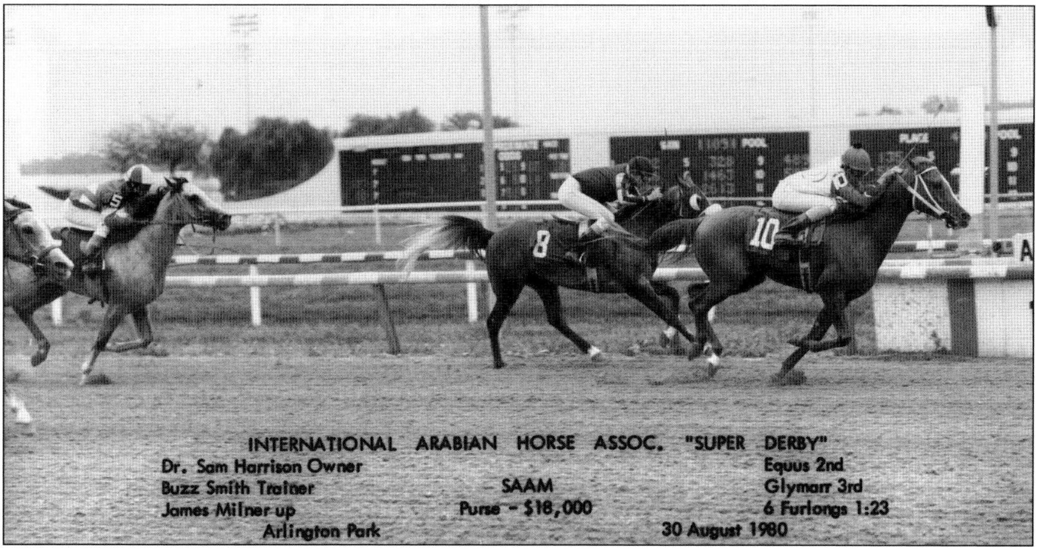

The year 1979 was a turning point for Arabian horse racing. Then began a shift from western to eastern venues, including Florida, Indiana, and Illinois, as well as greater exposure at top tracks and an increase in pari-mutuel races. Chicago's esteemed Arlington Park hosted an Arabian exhibition race in 1979. In 1980, the Arabian Super Derby was held at Arlington, and Harrison's first offspring, the stallion Saam from champion Samtyr, was the winner. In 1980, there was a symbolic changing of the guard as Samtyr surpassed Hazel Lucas's Nusabre as the perennial leading sire of racers when Saam became 1980's leading money winner, with $11,732.

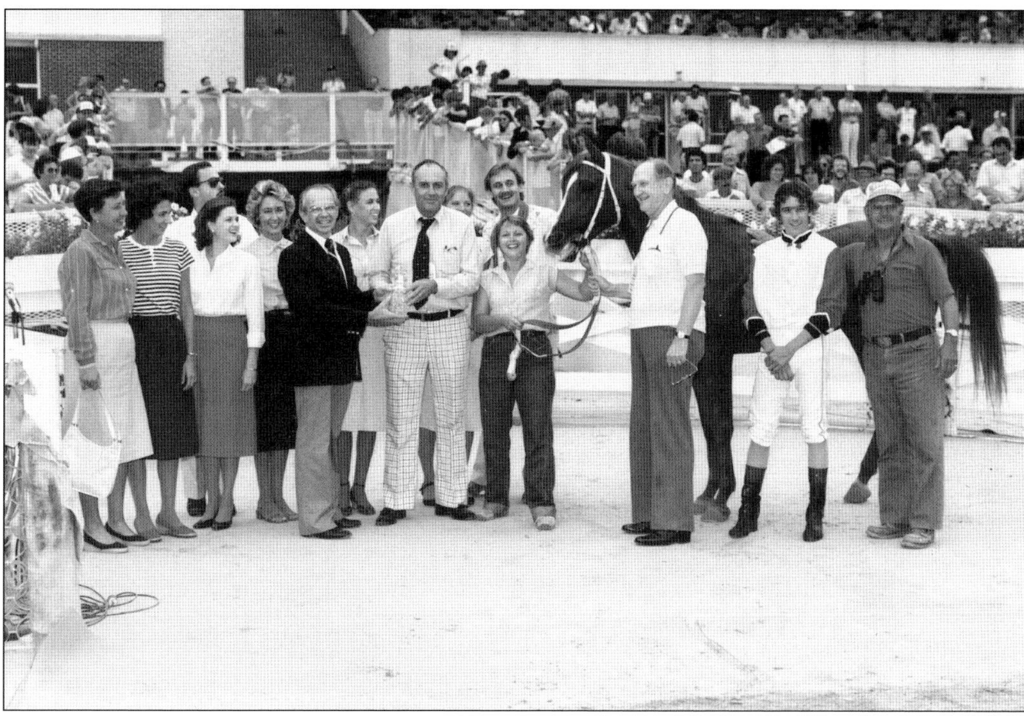

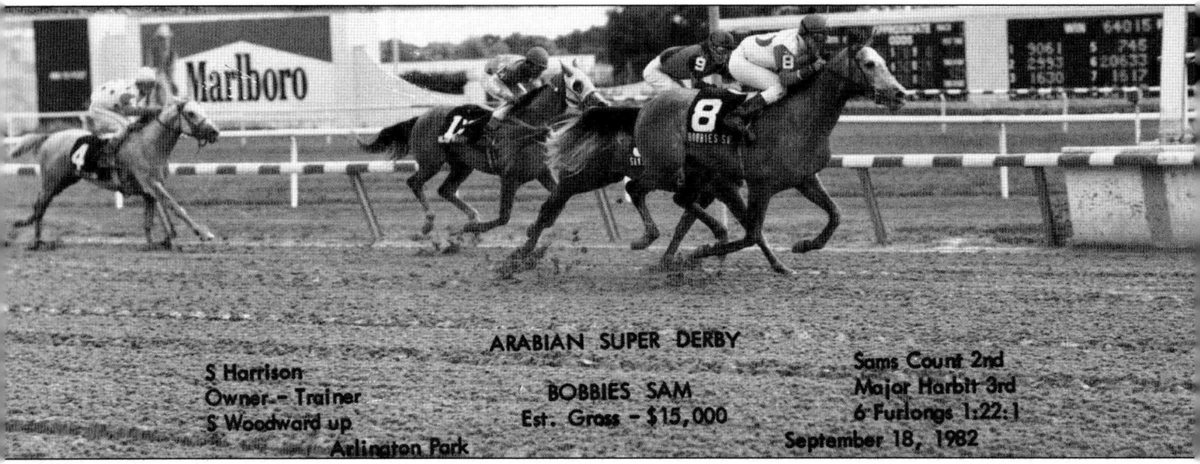

Samtyr's list of successful racers included Bobbies Sam, winner of the 1982 Super Derby, pictured above, and three Stakes races. Held again at Arlington, the derby was finally made pari-mutuel, another huge step for Arabian racing. Accepting the winner's trophy below are, from left to right, Martin Loeber, Sam Harrison, Susan Woodward, Paul Loeber, and Gail Becker.

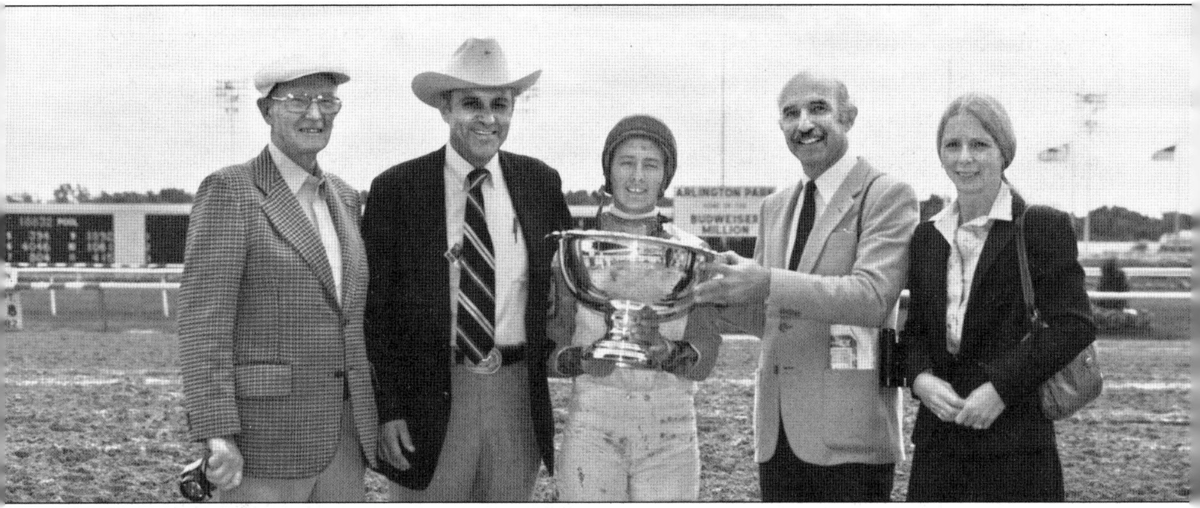

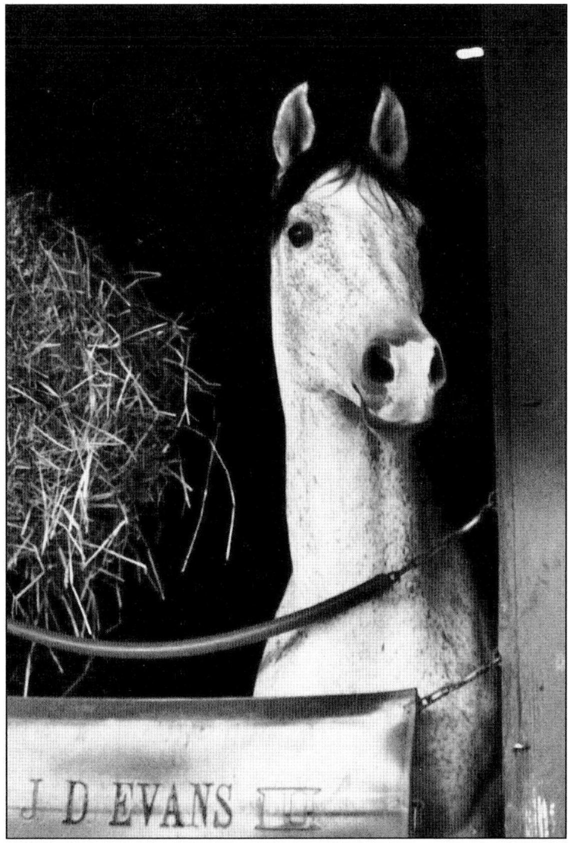

Bobbies Sam was named 1982 IAHA Colt of the Year and was 1983's leading money winner in Arabian racing with $28,842. Bobbies Sam's full brother Samorc had been named IAHA Colt of the Year in 1981, and Samorc was Horse of the Year in 1982. Also pictured is Eld Samarin, a daughter of Bobbies Sam.

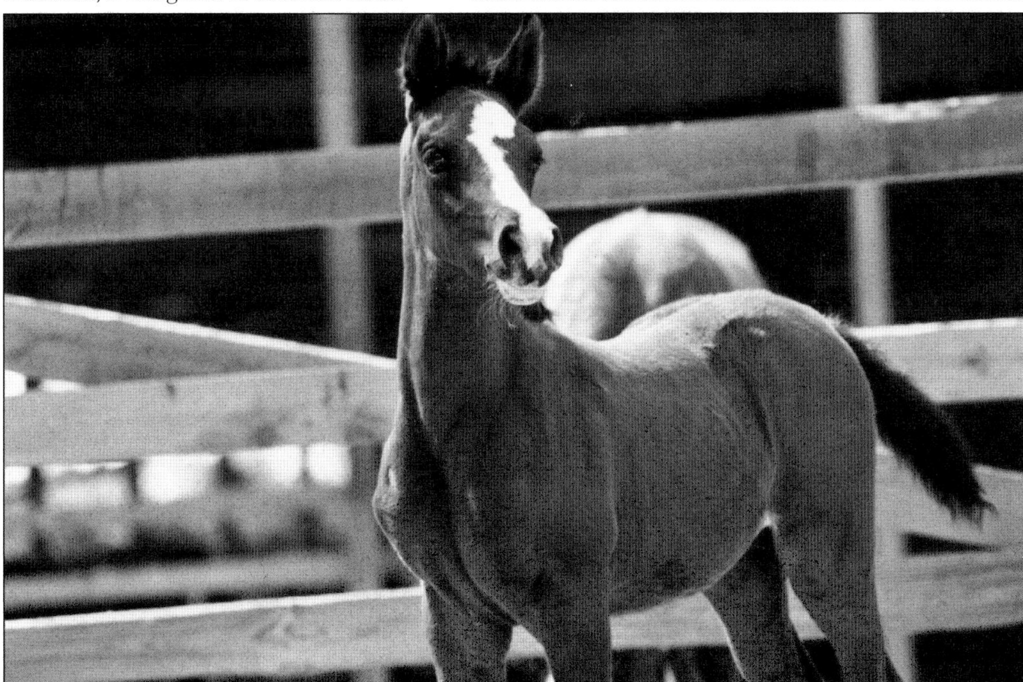

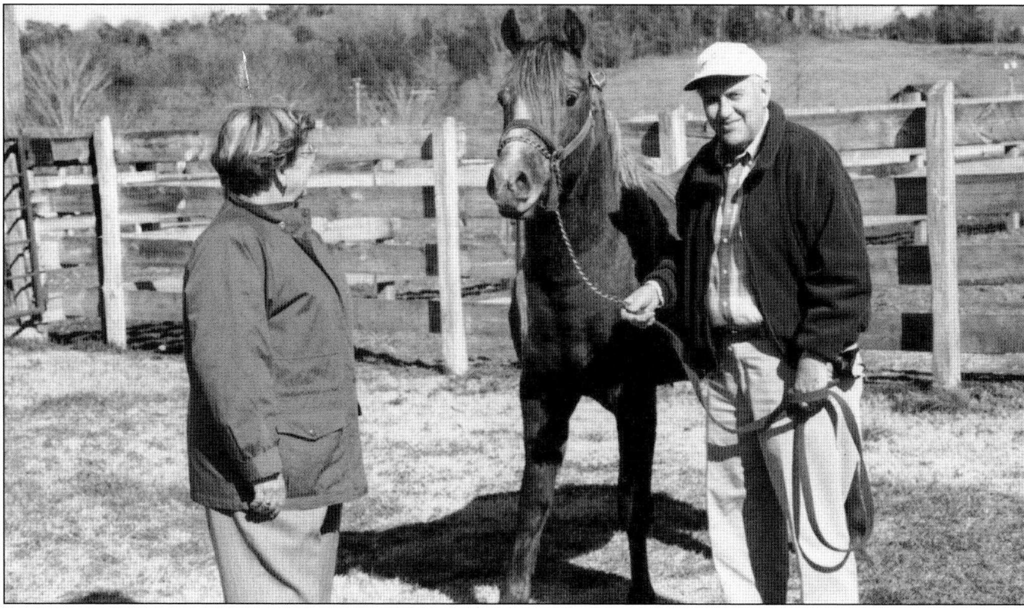

Two shots show Miss Bettye and Dr. Sam, at Sa-Arabet and at a parade in Loudon, were still enjoying regular farm life in a small town. Still practicing medicine, Dr. Sam promoted racing with devotion, and he and Miss Bettye traveled to races when possible. In 1980, they also had at least two horses running in Michigan with success, Mohak and Dimorca. The latter, by Harrison's *Dimrak, won that year's Michigan Derby and became a very valuable broodmare. The early years of exhibition racing—hard tracks, walk-up starts, and times clocked with hand-held stopwatches—began to pay off during the 1980s: a winter meet in Florida was started at Tampa Bay, and in the mid-1980s, Harrison assisted in pushing through legislation for Arabian pari-mutuel racing in Michigan.

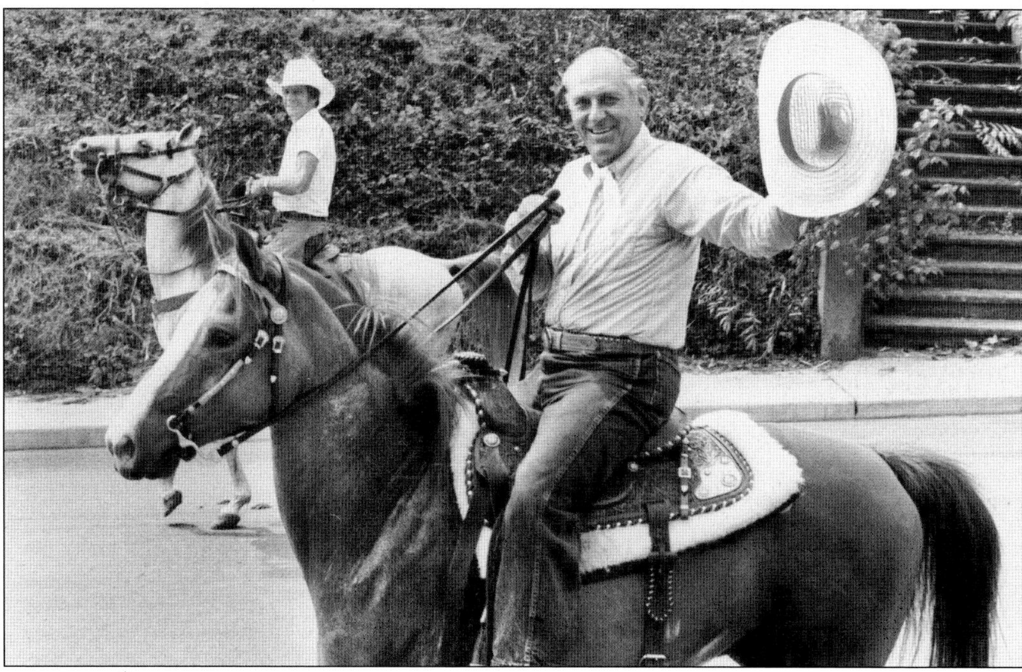

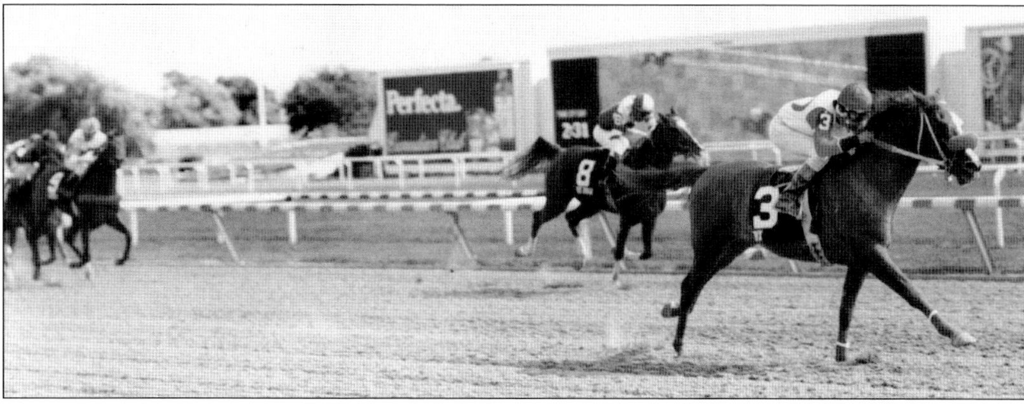

Tyrix, by Samtyr and out of the *Dimrak daughter Dimfixa, was the winner of the 1983 Arlington Super Derby. He was named Colt of the Year, earning over $23,000 that year, finishing in the money in 13 of 18 races.

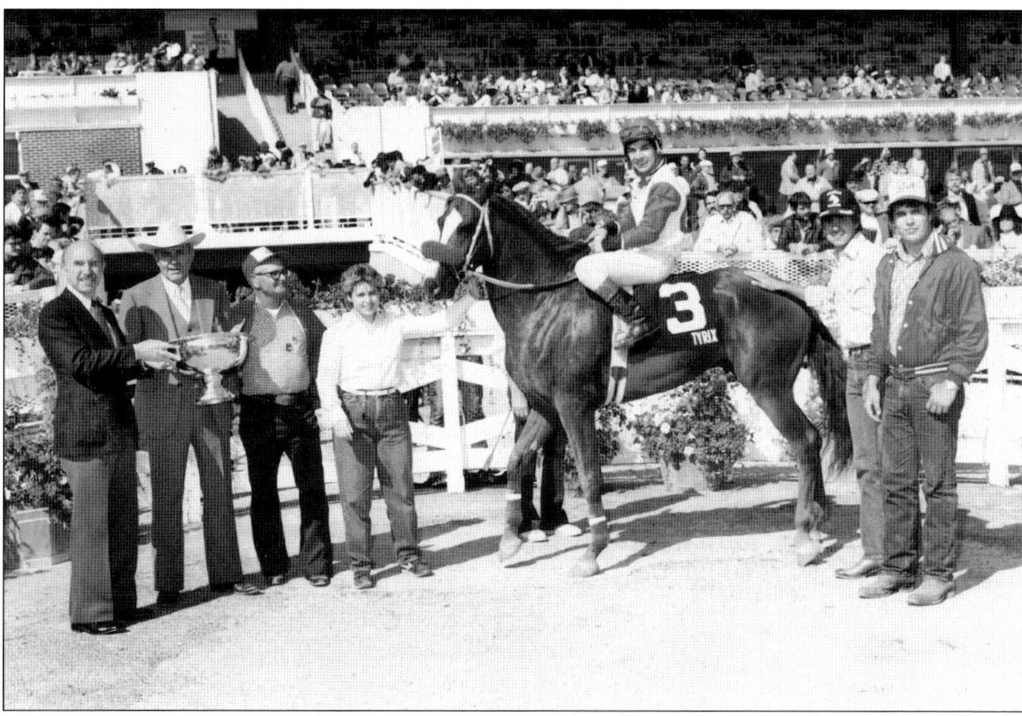

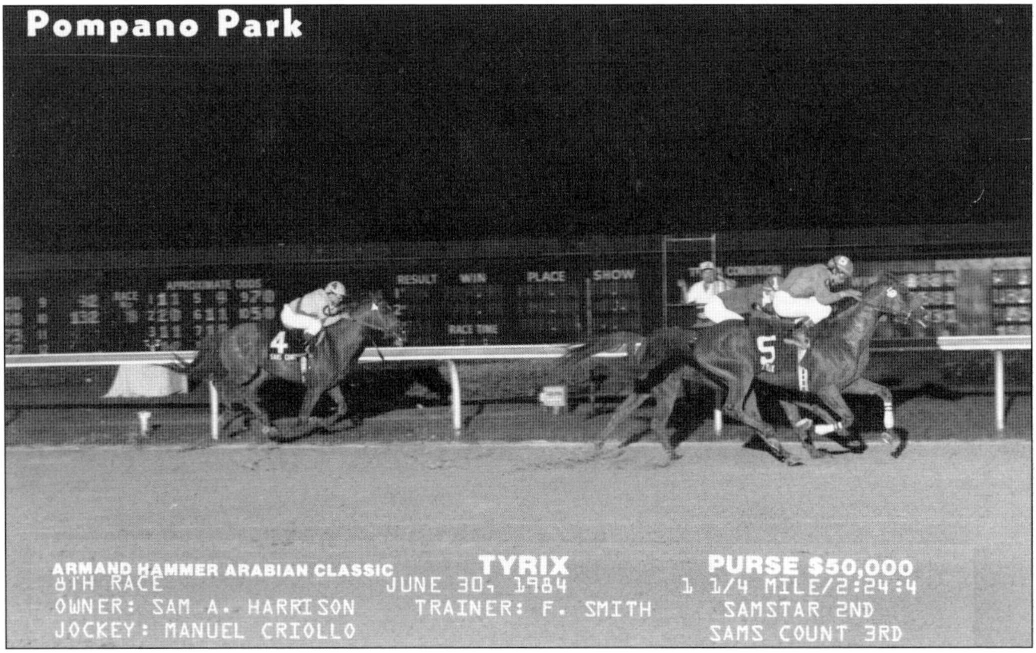

On June 30, 1984, Tyrix won the prestigious Armand Hammer Classic Stakes race at Pompano Park, Florida. In the race, he ran far behind the leader, as much as 15 lengths. Slowly he closed the gap for an exciting finish. In the final strides, he overtook his brothers Samstar, then owned by Robert Van Hoose, and Sams Count, owned by C. T. Williams, to win. All three horses were bred at Sa-Arabet in Loudon. In the winner's circle holding the trophy are Dr. Armand Hammer (left) and Merv Griffin.

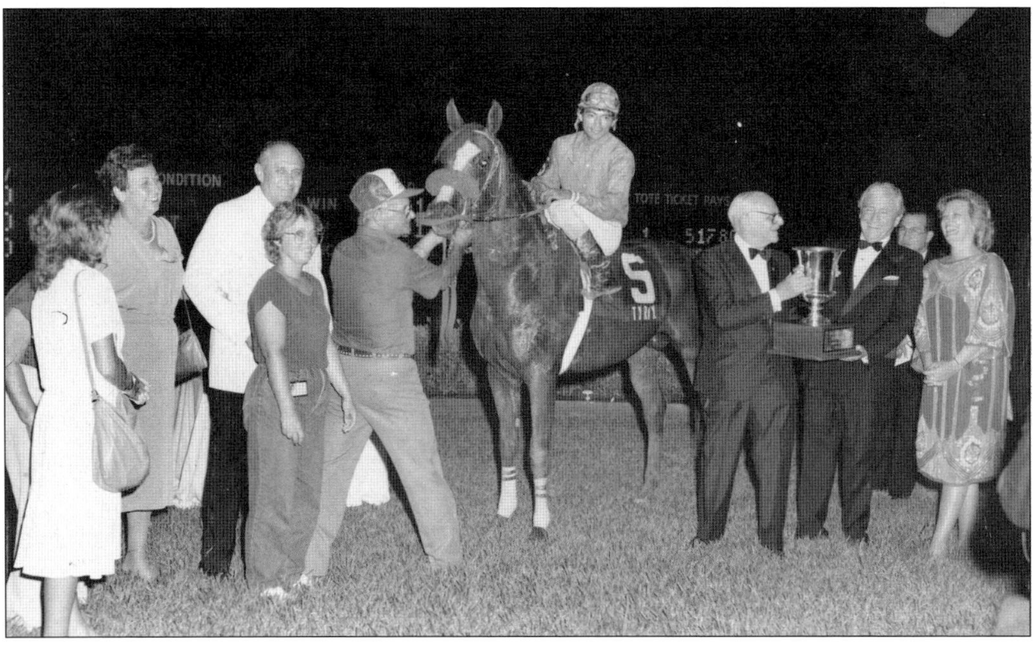

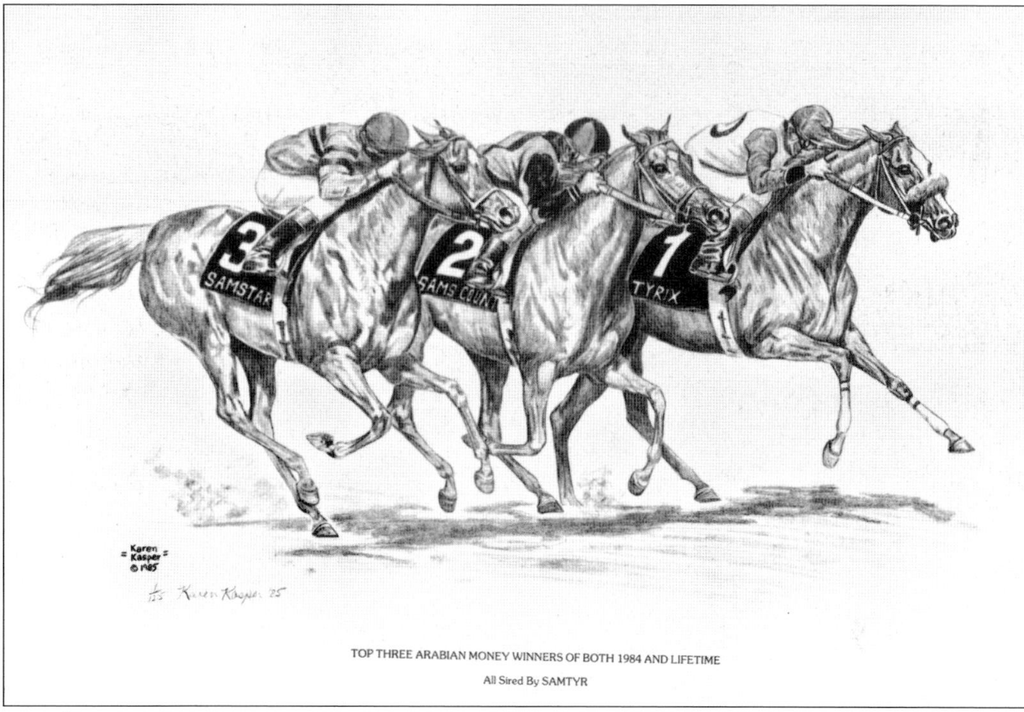

The three Samtyr sons winning in the money in the 1984 Armand Hammer Classic are depicted in artwork by Karen Kasper from 1985. From left to right are the top three Arabian money winners of 1984 and lifetime: Tyrix, Samstar, and Sams Count.

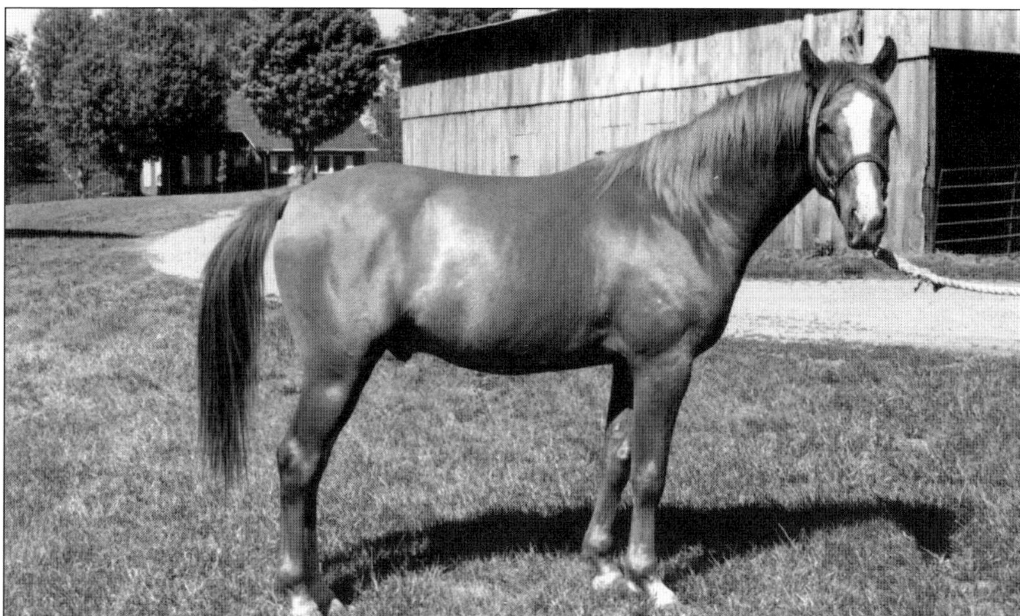

Back at Sa-Arabet, the retired racers were producing new generations of runners. Shown here is a son of the mare Ruraka, herself a daughter of *Dimrak. She was a valuable broodmare for the Harrisons.

The year 1984 was a big year for racing: Samtyr was the first Arabian racehorse to become syndicated, and a regular meet began at Delaware Park, today's premier Arabian racing track. By 1985, total purse money for Arabian racing topped $594,000, from $54,000 in 1978. Racing participants began discussing the idea of an organizational body outside of IAHA. Dr. Harrison began developing an outline for an Arabian Jockey Club (AJC). Begun in 1985, the AJC, a 501 nonprofit, still oversees and administers all aspects of Arabian horse racing. Its sister incorporation, the Arabian Racing Cup, Inc. (ARC), also began as a Tennessee nonprofit stewarded by Harrison. Owners enroll horses into the program for a lifetime opportunity at ARC purse money. Members elect directors to serve terms, and nomination payments are held in escrow to be used for purse monies.

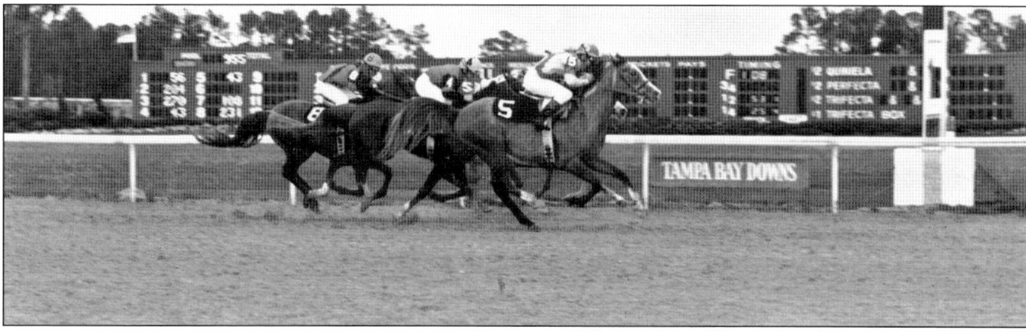

Kimorca, by Samtyr and out of the mare Dimorca, earned over $10,000 as a three-year-old. She is shown here winning at Tampa Bay Downs on March 10, 1986. Her trainer was Ike Pahlen, and she finished the five-furlong race (one furlong equals an eighth of a mile) in 1:08.4. Harrison sold Kimorca that year for $31,000 in a sale at Delaware Park near Wilmington, Delaware. He consigned two other horses to that sale. As Harrison's Sa-Arabet prospered, he was selling his stock to new racing enthusiasts, helping the sport continue to progress.

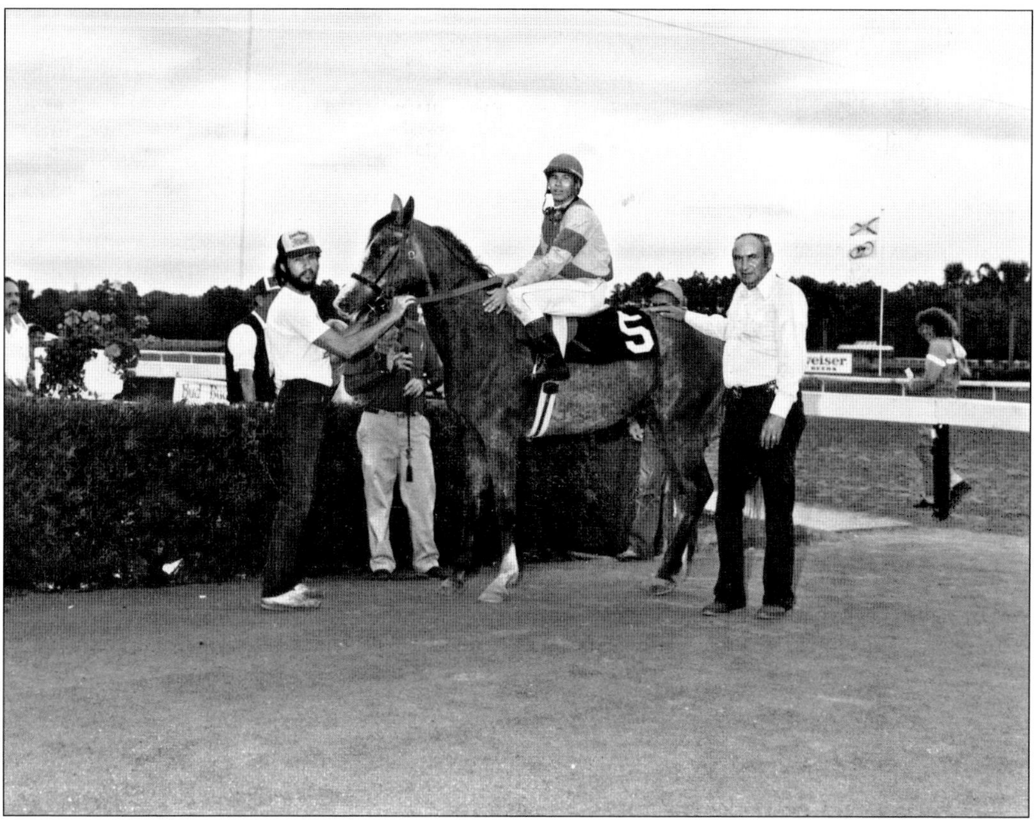

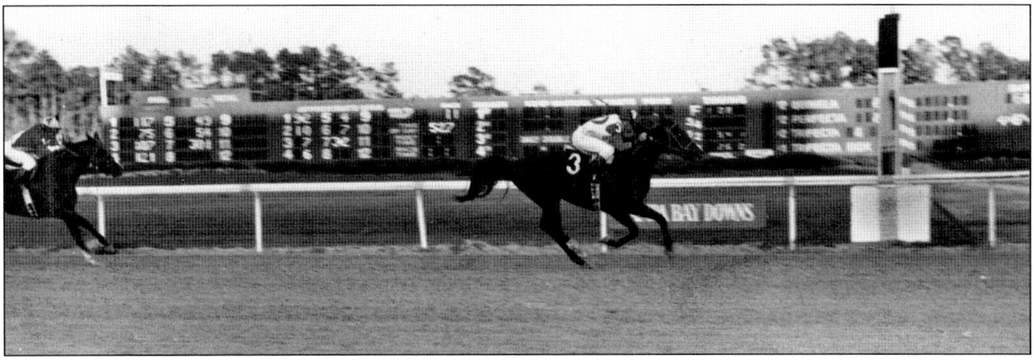

Tyrixa, a three-quarters sister to Kimorca, also raced in 1986 at Tampa Bay Downs. Her trainer was Russ Ragain, and this was the first year Harrison used Ragain as a trainer. This race, on January 23, marked his first win, with Tyrixa finishing the five-furlong distance in 1:05. Tyrixa finished the 1986 season earning $7,500.

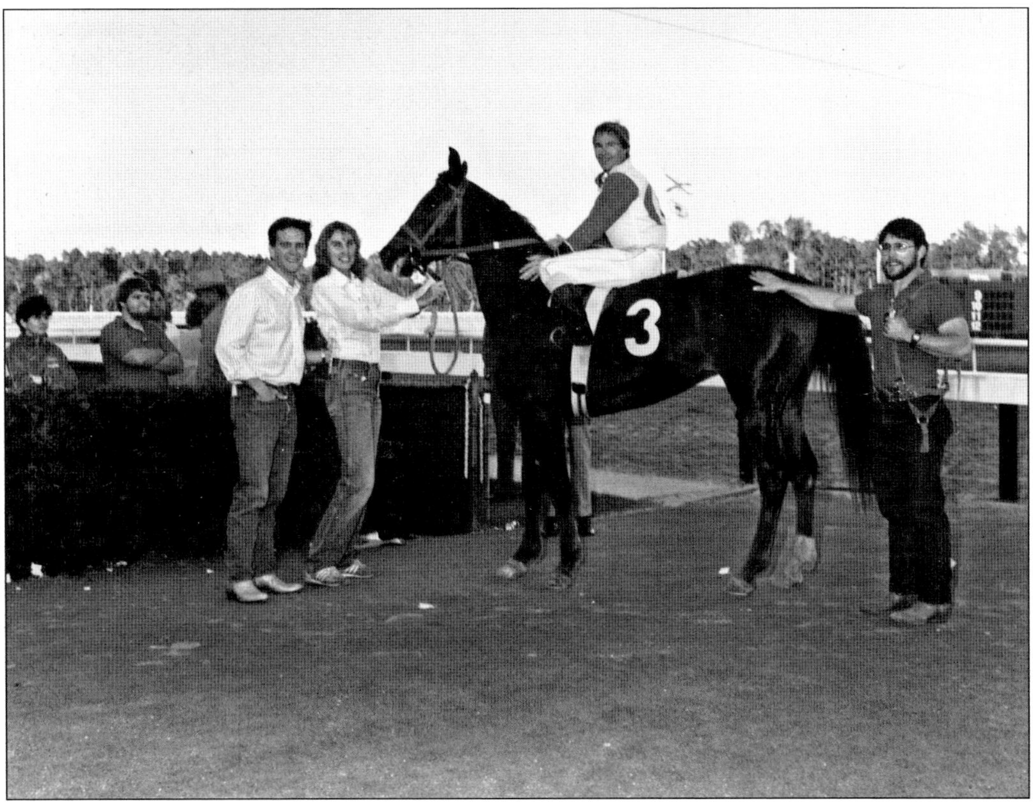

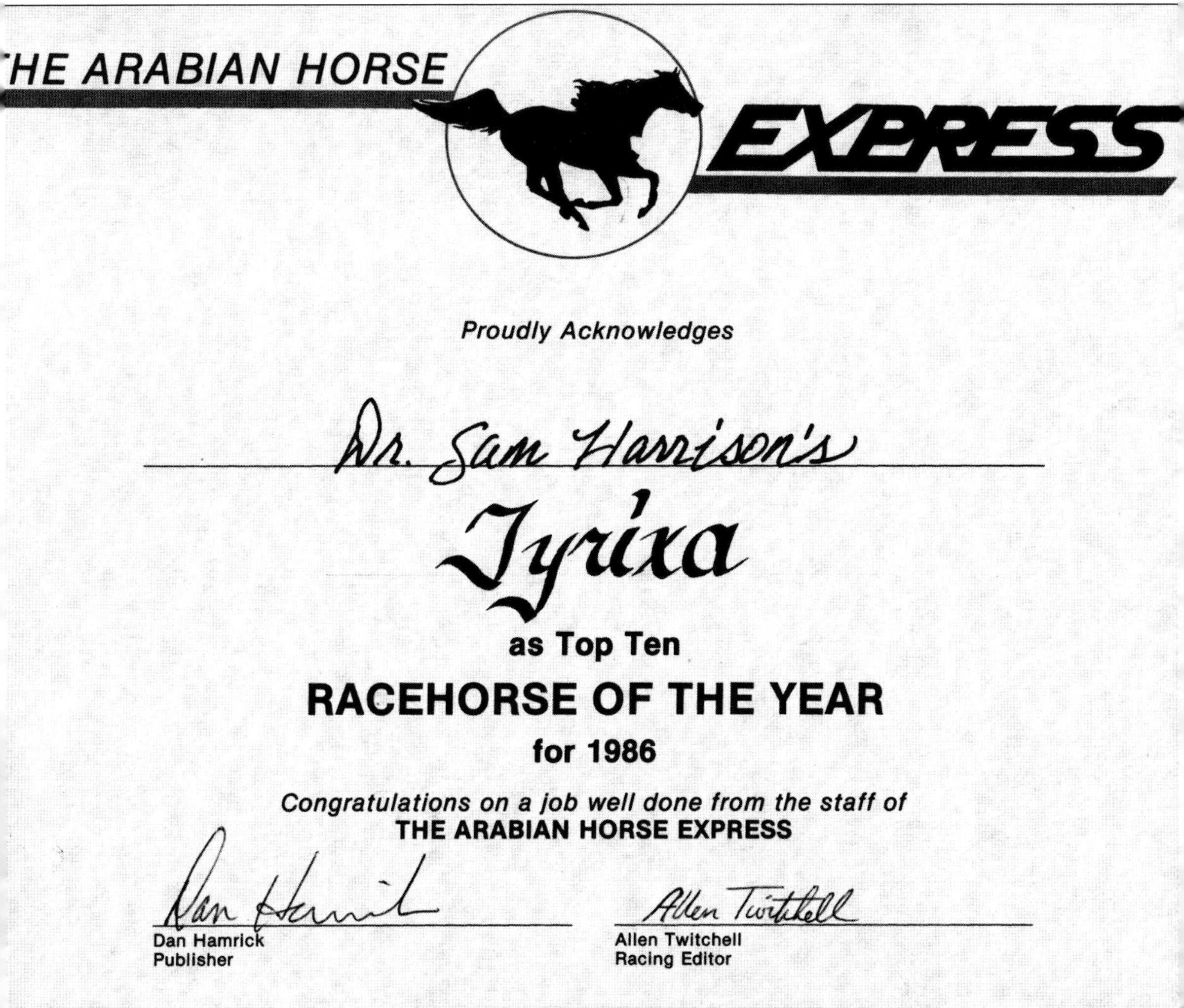

THE ARABIAN HORSE EXPRESS

Proudly Acknowledges

Dr. Sam Harrison's

Tyrixa

as Top Ten

RACEHORSE OF THE YEAR

for 1986

Congratulations on a job well done from the staff of
THE ARABIAN HORSE EXPRESS

Dan Hamrick
Publisher

Allen Twitchell
Racing Editor

The *Arabian Horse Express*, a trade publication, honored Tyrixa with a "Top Ten Racehorse of the Year" award.

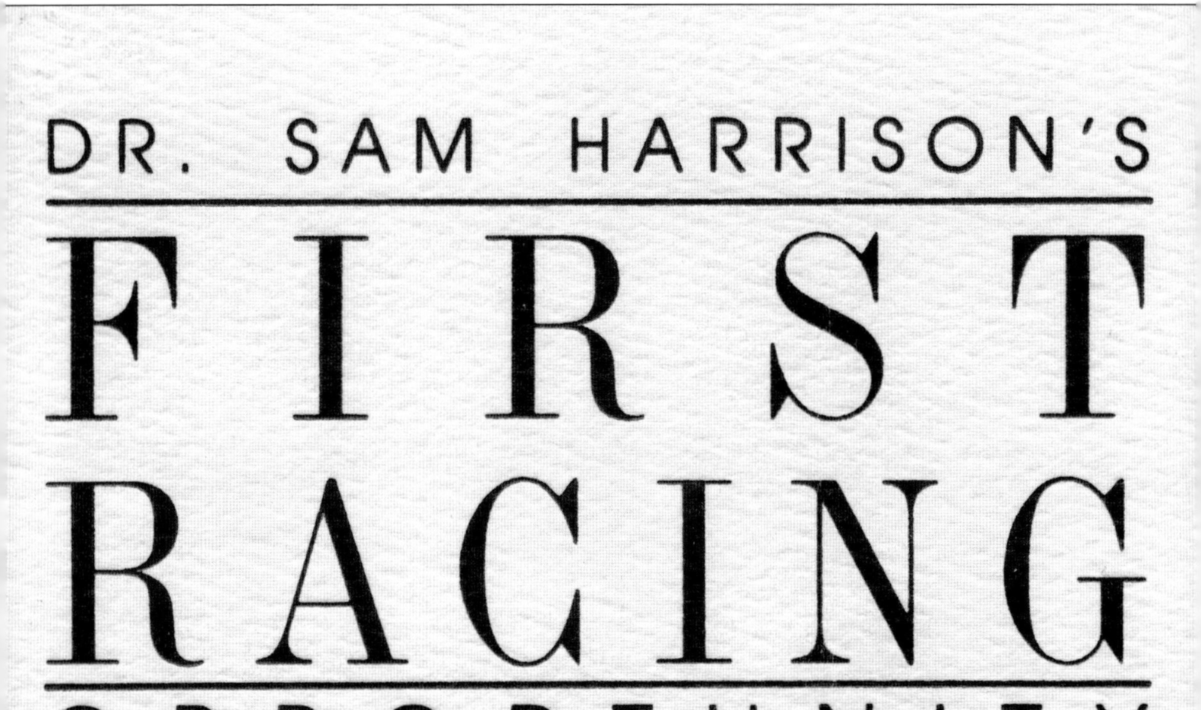

In 1987, maintaining his goal of increasing participation through sales, Harrison hosted an Easter weekend First Racing Opportunity Sale at his Loudon, Tennessee, farm. Every horse except Samtyr was for sale, with yearlings starting at $1,000. Dr. Sam and Miss Bettye hosted visitors from nine states. Sa-Arabet's finest runner and broodmares were available for purchase. The sale represented the development of the American Arabian racehorse.

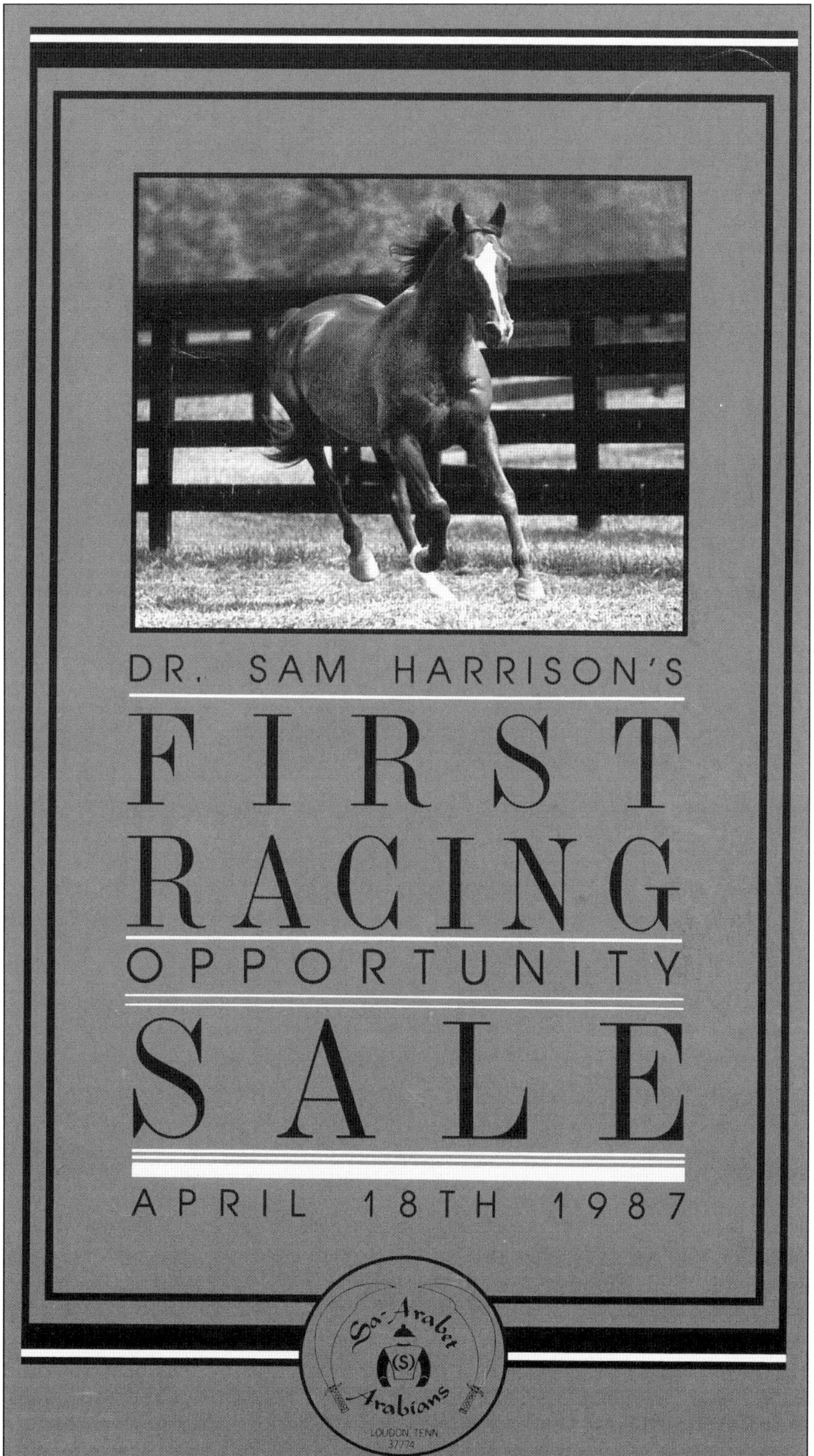

Though not for sale, Samtyr was the star, as many of the horses available were his offspring.

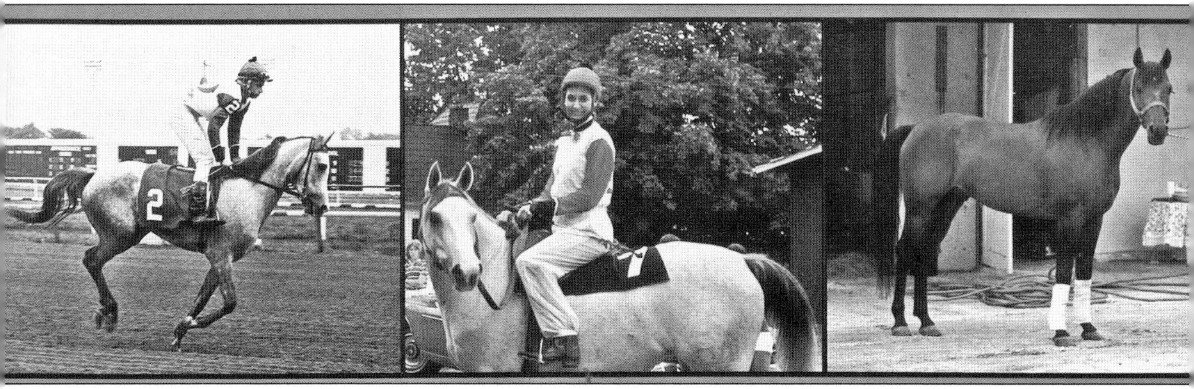

Shown in the sales catalog are, from left to right, the mares Dimorca and HCC Maloska and the stallion Samorc.

LOT 1

DIMORCA

RESERVE

1977 Grey Mare • In foal to Samtyr for March '87
Sells bred to Samtyr or with a 1987 breeding to Samtyr
Breeder: Dr. Sam Harrison

IAHA Filly of the Year 1980. Full sister to Mohak. Foals: Miss Reed '82, Kimorca '83 ($31,000), Jessorca '84, Cain '85, Camorca '86. Great race filly against colts and probably best race mare in North America.

			Faher
		El Azrak	
			Ellora
	*Dimrak		
			Wielki Szler
		*Dimatra	
			Imatra
DIMORCA 16 (3-4-5) $3,224			
			Trypolis
		*Mohacz	
			Mimonka
	Majorca de Washoe		
			Uad-El-Keb
		*Brussa II	
			Lakme

FOAL

Dimorca was not only a great broodmare, she had also raced in the earlier years. Born in 1977, she raced when purse money was still lacking. She ran in the money 12 of her 16 starts; her total earnings were $3,224. She was the 1980 IAHA Filly of the Year. As a broodmare, she produced Kimorca and Jessorca. Harrison considered her the best race mare in the country.

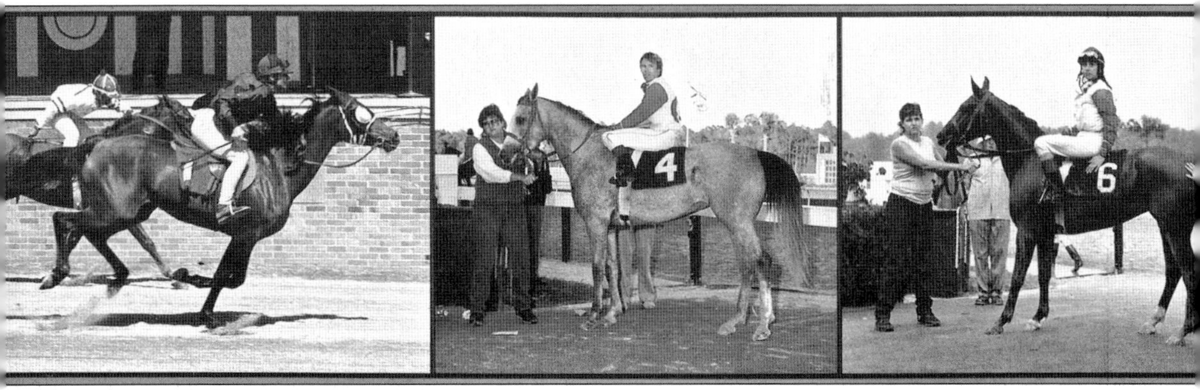

Shown in the sales catalog are, from left to right, Dimfixa, Bettye Sam, and Tyrixa.

LOT 3

DIMFIXA

ESERVE

975 Bay Mare • Bred to Samtyr for '88 foal
reeder: Dr. Sam Harrison

am of Tyrix (winner Armand Hammer) and Sams Fix
$10,000 claimer) and Tyrixa and Samtyra. Foals: Tyrix '80,
ams Fix '82, Tyrixa '83, Samtyra '84, Tyx '86.

DIMFIXA
8 (1-3-1) $995

DIMFIXA	*Dimrak	El Azrak	Faher
			Ellora
		*Dimatra	Wielki Szler
			Imatra
	Safixa	Witezfix	*Serafix
			Witeza
		Saja	Count Me
			Cool Jewe

ARC FOAL

The bay mare Dimfixa was born in 1975. Her sire was *Dimrak, and her dam went back to Harrison's first Arabian horses, Count Me and Cool Jewel. Another great broodmare, she produced Tyrix, Tyrixa, and Samtyra.

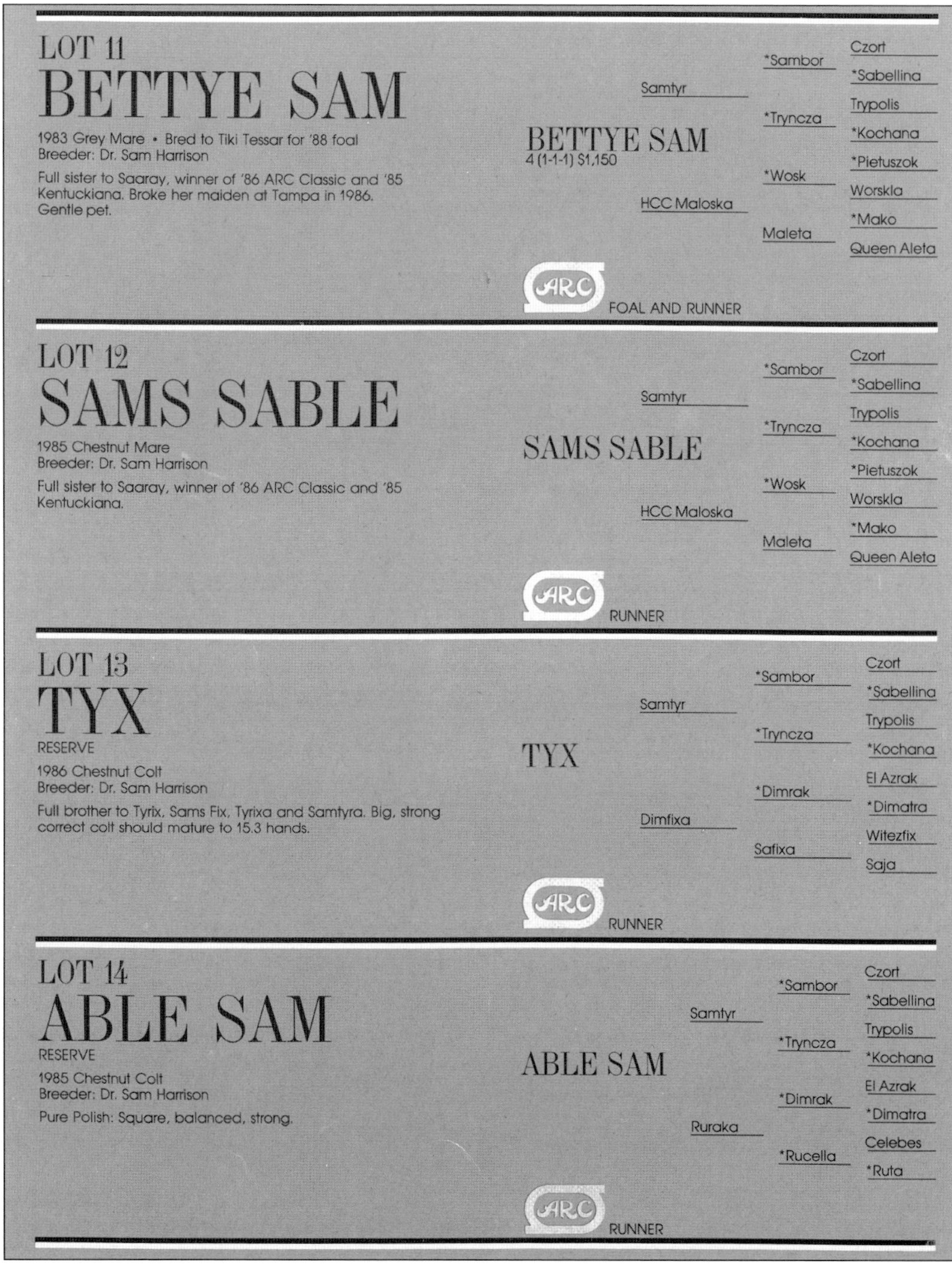

LOT 11
BETTYE SAM

1983 Grey Mare • Bred to Tiki Tessar for '88 foal
Breeder: Dr. Sam Harrison

Full sister to Saaray, winner of '86 ARC Classic and '85 Kentuckiana. Broke her maiden at Tampa in 1986. Gentle pet.

BETTYE SAM
4 (1-1-1) $1,150

- Samtyr
  - *Sambor
    - Czort
    - *Sabellina
  - *Tryncza
    - Trypolis
    - *Kochana
- HCC Maloska
  - *Wosk
    - *Pietuszok
    - Worskla
  - Maleta
    - *Mako
    - Queen Aleta

ARC FOAL AND RUNNER

LOT 12
SAMS SABLE

1985 Chestnut Mare
Breeder: Dr. Sam Harrison

Full sister to Saaray, winner of '86 ARC Classic and '85 Kentuckiana.

SAMS SABLE

- Samtyr
  - *Sambor
    - Czort
    - *Sabellina
  - *Tryncza
    - Trypolis
    - *Kochana
- HCC Maloska
  - *Wosk
    - *Pietuszok
    - Worskla
  - Maleta
    - *Mako
    - Queen Aleta

ARC RUNNER

LOT 13
TYX

RESERVE
1986 Chestnut Colt
Breeder: Dr. Sam Harrison

Full brother to Tyrix, Sams Fix, Tyrixa and Samtyra. Big, strong correct colt should mature to 15.3 hands.

TYX

- Samtyr
  - *Sambor
    - Czort
    - *Sabellina
  - *Tryncza
    - Trypolis
    - *Kochana
- Dimfixa
  - *Dimrak
    - El Azrak
    - *Dimatra
  - Safixa
    - Witezfix
    - Saja

ARC RUNNER

LOT 14
ABLE SAM

RESERVE
1985 Chestnut Colt
Breeder: Dr. Sam Harrison

Pure Polish: Square, balanced, strong.

ABLE SAM

- Samtyr
  - *Sambor
    - Czort
    - *Sabellina
  - *Tryncza
    - Trypolis
    - *Kochana
- Ruraka
  - *Dimrak
    - El Azrak
    - *Dimatra
  - *Rucella
    - Celebes
    - *Ruta

ARC RUNNER

Sales pages from Dr. Sam's First Opportunity Sale showed each horse's pedigree and supplied

LOT 15
SHOSAMA

1983 Chestnut Mare
In foal to *Wiking for March '87 (Samtyr/*Wiking cross)
Breeder: Dr. Sam Harrison

Full sister to Bobbies Sam, Samorc, Abac. Dam produced Mohak and Dimorca.

SHOSAMA		
Samtyr	*Sambor	Czort
		*Sabellina
	*Tryncza	Trypolis
		*Kochana
Majorca de Washoe	*Mohacz	Trypolis
		Mimonka
	*Brussa II	Uad-El-Kebir
		Lakme

ARC FOAL AND RUNNER

LOT 16
GAIETI

RESERVE

1983 Chestnut Mare • In foal to Samtyr for March '87
Sells bred to Samtyr or with a 1987 breeding to Samtyr
Breeder: Jim Brown, Paramont

Very gentle. Child broke and a pet. Pretty with Samtyr-English cross which produced Saam, Sams Count, etc.

GAIETI		
Kadence	*Bask	Witraz
		Balalajka
	Four Winds Kalifa	*Cytrys
		Four Winds Kitkat
Griffin Gaiety	Gazon	Ferzon
		Scheraff
	Ala-Ed-Din-Cindi	Geym
		Gasaraff

ARC FOAL

LOT 17
TESHAWNA

1980 Grey Mare • In foal to Samtyr for June '87
Sells with 1987 breeding to Samtyr
Breeder: Robbie Rogers

Up close to By Golly. Foals, Saatesha '85, Tabella '86.

TESHAWNA		
Juan de Shawn	*Mohacz	Trypolis
		Mimonka
	*Salina	Aboukir
		Famula
Metessa Ku	Meteor	*Serafix
		*Thorayyah
	Kartessa	Izkar
		Tezeyna

ARC FOAL

LOT 18
SAAM

1977 Chestnut Horse
Breeder: Dr. Sam Harrison

Winner 1980 IAHA Derby; '81, '82 Paramont, Florida Derby, Ocala Derby, Michigan Derby, '81 and '82 Ocala Classic Mile. 1980 IAHA Racing Colt of the Year. '81 IAHA Racehorse of the Year. Full brother Sams Count and Samstar. Samtyr's first foal. Classic Polish-English cross. Proven sire. Saam's oldest son broke his maiden at Del Park in 1986 (Hala Saamrock). Saam won 25-mile Tennessee Endurance ride two weeks after running at Latonia, Cincinnati in 1984.

SAAM
38 (20-10-3) D+5 $24,761

SAAM		
Samtyr	*Sambor	Czort
		*Sabellina
	*Tryncza	Trypolis
		*Kochana
Counts Jewel	Count Me	Count Thirteen
		Rififfi
	Cool Jewel	Ruffles
		Desert Jewel

ARC SIRE

information about each one's racing record and information about any offspring.

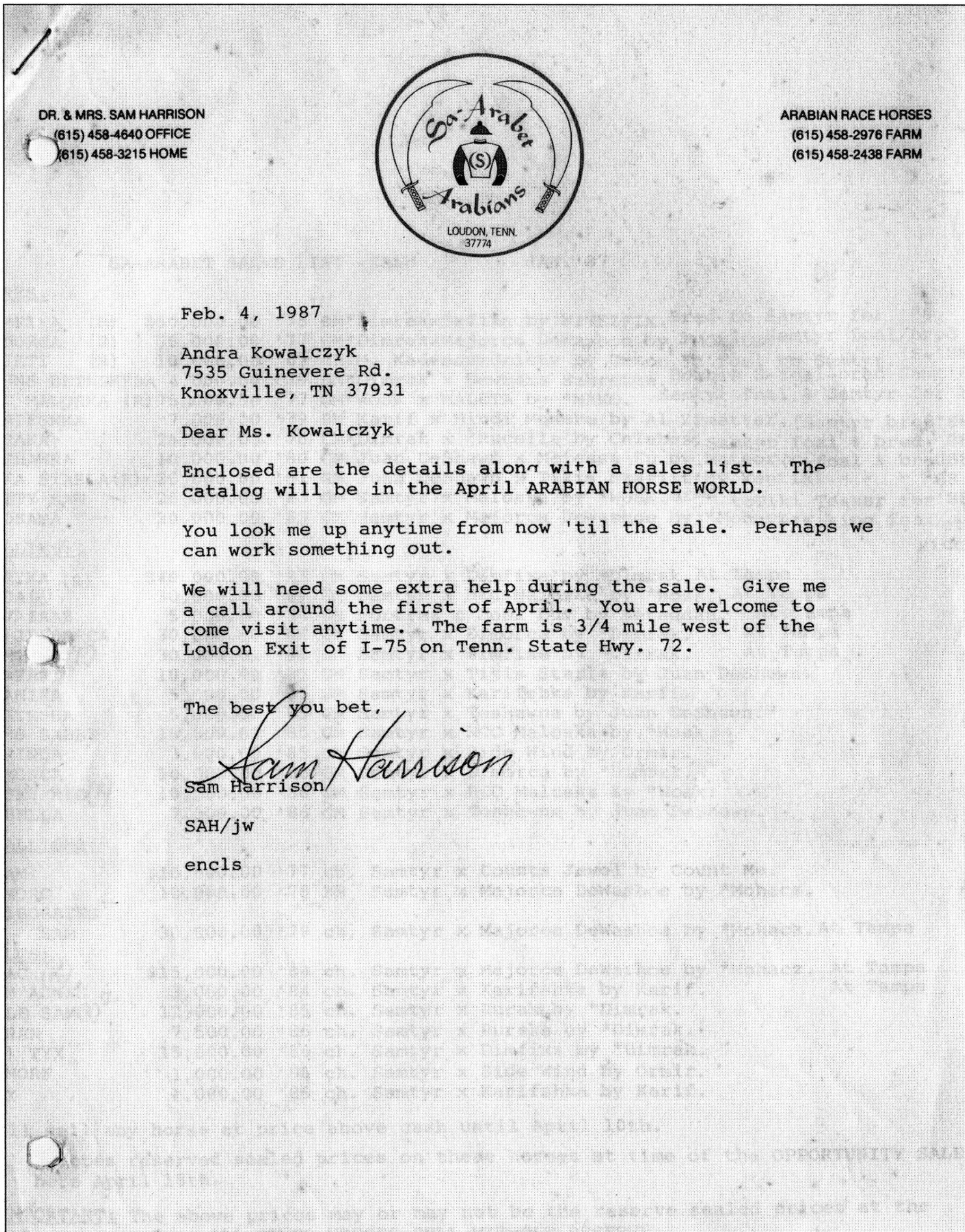

DR. & MRS. SAM HARRISON
(615) 458-4640 OFFICE
(615) 458-3215 HOME

Sa-Arabet Arabians
LOUDON, TENN. 37774

ARABIAN RACE HORSES
(615) 458-2976 FARM
(615) 458-2438 FARM

Feb. 4, 1987

Andra Kowalczyk
7535 Guinevere Rd.
Knoxville, TN 37931

Dear Ms. Kowalczyk

Enclosed are the details along with a sales list. The catalog will be in the April ARABIAN HORSE WORLD.

You look me up anytime from now 'til the sale. Perhaps we can work something out.

We will need some extra help during the sale. Give me a call around the first of April. You are welcome to come visit anytime. The farm is 3/4 mile west of the Loudon Exit of I-75 on Tenn. State Hwy. 72.

The best you bet,

Sam Harrison

Sam Harrison

SAH/jw

encls

This is a letter in reply to an inquiry from the author, then a teenager unable to afford a horse but interested in coming to Sa-Arabet to witness the sale.

DR. & MRS. SAM HARRISON
(615) 458-4640 OFFICE
(615) 458-3215 HOME

Sa-Arabet Arabians
LOUDON, TENN. 37774

ARABIAN RACE HORSES
(615) 458-2976 FARM
(615) 458-2438 FARM

January 15, 1987

Dear Friends,

For the past 25 years Sa-Arabet has bred, owned, raced and sold many winners (some of the best).

I have long advocated and encouraged racehorse sales. The Delaware Park Sale (I sold 3 lots of the 18 for $65,000) broke the ice and I believe that the time has come to continue with more and more sales getting Arabian racehorses into more and more hands thereby increasing the numbers at the track which we need.

So my First RACING OPPORTUNITY SALE is set for Easter weekend. The time is right to buy foundation breeding stock capable of racing well and then going on to the breeding shed. All the horses have top racing pedigrees, the best racing conformation and famous racing sires and dams and brothers and sisters.

All horses will go across the block. A few will have reasonable reserves. The others sell without reserve. Most are young ARABIAN CUP runners eligible for those rich CUP races and the three year olds are Tampa Bay trained, raced and ready for Delaware Park and the rich stakes races for 3yos. Most are sired by Samtyr.

Buzz and Sandy Smith, Tim Kelly and Russ Ragain will be here beginning Friday afternoon to answer your questions about racing and demonstrate training techniques and conformation. This is your OPPORTUNITY. TAKE IT!

Come see Samtyr

The best you bet,

Sam Harrison

Sam Harrison

PLEASE WRITE OR CALL FOR CATALOGS.

An invitational form letter was sent out to advertise the sale, its events, and guest speakers. Dr. Sam wanted visitors and potential buyers to have access to professional trainers involved in racing, as well as to enjoy some Tennessee hospitality.

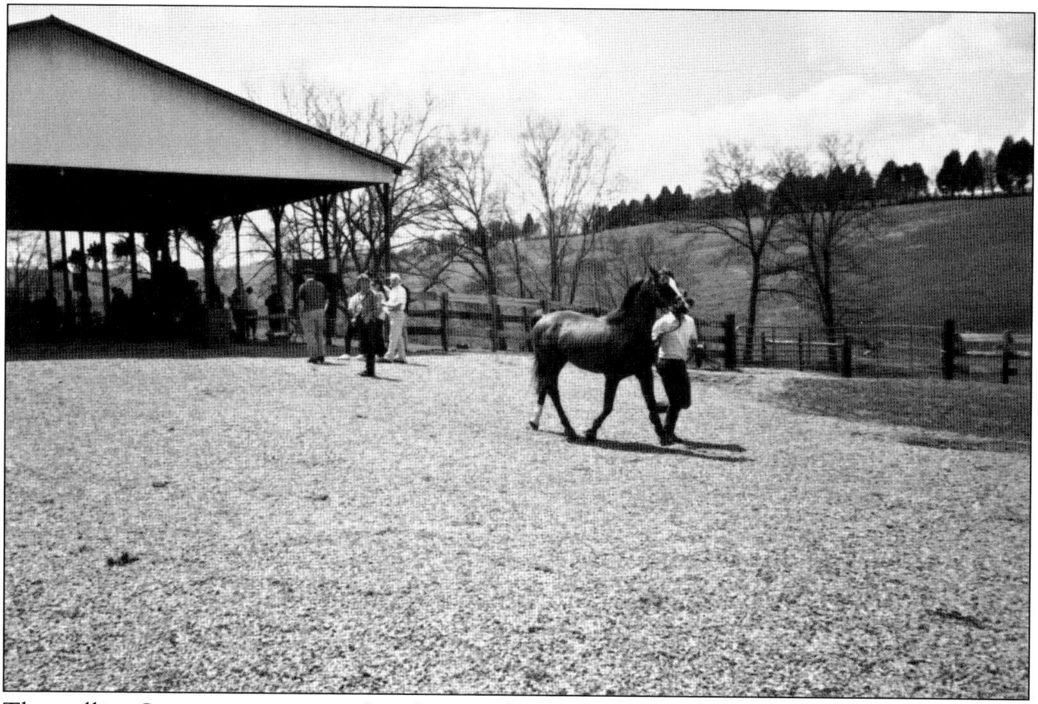

The stallion Samtyr was presented to the crowd and then returned to his stall while the auction began. His daughter Bettye Sam is being groomed for her turn in the sales ring. Most of the horses went to the highest bidders, although the most valuable broodmares, such as Dimorca and HCC Maloska were "no saled," as their reserve bids were not met.

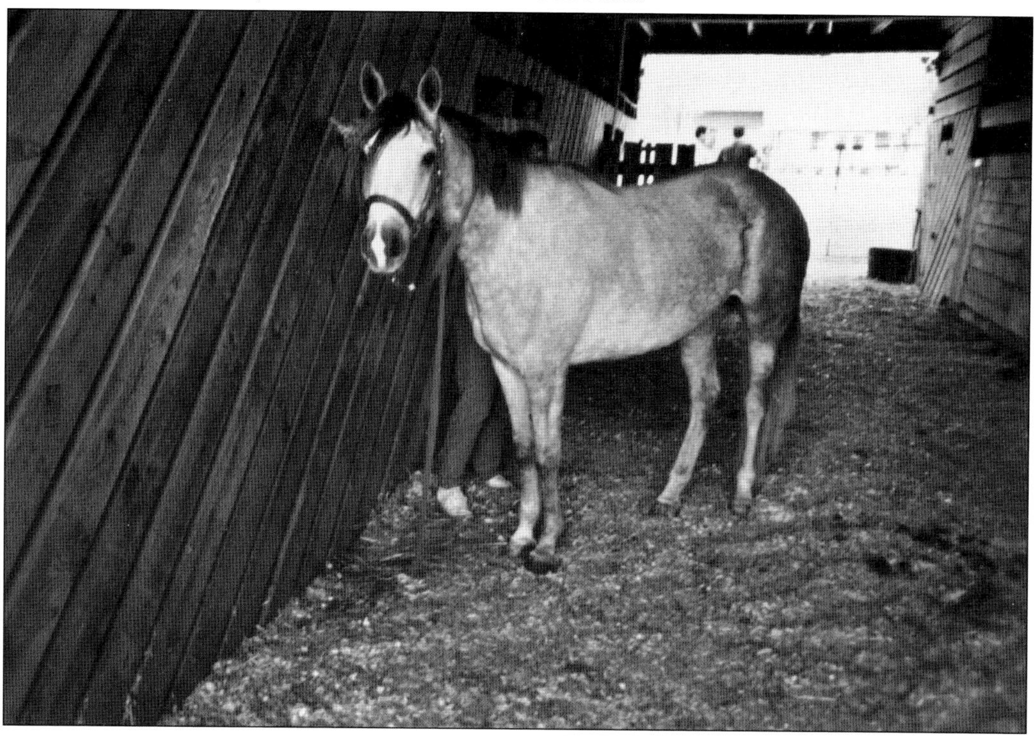

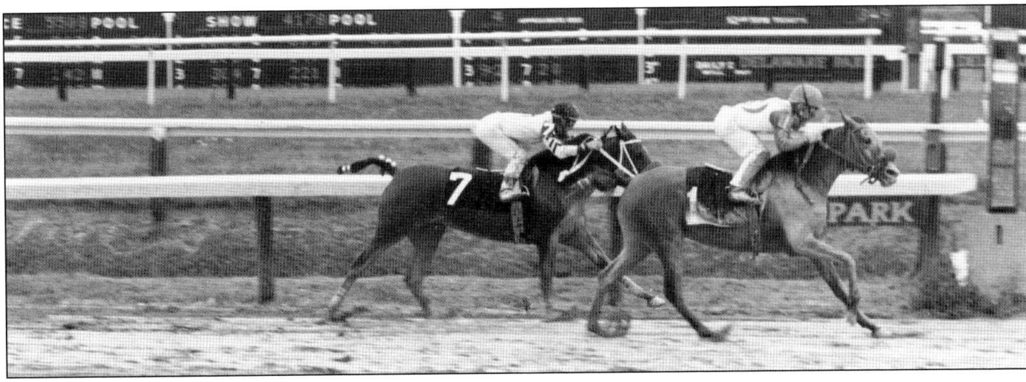

Dr. Sam and Miss Bettye were in attendance on September 7, 1987, when Samtyra won the $30,000 Gladys Brown Edwards Stakes race in Delaware. Edwards had been the secretary at the Pomona Remount Depot during World War II and was a worldly traveler and scholar on Arabian horses. She was an advocate of the Polish system of race training of all breeding stock and wrote an Arabian horse racing column for a national horse magazine after Dr. Sam no longer published his *Arabian Racing News*.

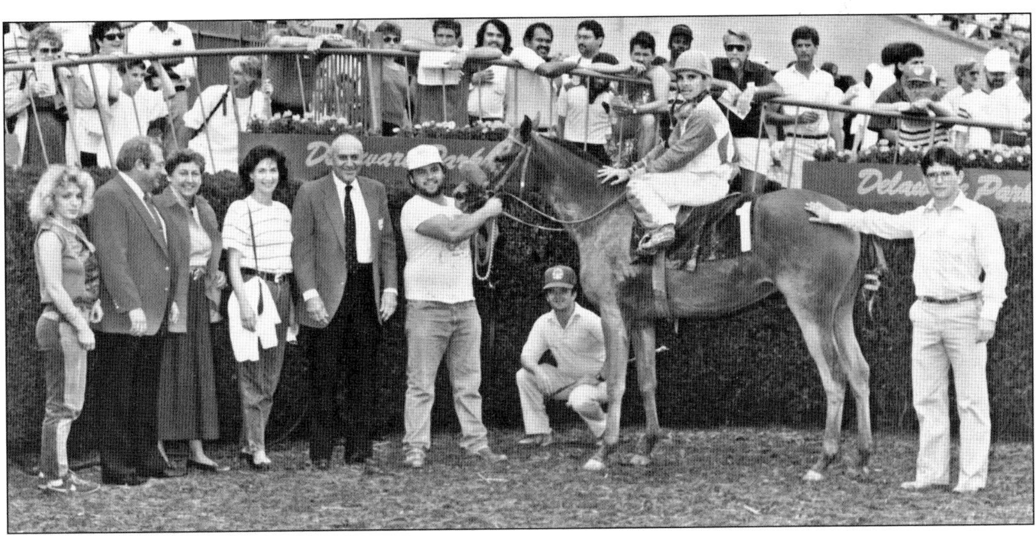

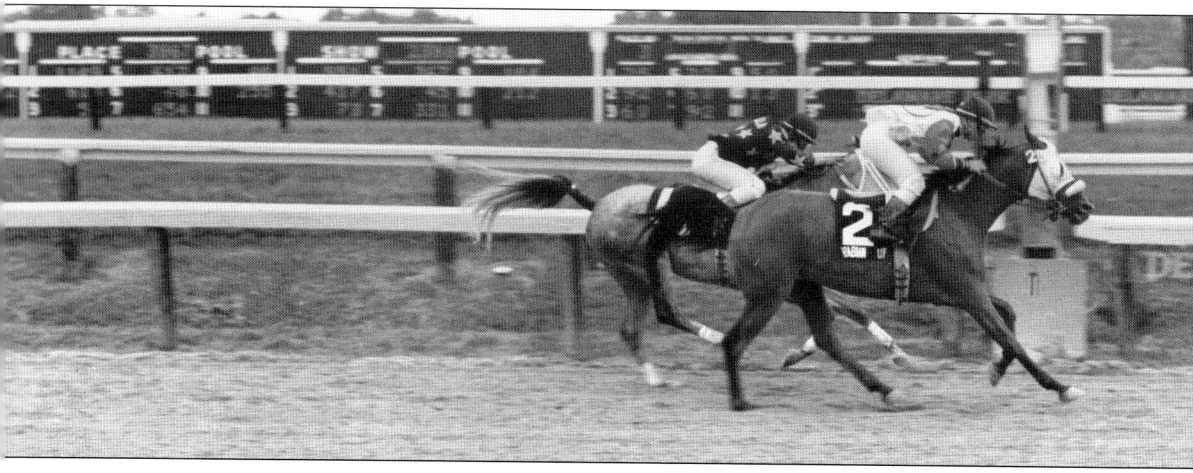

Samtyra continued to shine throughout 1987, winning the Arabian Racing Cup Distaff, shown here, as well as the $15,000 Julie Wrigley Arabian Cup Juveniles for fillies and the $10,000 Juan de Shawn Matchmaker Handicap. That year, the ARC (the nonprofit originally started by Harrison) created the Darley Awards to honor the racing community's best horses, trainers, and breeders. At the first Darley Awards ceremony on January 23, 1988, Samtyra won Race Filly of the Year. Dimfixa was named Racing Broodmare of the Year, meaning top producer of current racers. At the event, Harrison declared that the racing industry as a whole had come of age.

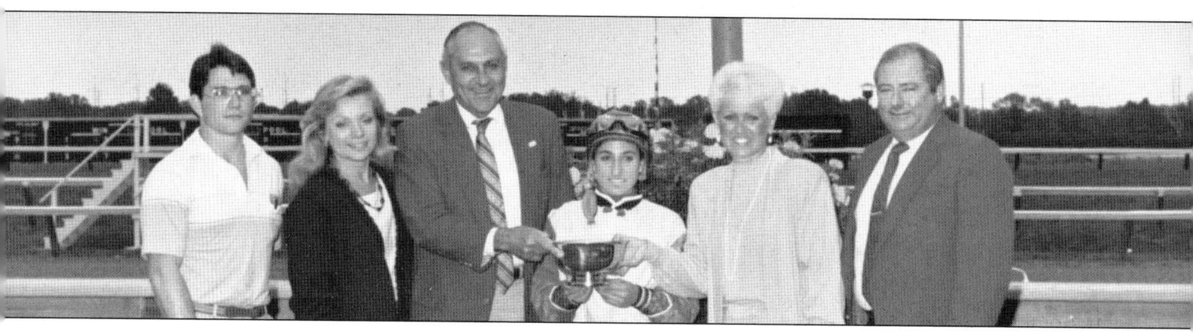

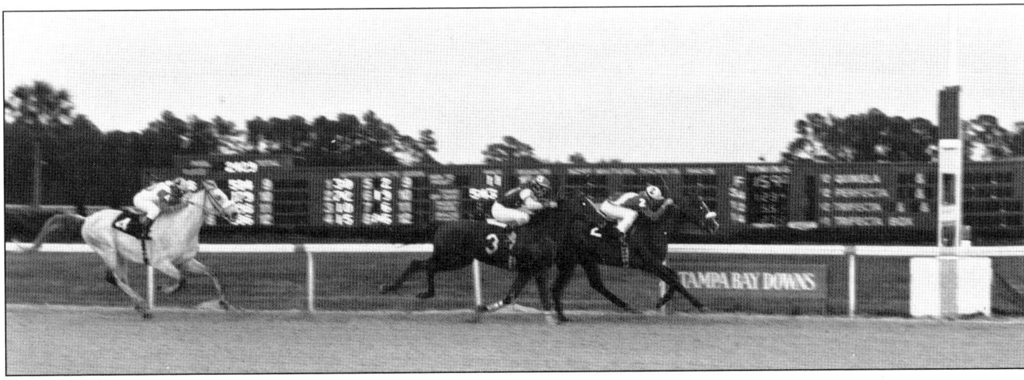

Sams Fix, by Samtyr and out of the mare Dimfixa, is pictured winning at Tampa Bay Downs. The colt was the first Arabian racehorse ever "claimed," meaning he was entered in a "claiming race," in which every horse can be purchased if an interested party contacts the track office and pays a set fee. The claiming system is considered the backbone of the sport of racing, allowing for the opportunity to purchase a race-ready horse for a fee much less than the cost of raising and training one. Finishing second in this race was Tyrix, and third was Bobbies Sam.

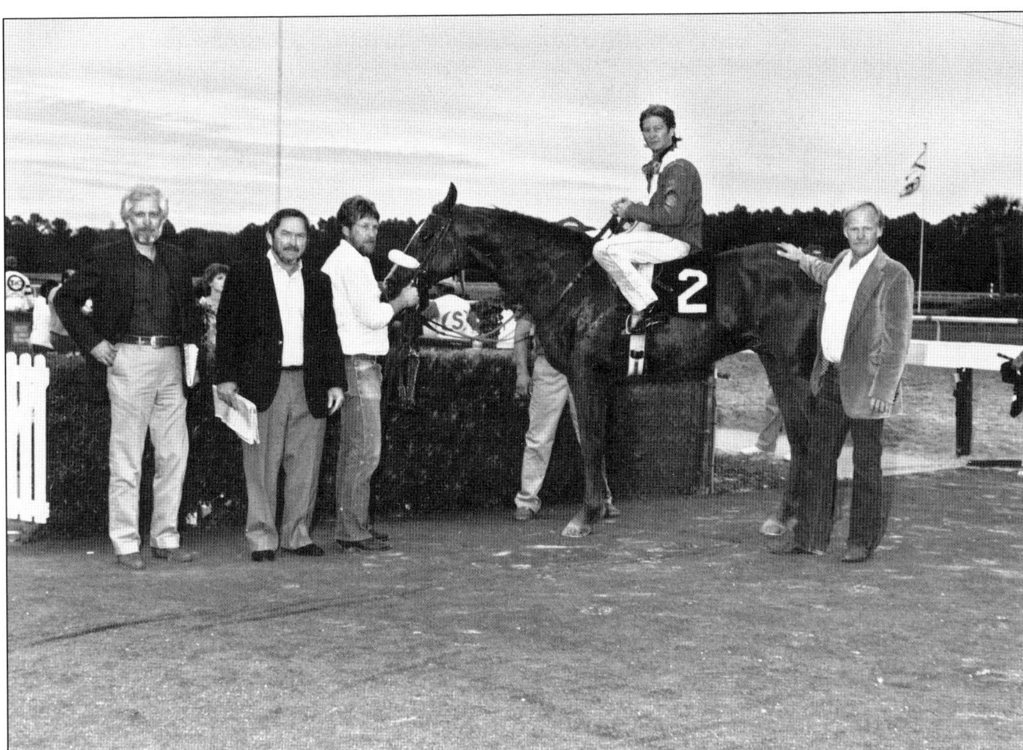

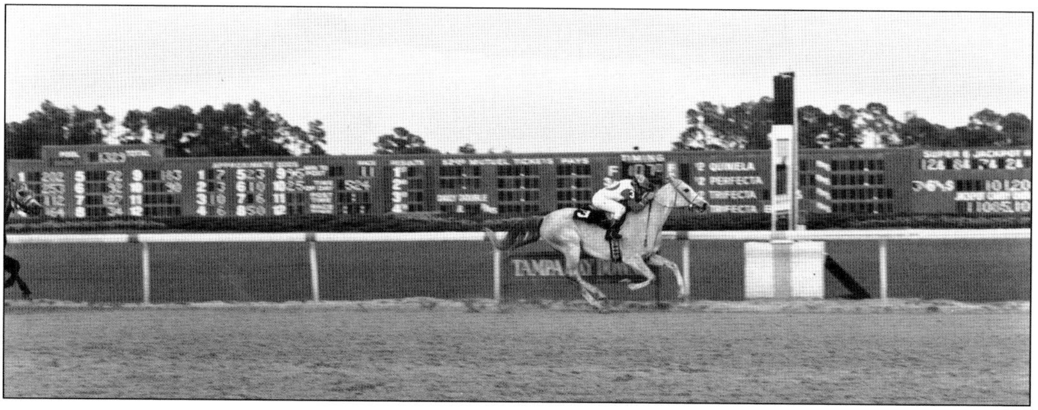

The colt Abda, by Samtyr and out of the mare HCC Maloska, wins a 1988 race at Tampa Bay Downs. The origin of Arabian horse racing at the track has an interesting story behind it. In 1978, Dr. Sam and Florida horse owner Robert Van Hoose had scheduled two exhibition races at the Florida State Fairgrounds only to learn the track was for stock cars, not horses. In his typical tenacious fashion, Dr. Sam would not be deterred and used a tractor to plow up an impromptu race course in the gravel parking lot. Among the crowd in attendance for the races was George Steinbrenner, of New York Yankees fame and also owner of Tampa Bay Downs. The chance happening opened the way for Arabian horses at Steinbrenner's track by 1983.

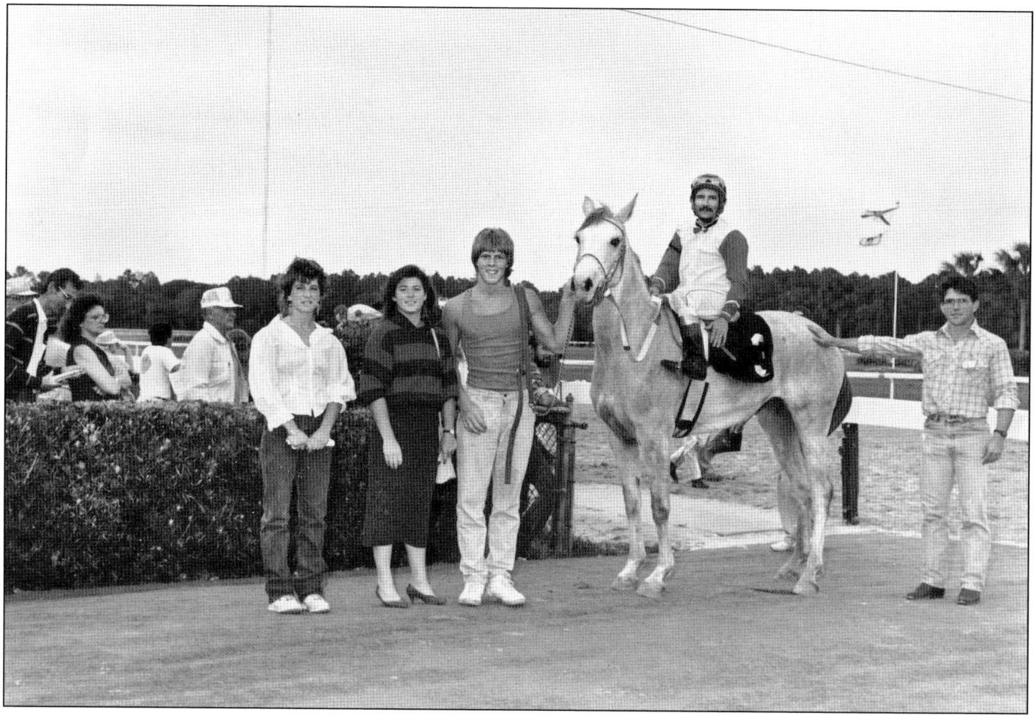

With dogged determination, Dr. Sam finally fulfilled a goal of seeing an Arabian horse race with a $100,000 purse. Advertised as the first and world's richest Arabian horse race, the Blackheath Arabian Cup, sponsored by Blackheath Farms of Atascadero, California, was scheduled for August 20, 1988. Hosting the race was the Bay Meadows track in San Mateo County, California.

ARABIAN

$2 EXACTA WAGERING

1¼ MILES

WIN	PLACE	SHOW	NO.
EX.			

ARC
ARABIAN RACING CUP

12TH RACE

First Running

BLACKHEATH ARABIAN CUP

$100,000

For three-year-olds and upward. By subscription of $400 for ARC nominated horses; $1,000 for horses by ARC nominated horses; or $2,000 for other horses, to accompany the nomination. $600 additional to pass the entry box, for ARC nominated horses; $2,000 for horses by ARC nominated horses or $3,000 for other horses. With $100,000, of which 40% to first, 20% to second, 10% to third, 8% to fourth, 7% to fifth, 6% to sixth, 5% to seventh, 4% to eighth. Weights, three-year-olds, 118 lbs.; four-year-olds, 122 lbs.; older, 126 lbs. Field to be chosen by the Racing Secretary. Starters to be named through the entry box by usual time of closing. Closed Sataurday, August 13, 1988 with twelve nominations.

No.	Owner / Trainer / Colors / Horse / Breeding	Weight	Jockey	Odds
1 Black	Pam Karlsgodt Roylance — Jesse Maldonado Royal blue, tartan plaid sash, bars on sleeves **B W RASPUTIN** Gr.h.82, Princip—HT Bint Soqa	126	Lute Proctor	20
2 Yellow	James A. Wagner — Robert Knight Maroon, gray "CR" on back, gray sleeves **CHARLIE VALENTINE** Ch.c.84, Samstar—Silver Dahl	122	Willie Rodriguez	8/5
3 Blue	Brent Crowley Arabian — Bobby Martin Yellow, blue cross sashes **SAMS FIX** (ARC) Ch.h.82, Samtyr—Dimfixa	126	Billy Lewis	20
4 Pink	Charles T. Williams — Bobby Martin Red, black cross sashes **SAMS COUNT** (ARC) Ch.h.79, Samtyr—Counts Jewell	126	Alan Sherman	20
5 Red	Robert or Judith Wey — Charles O. Pollard, Asst. Tr. Maria Deason Pink and black diamonds, black brand on pink sleeves **PLAKAN** Gr.h.83, Plakat—Kaluahh	126	Cheryl White	12
6 Green	Cain or McDonald — Charles O. Pollard, Asst. Tr. Maria Deason Pink and black diamonds, black brand on pink sleeves **MG TUTS MIRAGE** (ARC) Gr.g.84, Tuts Mira Image—Seven Lakes Rolla	122	Elizabeth Daniels	30
7 Orange	Dianne K. Monte (Lessee) — Gary Brislawn Black and tan halves, white grape leaf **HARBOR LIGHTS** B.h.83, Bajdak—Harbonet	126	Jeff Gee	15
8 White	Raymond Arana (Lessee) — Renee Glass White, green diamond braces, "RVR" on back, diamond stripe on sleeves **HAWK HILL ROYAL** Gr.h.83, Hawk Hill Cyczark—Surnetta	126	Bruno Maelfeyt	20
9 Turquoise	Virginia Barkley — Lynn Ashby Lime green, green trees on silver ball on back, silver diamond on sleeves **PARKWOOD SAMPSON** Gr.h.82, Kassadd—Parkwood Naiad	126	Victor Miranda	10
10 Gold	John A. or Peggy Yates — Robert Knight Gray, blue triangle on back, blue sleeves **VLADIN** Gr.c.83, Mc-Bask—SW Tyncza	126	Ron English	3
11 Maroon	Tim Kelley (Lessee) — Tim Kelley White, blue circle "TC" on back, bars on sleeves **FLAMING TRON KU** Gr.h.82, Ibn Kontiki—Flaming Emotion	126	Brenda Zoppo	6
12 Lavender	Bergstrom, Pacheco & Rust (Lessee) — Jean Pacheco Black, red and gray hoops, gray horse on back **BAJA DANSK** Gr.c.84, Goansk—Dunabajrama	122	Severiano Martinez	20

(ARC) Arabian Racing Cup.

Latest workouts not appearing in The Daily Racing Form:
MG TUTS MIRAGE, Aug 16 BM 6f 1:25⅘h.; Aug 13 BM 3f :38⅘hg.

Last Race Omitted from Daily Racing Form:
B W RASPUTIN, Jul 31 1m 1.58 1' Stk. HAP B W Rasputin, Kishstar, Pterski.

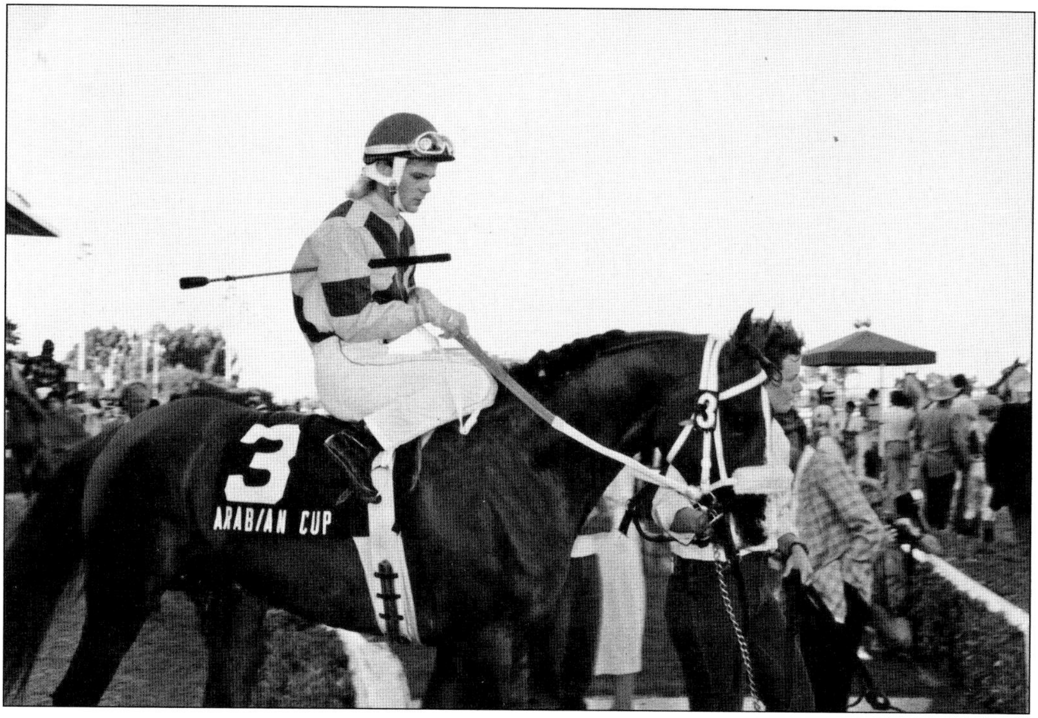

Harrison sent two horses from Delaware Park to compete in the race. The competition was stiff, and even Sams Fix (Number 3) and Sams Count (Number 4) were longshots at 20-1 odds.

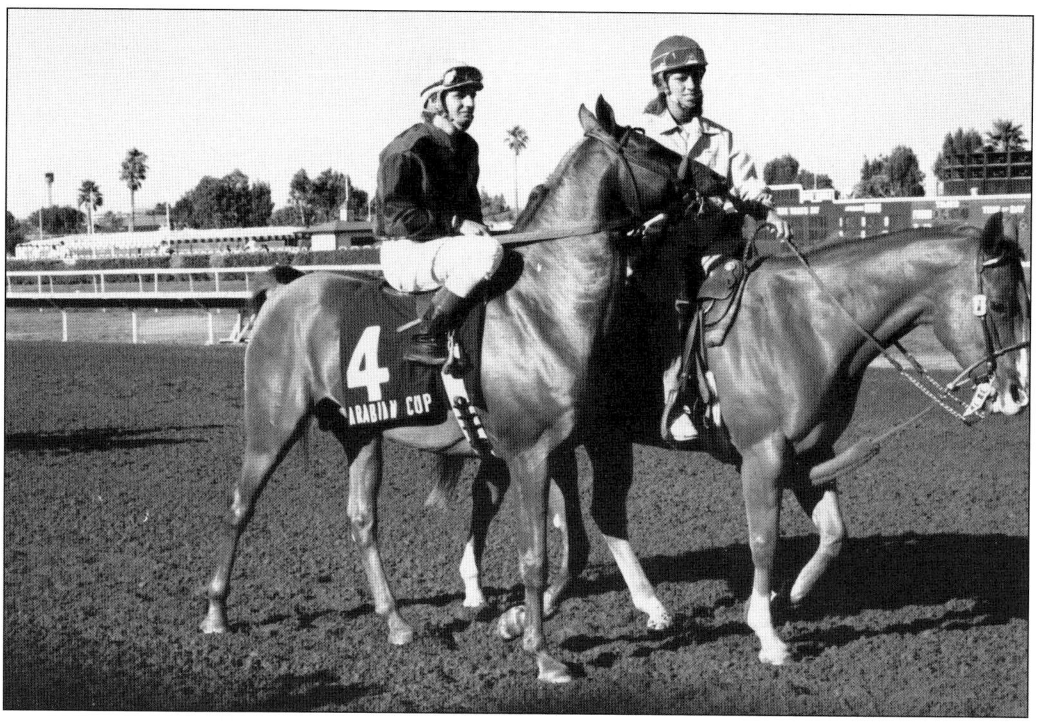

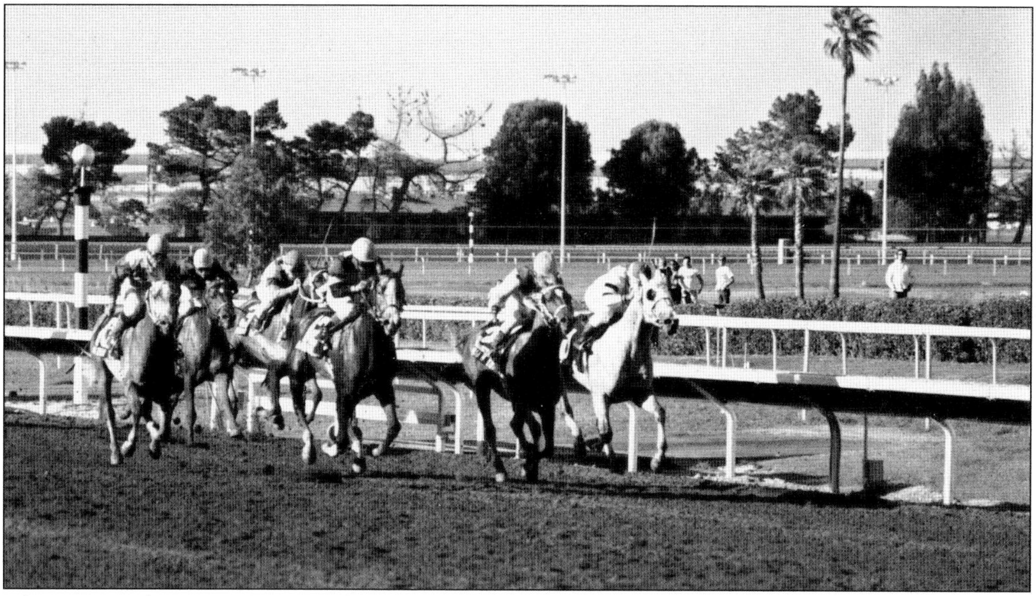

The eventual winner was another longshot, Baja Dansk. A minimum $2 bet on Baja Dansk returned $76 to the bettor. Though Dr. Sam didn't walk away with the victory, he and Miss Bettye, and a large group of other friends of the winning owner, crowded in for the winner's circle photograph. The year 1988 was another year of honor: at the second annual Darley Awards, Dr. Harrison was honored with the Award of Merit, for his efforts over the years to promote racing, and with the Breeder of the Year Award, in light of Samtyr's offsprings' many victories, earning $750,000 through the 1988 season. (It was Samtyr's eighth consecutive year as Racehorse Sire of the Year.) Harrison's Samtyra was named the Darley Four Year Old Filly of the Year.

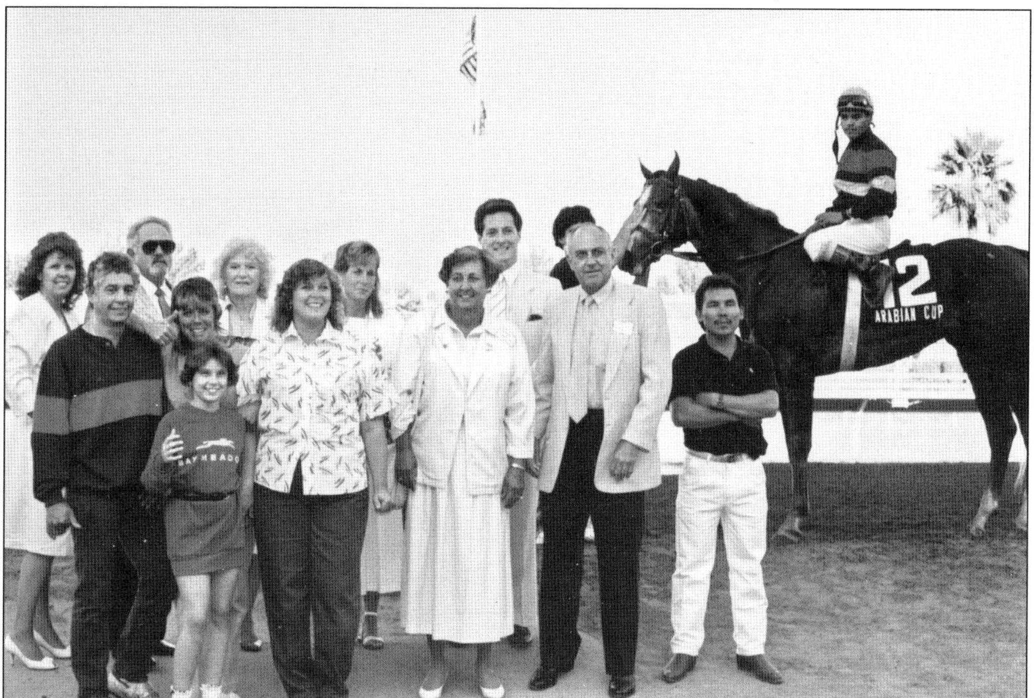

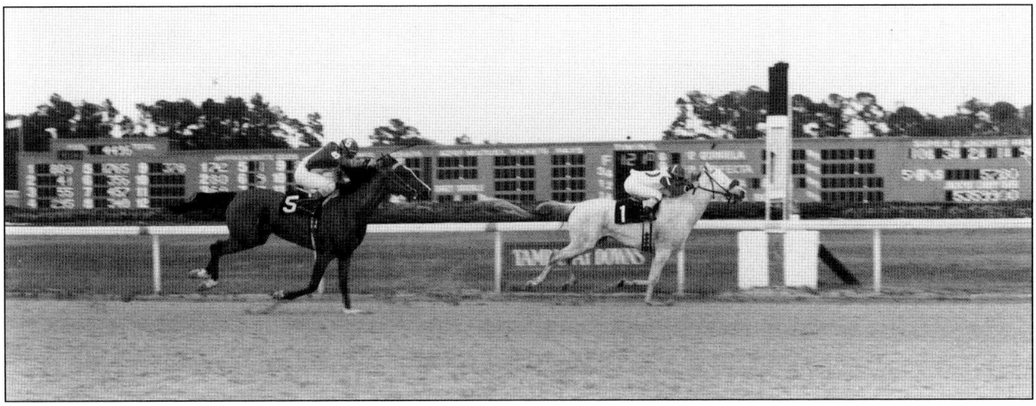

The mare Jessorca, a Samtyr daughter out of the esteemed Dimorca, was Dr. Sam's winner at Tampa Bay Downs on March 3, 1989. Russ Ragain was the trainer, and the jockey was Paula Fogle. She won the six-furlong race in 1:22.

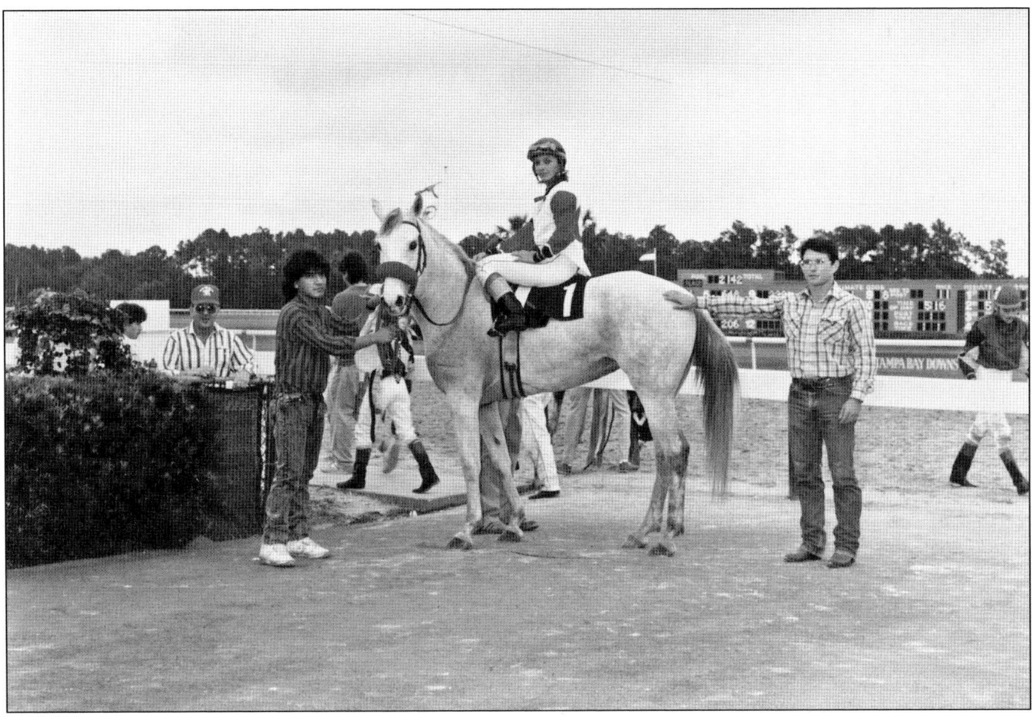

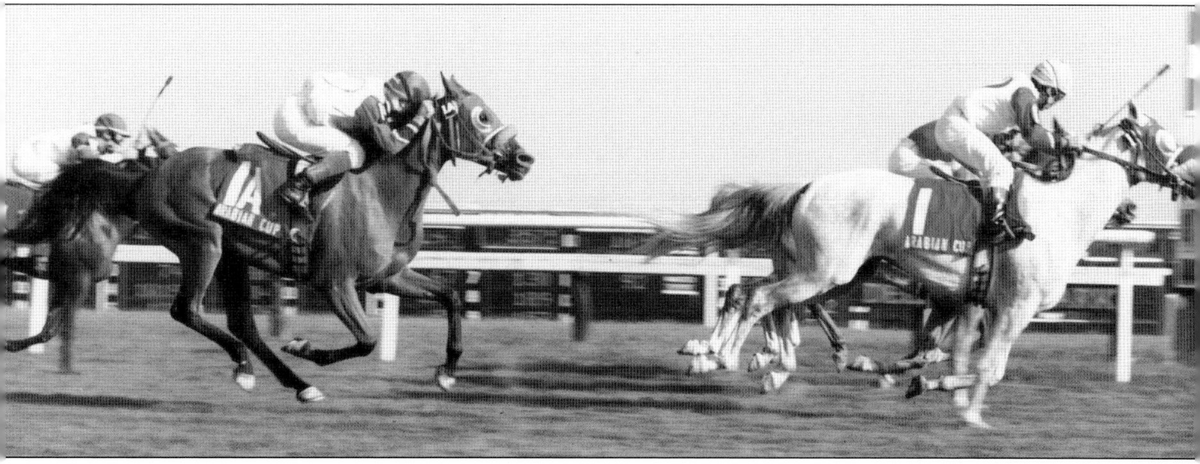

Dr. Sam was in attendance to witness Jessorca's victory in the prestigious $50,000 Gladys Brown Edwards Stakes race in Delaware. The race, a mile and one-sixteenth in distance over turf (grass), was a close call, with three across at the finish line. Placing second was another Sa-Arabet filly, Saafari, who was purchased from Dr. Sam at the First Opportunity sale for $4,500. As the second-place horse in the race, she won 20 percent of the $50,000 purse. At the end of the season, Jessorca was named the Darley Older Mare of the Year.

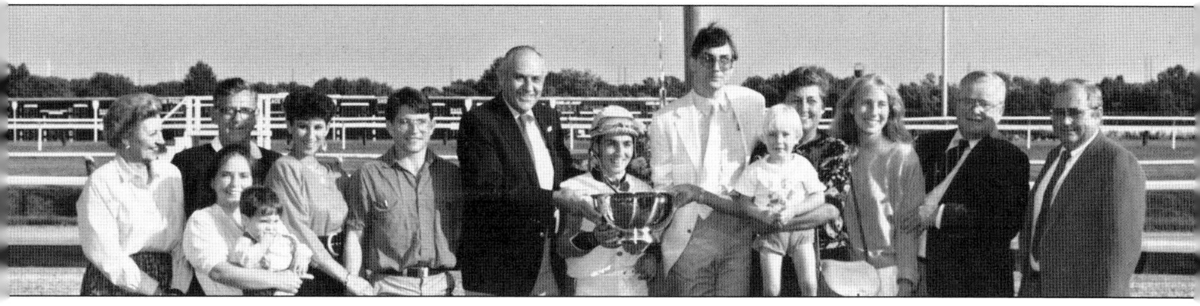

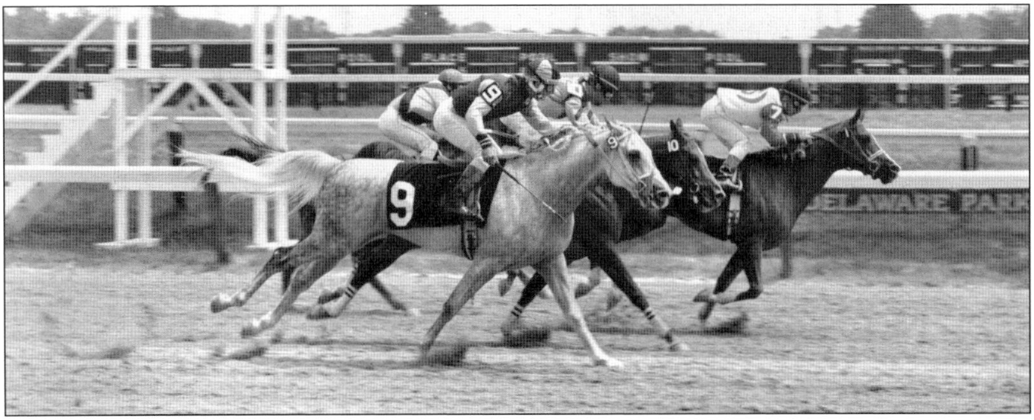

Able Sam, by Samtyr and out of Ruraka, was one of few Sa-Arabet horses all-Polish in pedigree. He is pictured here, on July 10, 1988, "breaking his maiden," or winning his first race, finishing one mile in 1:55.3.

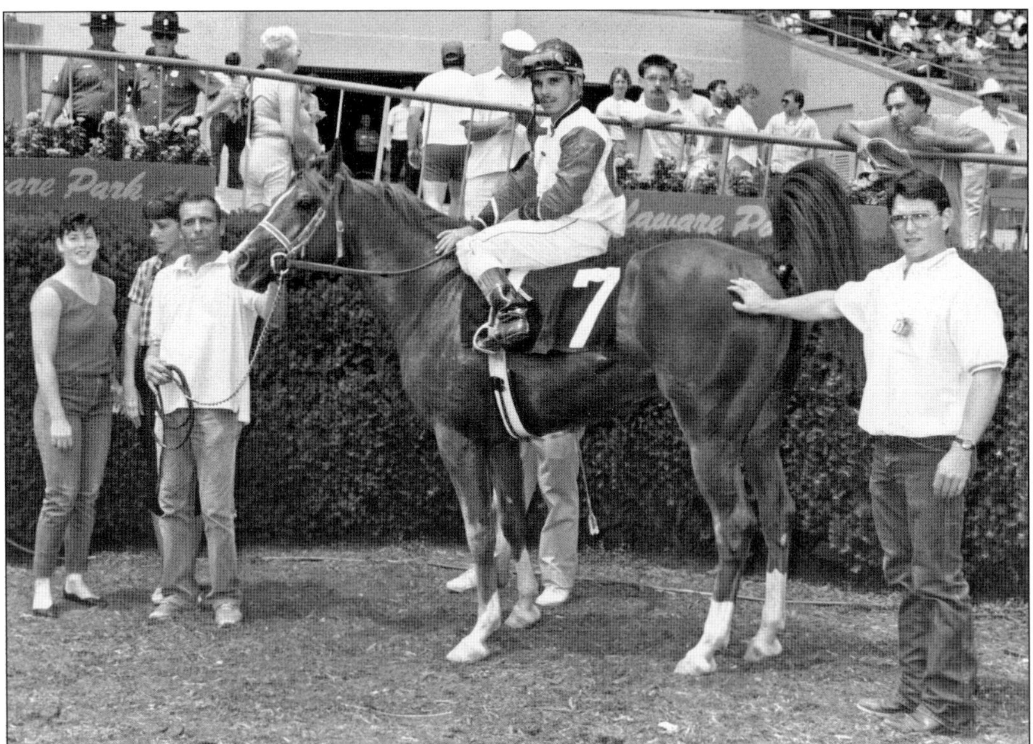

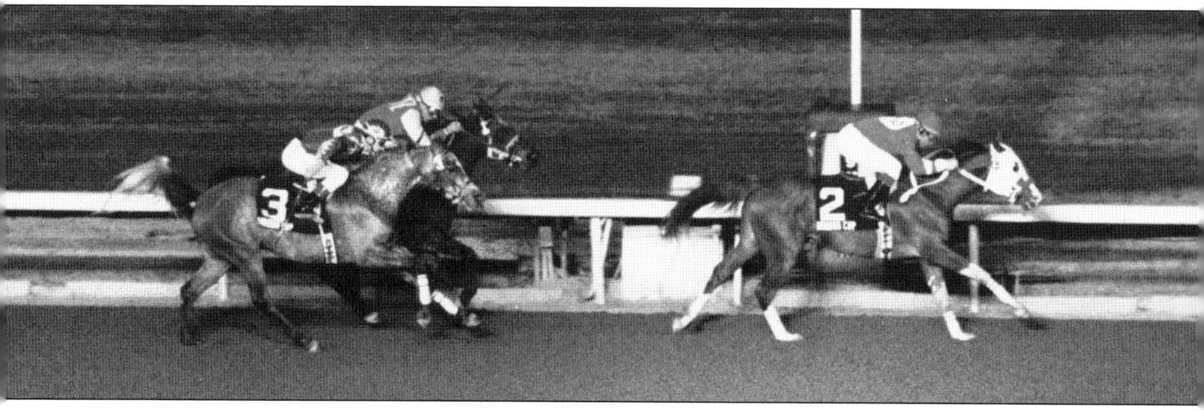

In 1990, Stiltz, owned by Roger D. Lang, won the seven-furlong, $15,000 Arabian Cup for Juveniles at the Los Alamitos racetrack in California. His full brother Styxx was California's Champion Four Year Old for 1992. This cross of Samtyr on the mare HCC Maloska proved successful. Harrison bred 10 full siblings, including Saaray, Sams Sable, Abda, and Bettye Sam. Eight of the 10 ran in the money, six of those earning over $10,000 each. Saaray won $42,000 in three seasons, including the Kentuckiana Futurity in 1985 and the Armand Hammer Classic.

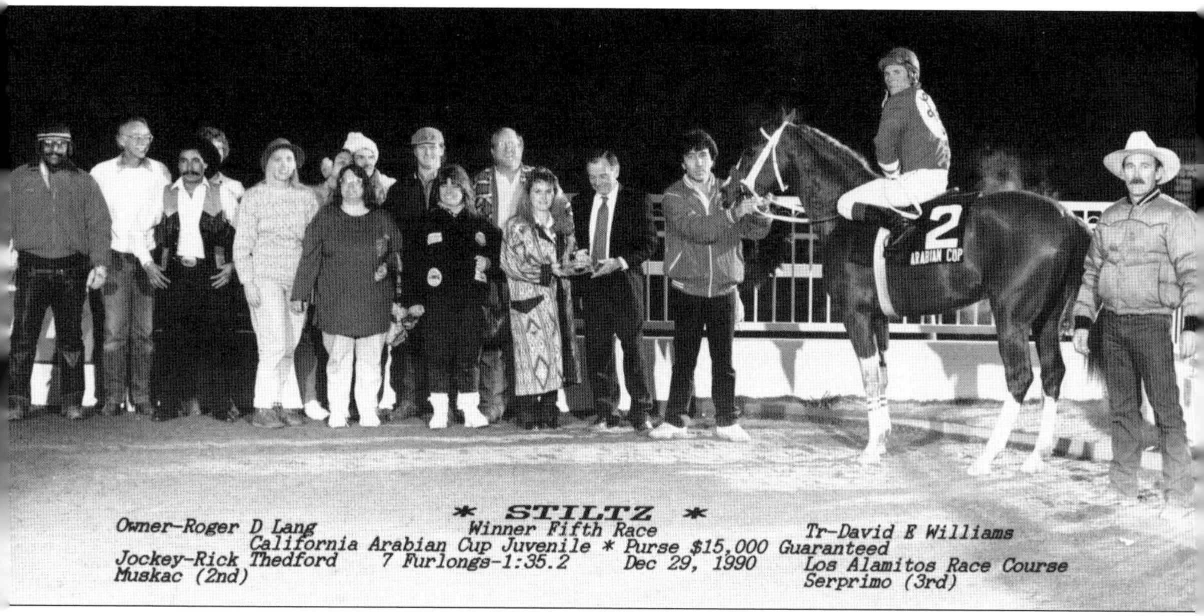

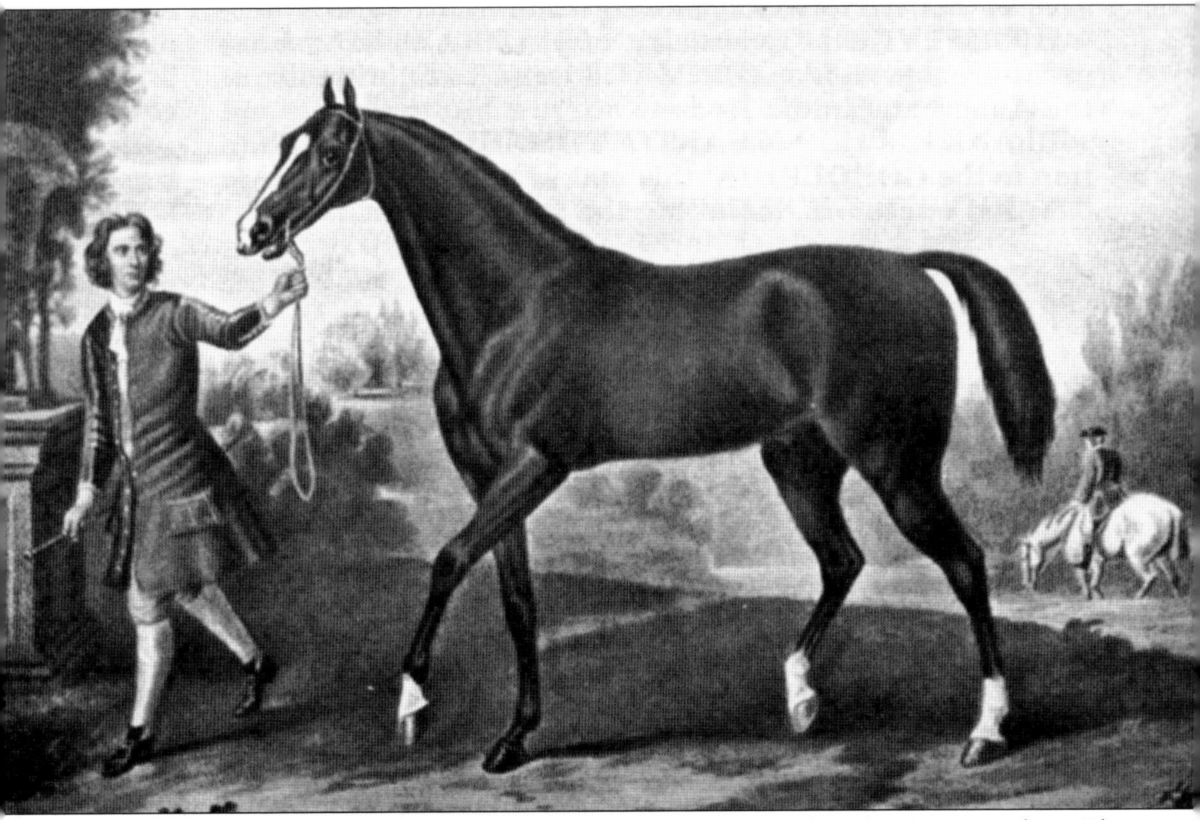

In the late 1980s, the Darley Awards were created to honor Arabian horse racing's best. The Darley Arabian, depicted in a painting, was imported to England from the Syrian desert in 1704. The stallion sired a number of excellent racers in England, where the Thoroughbred racehorse was developed as it own distinct breed. The Darley Awards, for Arabian racehorses, allude to the famous progenitor of the Thoroughbred breed and honor each year's best in categories including Breeder of the Year, Trainer of the Year, Horse of the Year, Sprinter, Older Mare, Four Year Olds, and several others.

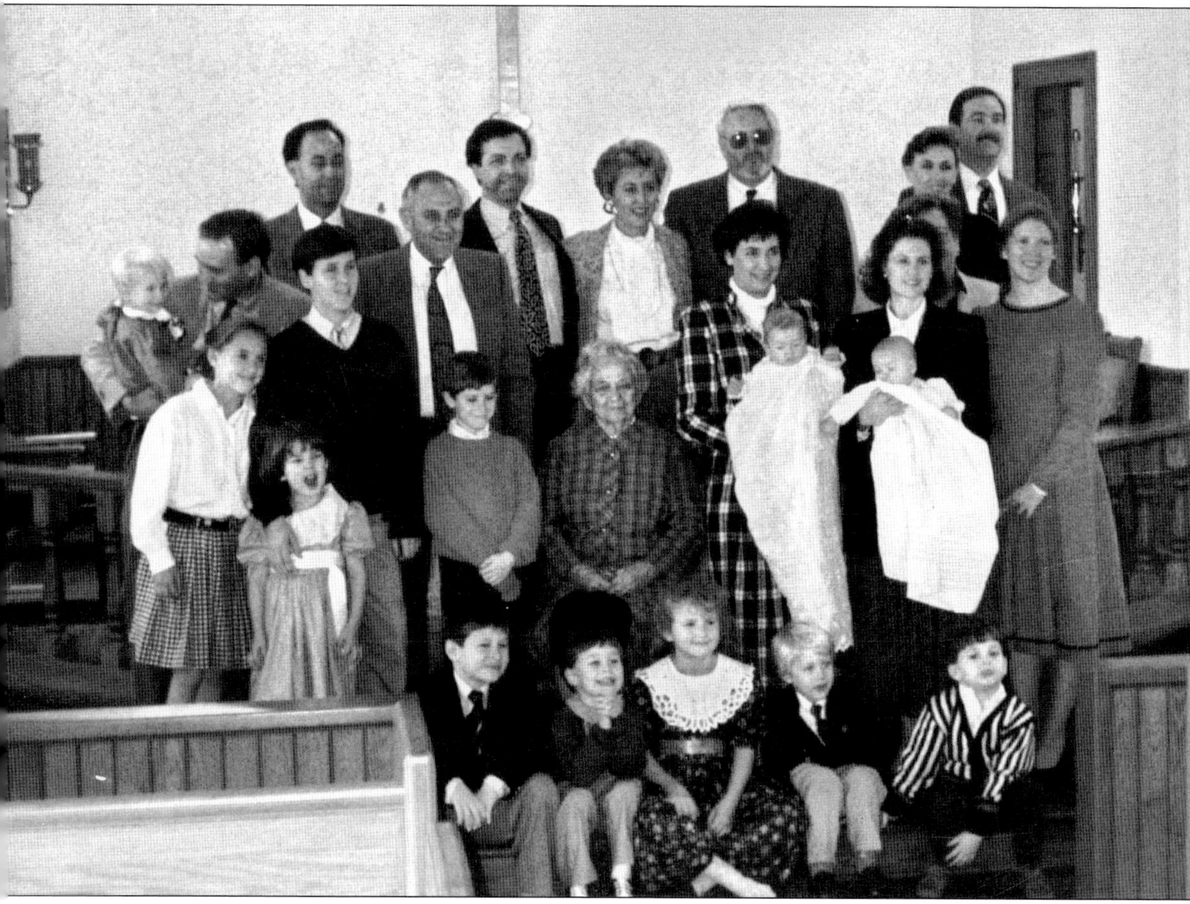

Dr. Sam stands among his many children and grandchildren, gathered together at the Church of the Resurrection in Loudon for the occasion of a baptism of twins in the family in November 1993.

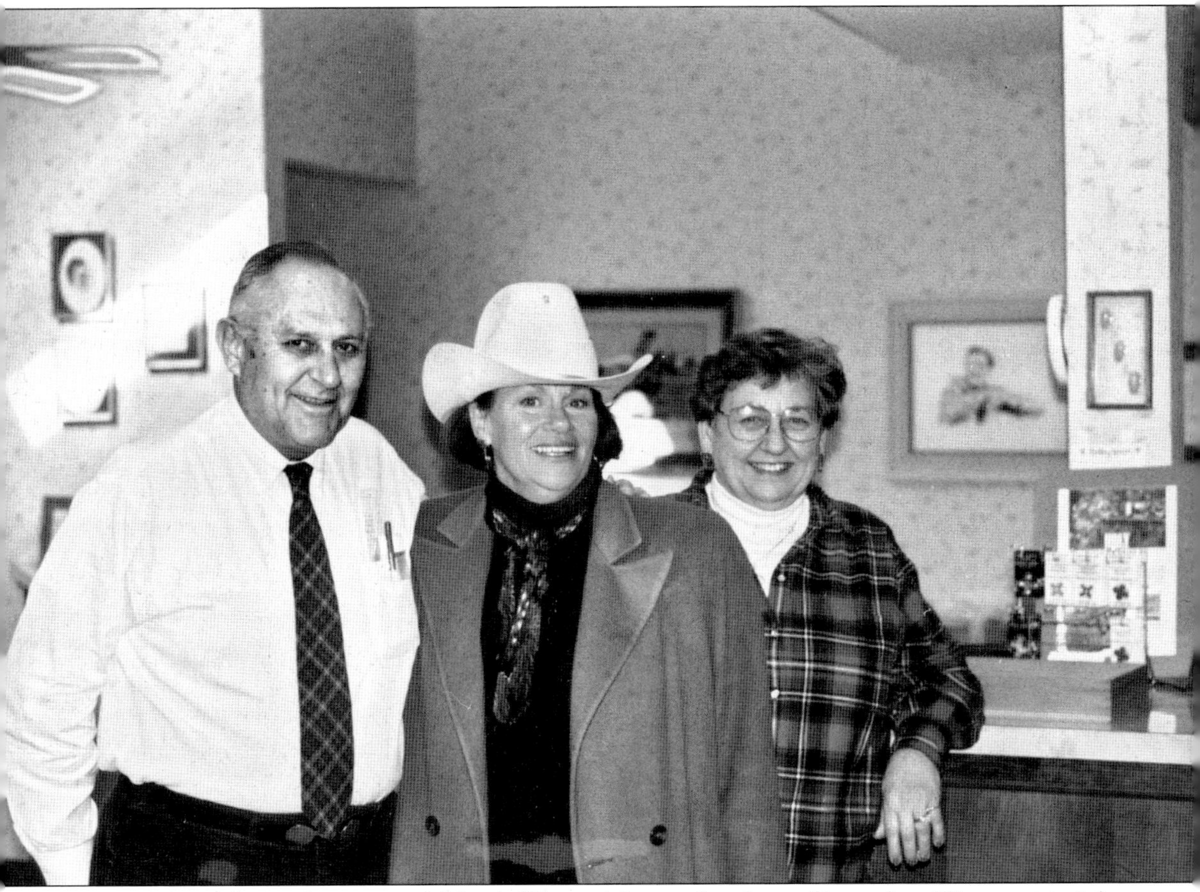

Dr. Sam and Miss Bettye met Melinda Wayne Munoz, daughter of legendary Western star John Wayne, through some mutual horse friends at Delaware Park. Here the couple enjoys a visit with Munoz in their Loudon home. The three traveled together, visiting places from New Orleans to South America. One of their adventures involved Dr. Sam's purchase of a drawing of "The Duke" at the John Wayne Cancer Institute Auxiliary Odyssey Ball in California. As a fan of John Wayne, Harrison bought the drawing because of a quote written on it, "Get out of here Sam." Munoz later informed Harrison that the "Sam" referred to was a dog, which only added humor to the purchase. Munoz likened Dr. Sam to her father, noting that she was raised in a similar family-oriented home with middle-class values, despite the occasional brushes with celebrities.

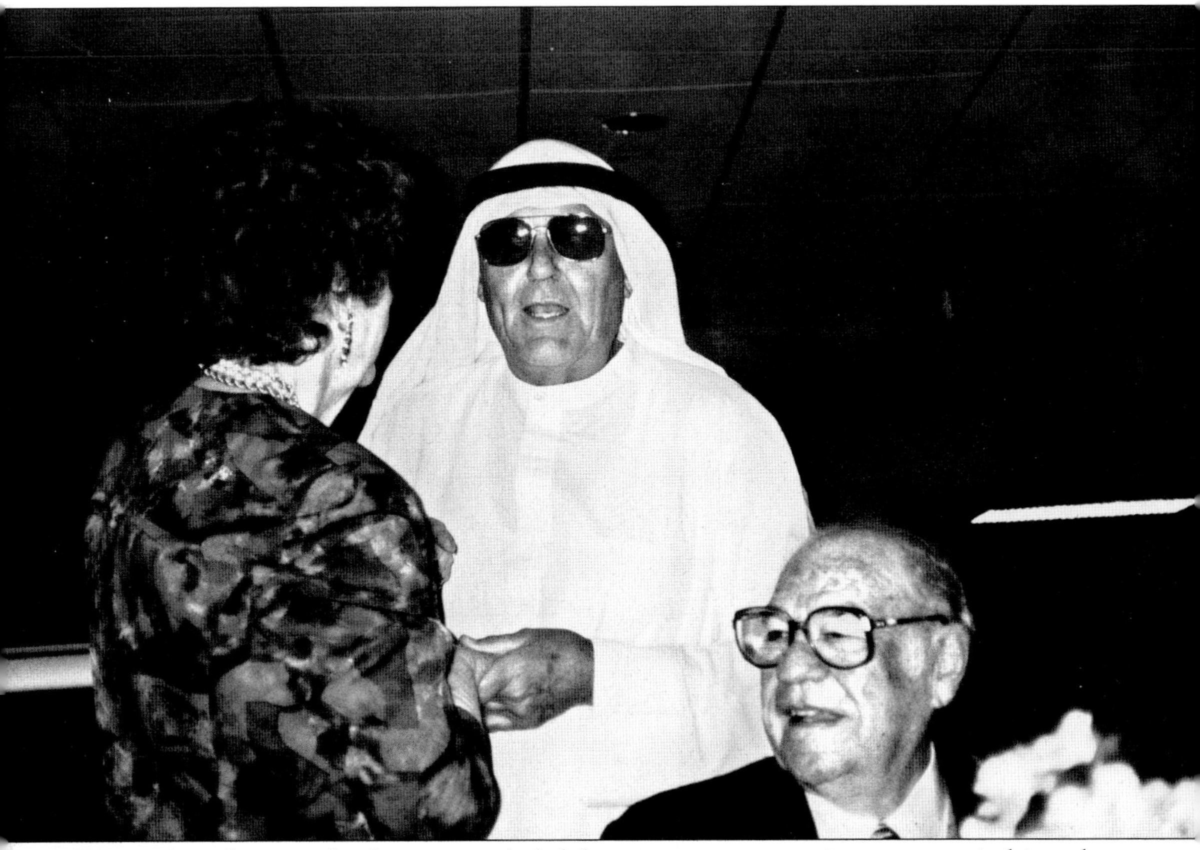

Harrison's enthusiasm for the sport included donning costumes at times, as seen in his early years parading through Loudon in a home-made bedouin's outfit. During the years of stumping for Arabian racing, in 1976, he had attended the first Arabian Horse Fair in Louisville dressed in jockey silks and helmet, which was surely a humorous sight, given Harrison's six-foot frame. He handed out flyers to anyone who would take them. In 1995, after racing had taken off in California, Harrison attended an event by ARAC, the Arabian Racing Association of California, dressed as a sheik. Sam Harrison was inducted into the Racing Hall of Fame that year, as was Samtyr. The following year, the *Dimrak daughter Dimorca was inducted.

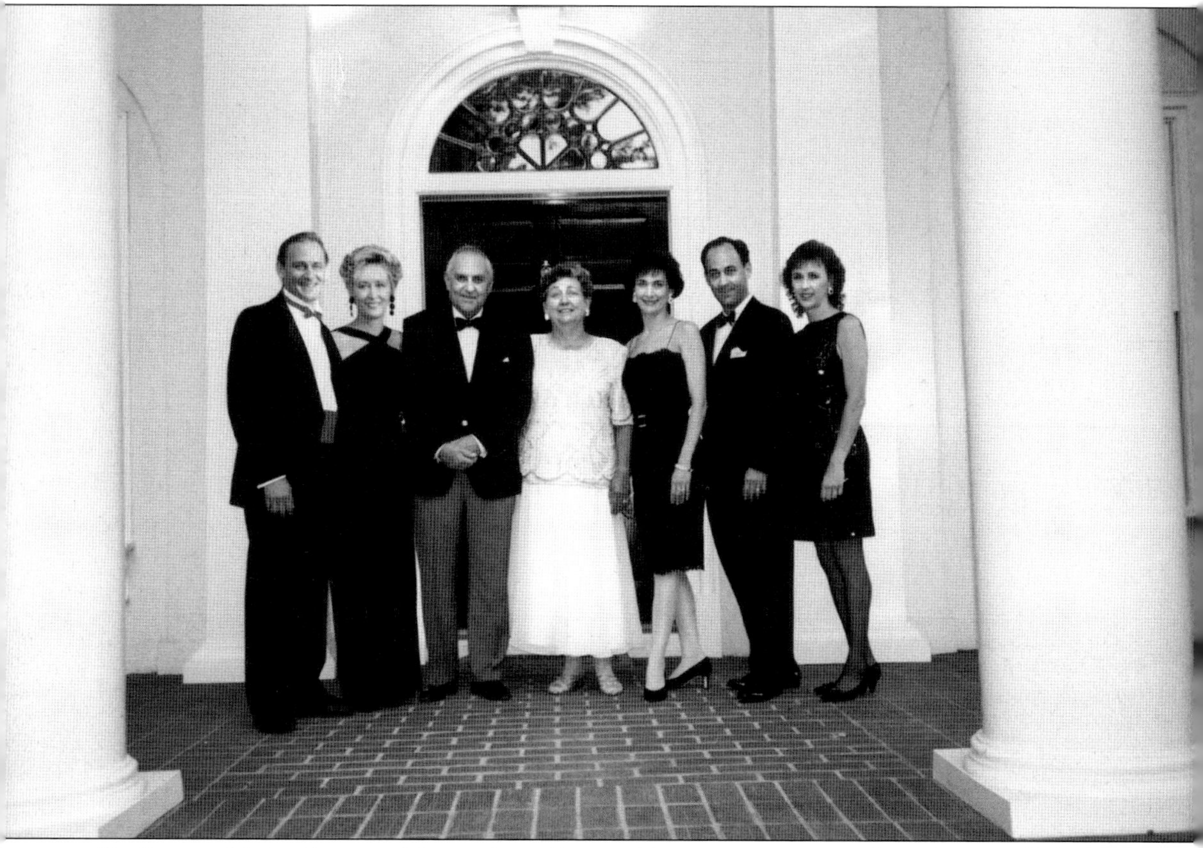

Dr. Sam and Miss Bettye celebrate their 50th wedding anniversary at their daughter Whitney Wheaton's home in Griffin, Georgia, in June 1996.

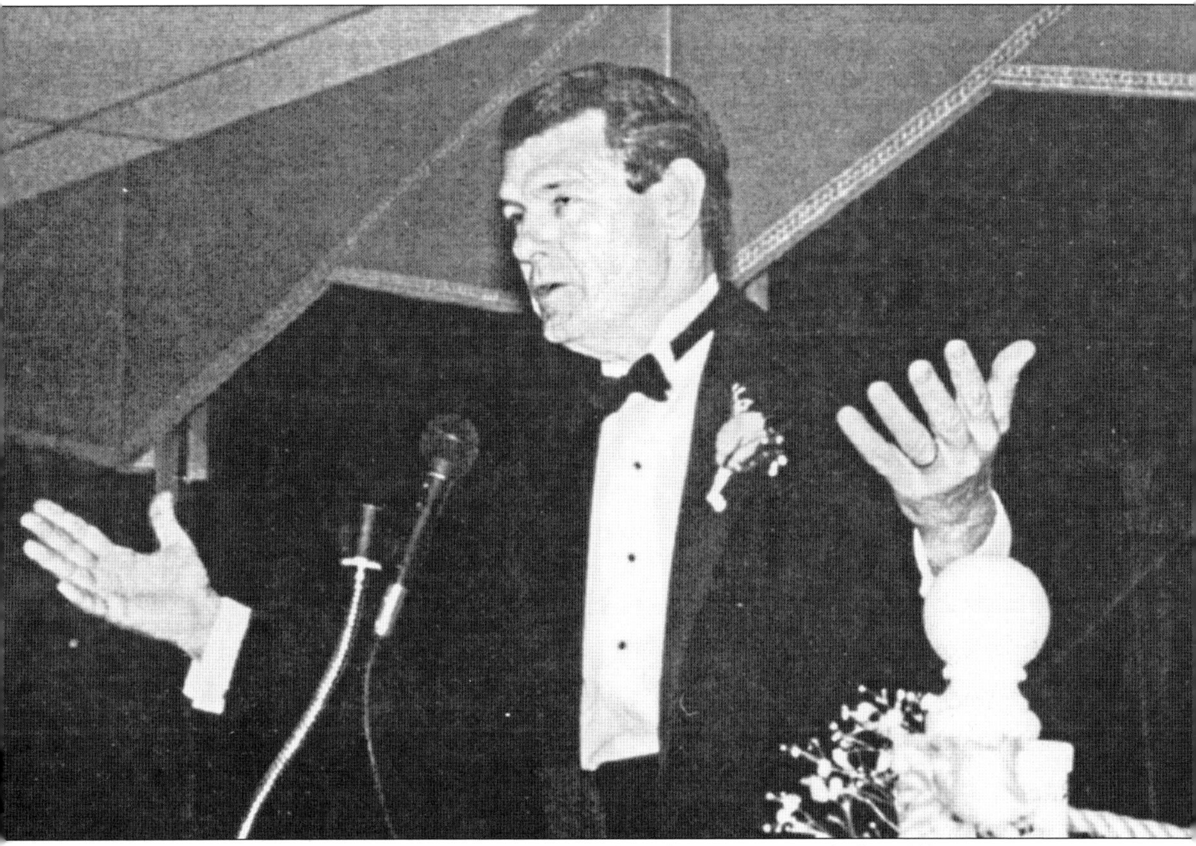

Dr. Sam Harrison initiated many newcomers into Arabian horse racing, including fellow Tennesseans. When Hamp and Ginnie Johnston moved to Chattanooga in the early 1970s, they attended one of Harrison's consignment sales, just "window shopping." Twenty years later, the couple purchased their first Arabian horses, one of which had been bred by Harrison. Its registration papers noted ARC enrollment, and the Johnstons contacted Harrison for an explanation. Harrison instructed the Johnstons to be at his farm the next weekend, and a subsequent trip to a Louisville sale put them into a partnership on a young racehorse. Hamp laughs at Harrison's persuasive method for involving newcomers in the sport of racing, almost a directive rather than a suggestion. The couple never even intended to become involved in Arabian horse racing with their first purchase. They are still active in racing today, and Hamp served as president of the Arabian Jockey Club. (Courtesy of *Arabian Finish Line*.)

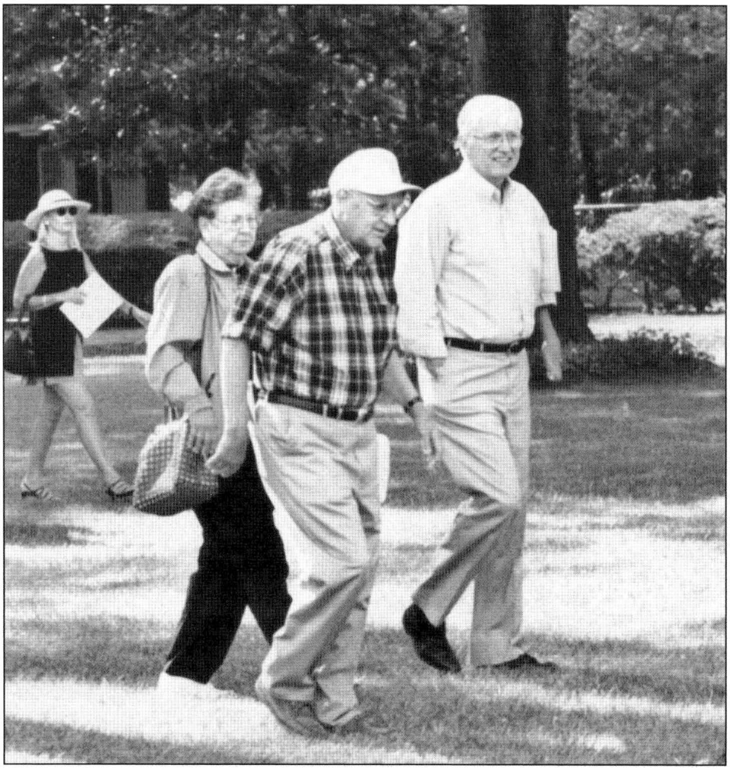

Another recruit of Dr. Sam's is Dr. Ted Wright (right) of Ooltewah, Tennessee, pictured here at Delaware Park with Miss Bettye (left) and Dr. Sam (center). Wright's first horse was Sam Taire, from Sa-Arabet breeding, and he owned other offspring of Samtyr. Wright has had much success in Arabian horse racing and serves as the Arabian Racing Cup Chief Steward. (Patschedier photograph courtesy of *Arabian Finish Line* magazine.)

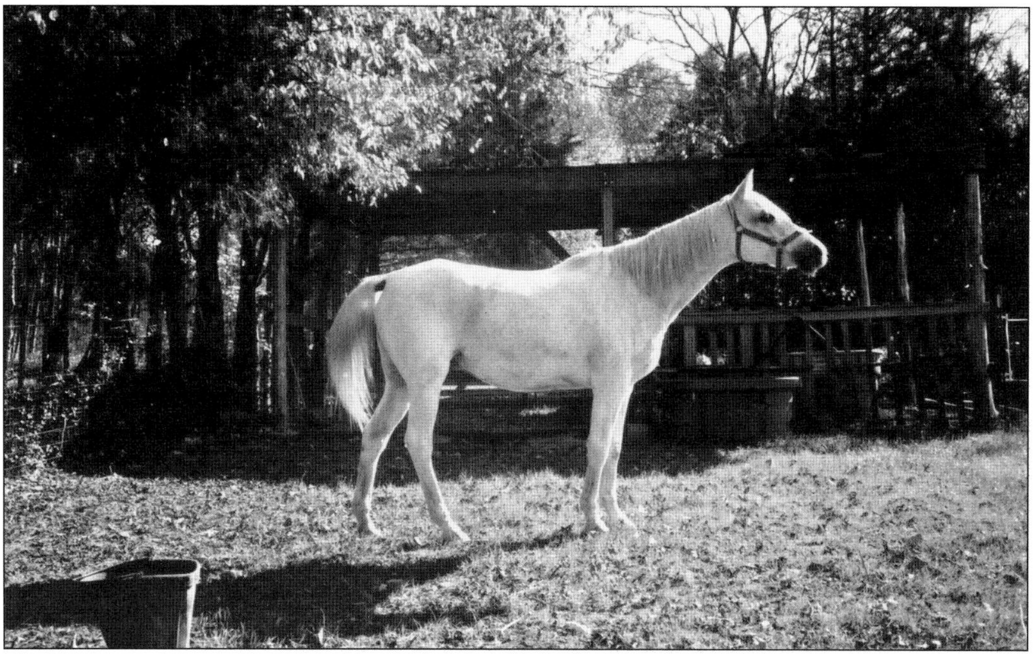

The Samtyr daughter Bettye Sam was considered something of a celebrity at the track, as, by name, she was easily identified not just with Dr. Sam, but Miss Bettye, too. Offered for sale by a large Florida breeding farm, the aged mare found her last home back in the hills of Tennessee, under this author's ownership.

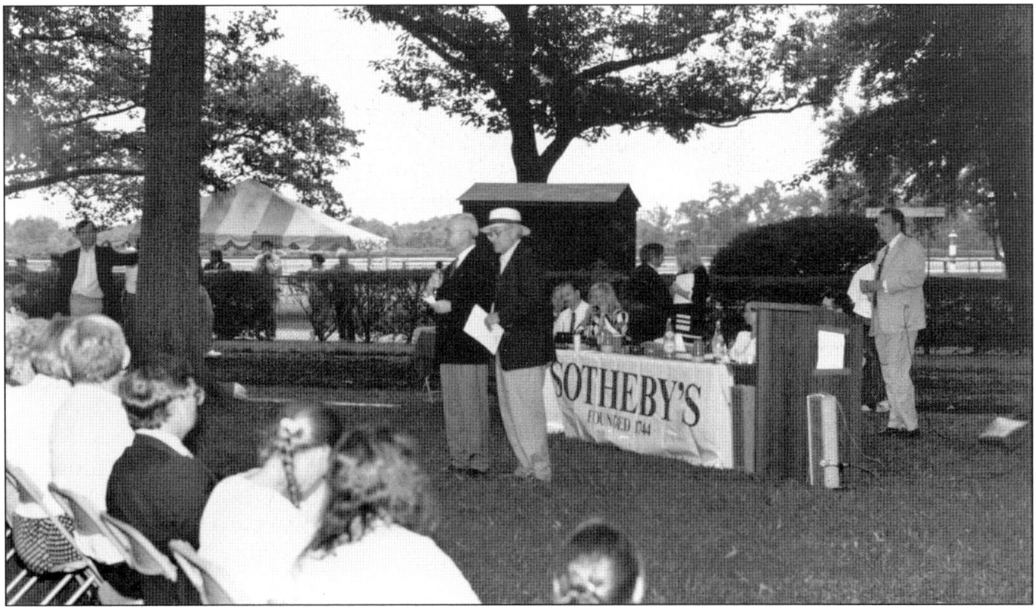

Dr. Sam believed in breeding the best horses and selling quality stock to new owners. He believed that public sales of racehorses were the best indicator of the state of the sport, where the public could evaluate racing stock and influence the future by changing ownership and increasing participation. He consigned his horses to racehorse sales, such as the one above at Delaware Park at which two brothers from the Middle East volleyed the bidding on one of Dr. Sam's horses, and he held sales back at Sa-Arabet in Loudon, proud to showcase the beauty and simplicity of his Tennessee farm and his roots. The photograph below captures a moment between good friends in the horse business, taken in the summer of 1997 at Dr. Sam's last sale.

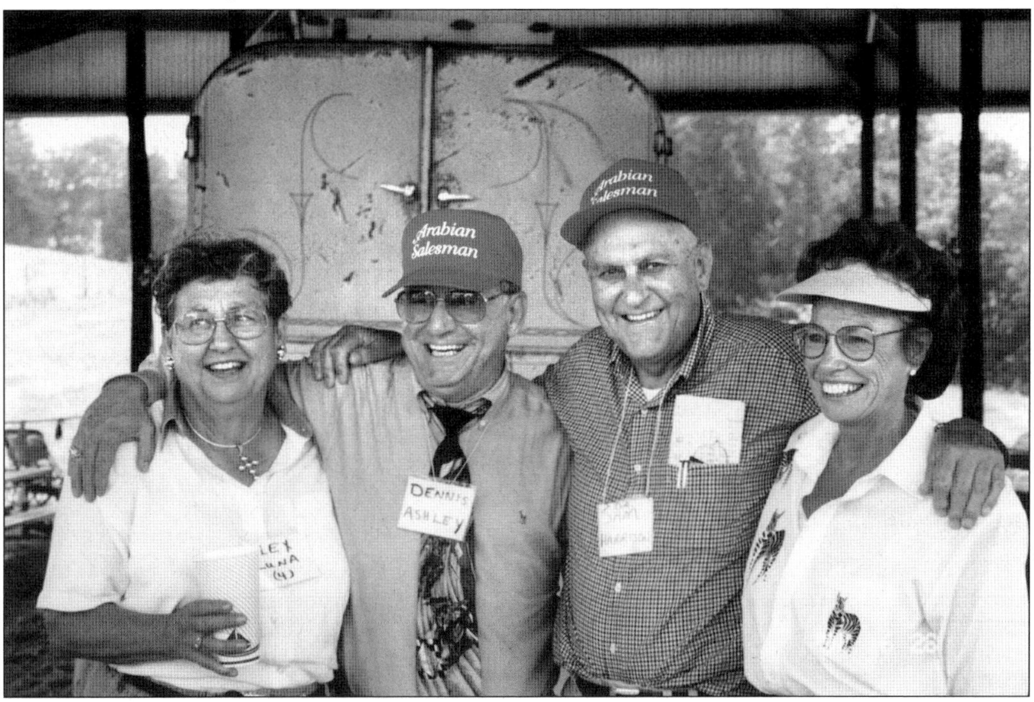

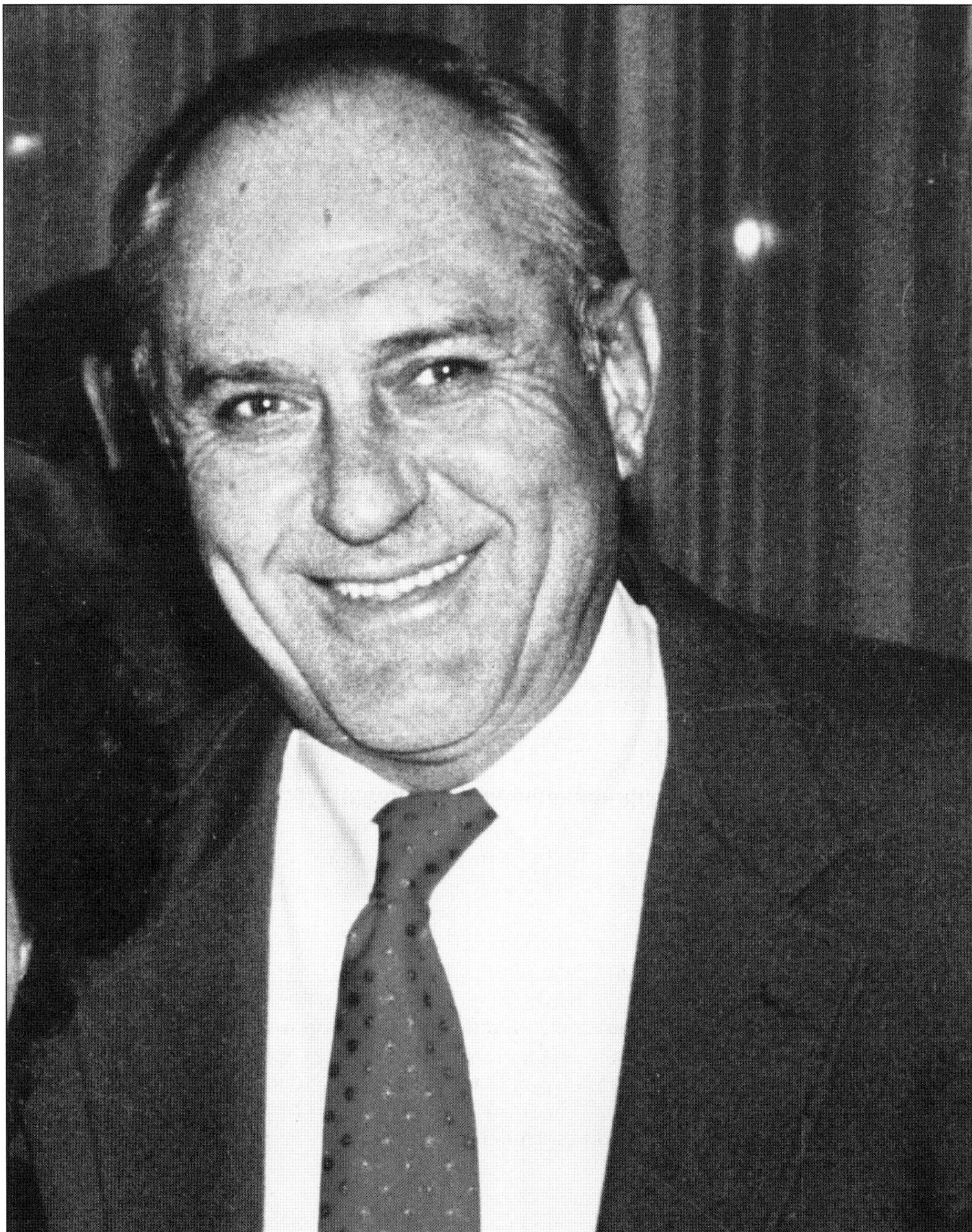

Dr. Sam was always where the action was in Arabian horse racing, often making the action happen. He was eager to meet people and encourage them to join in the fun and sport of Arabian horse racing. He was an ambassador for the Arabian breed and for their racing, traveling across the country and even the world to promote the sport. His programs helped the sport increase in number of owners and in purse money of races. At the same time, the sport has not become out of reach to newcomers, maintaining strong ties with its middle-class origins. Today it is not uncommon for Arabian racehorse owners to do preliminary conditioning at home, just as Hazel Lucas did and just as Dr. Sam had local teenagers do for him.

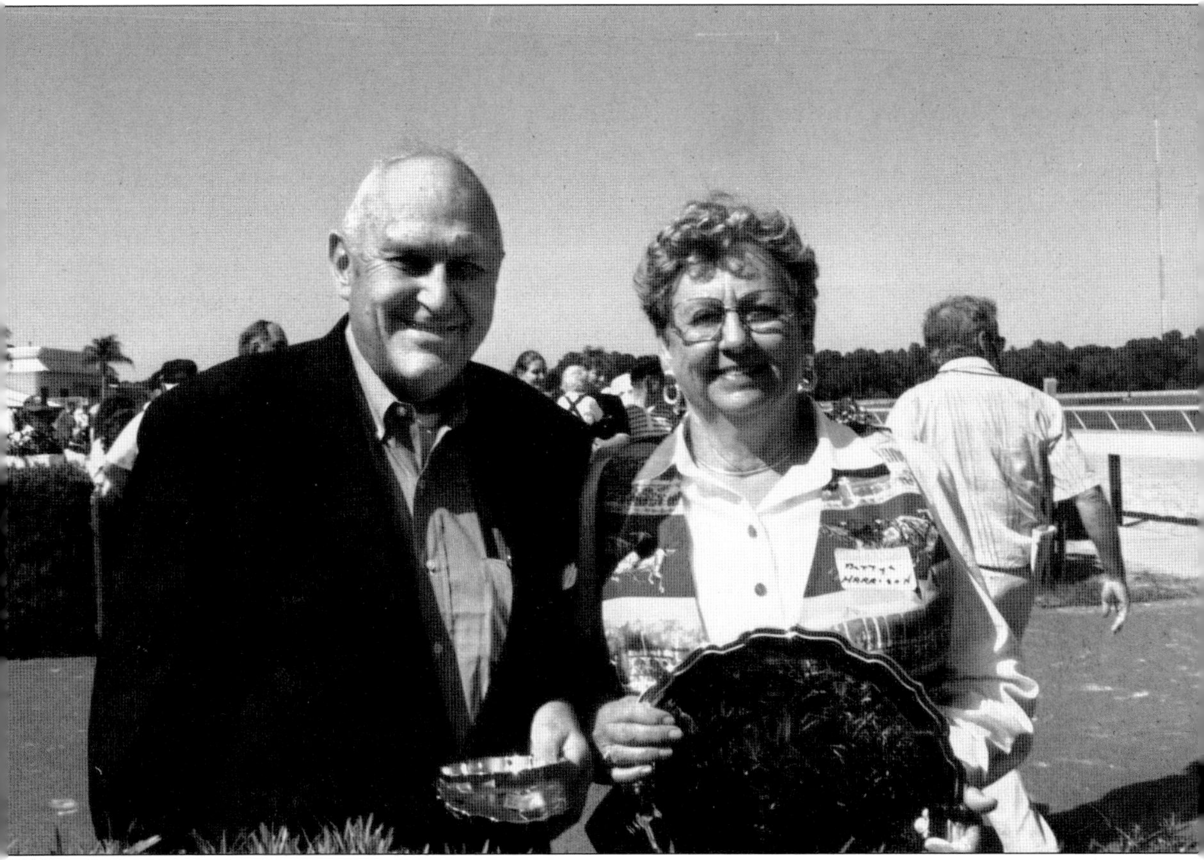

As the saying goes, behind every great man is a great woman, and Dr. Sam and Miss Bettye together devoted their lives to Arabian horse racing. It would be difficult to imagine that Dr. Sam could have achieved so much for his beloved sport if Miss Bettye did not offer her support and enthusiasm. They were a lively couple who were equally at home in small-town Loudon as at gala balls and awards banquets. Harrison entered the sport of Arabian horse racing when races were exhibition and very little purse money was involved. At times, he wondered if the sport would ever evolve. To engender momentum, he developed incentive programs, sold his own superior stock instead of hoarding, and helped grow an amateur recreation into a bona fide professional sport. From $54,000 in 1978, annual purse money increased to $1 million by 1988. Today that amount approaches $5 million. Though Dr. Sam passed away in November 1997, he created the energy for continued growth. Dr. Sam Harrison, like Gen. Jacob McGavock Dickinson before him, perpetuated Tennessee's long and esteemed horse breeding and racing tradition, leaving a worldwide legacy.